CLAUDE LÉVI-STRAUSS:
THE ANTHROPOLOGIST AS HERO

CLAUDE LÉVI-STRAUSS:
THE ANTHROPOLOGIST AS HERO

EDITED BY
E. NELSON HAYES
AND TANYA HAYES

THE M.I.T. PRESS
CAMBRIDGE, MASSACHUSETTS,
AND LONDON, ENGLAND

Preface copyright © 1970 by
The Massachusetts Institute of Technology

Set in Linotype Electra
Printed and bound in the United States of America by
Halliday Lithograph Corporation, Hanover, Massachusetts

Previously published material has been reprinted with permission
of authors and publishers, as noted in each chapter.

First paperback printing, April 1970
Second printing, July 1972

ISBN 0 262 08038 9 (hardcover)
ISBN 0 262 58016 0 (paperback)

Library of Congress catalog card number: 72–103897

CONTENTS

PREFACE

In Susan Sontag's phrase, structuralist Claude Lévi-Strauss has become "anthropologist as hero," not only in his native country of France but also throughout much of the Western world, and especially in the United States. Translations of six of his books have sold remarkably well on American campuses. References to him appear again and again in the intellectual media and sometimes even in the popular. In the phrase used by Robert Murphy, the "established literati" have especially made of him a hero, so that there is even a mention of him in such an outrageous put-on as Myra Breckinridge by Gore Vidal.

Some of the reasons for this extreme interest are readily identified. In his seeming rejection of history and humanism, in his refusal to see Western civilization as privileged and unique, in his view of the human mind as programed, in his emphasis on form over content, and in his insistence that the savage mind is not inferior to the civilized, Lévi-Strauss appeals to the deepest feelings among the alienated and disenchanted intellectuals of our society.

Yet the thought of no other *philosophe* of the twentieth century is more subtle, more complex, more convoluted. His critics even claim that his methodology and models deny his own theses.

This collection came about through our reading the first article reprinted here. It seemed significant to us that a newspaper, albeit the nation's most respected, should carry an essay of such length and depth on an anthropologist until then little known except on the campuses. This led us to survey what else on him had appeared in this country and to begin the choice of materials for this volume. Although some of the pieces originally appeared abroad, we have confined ourselves to materials published in the United States, a somewhat artificial restriction made necessary by the extraordinary wealth of essays and reviews that have appeared in the last decade or so. A few pieces we wished to include we could not because of legal restrictions or the peccadillos of authors.

The focus is on the writings of Lévi-Strauss and their reception in the United States, not on structuralism itself. For aspects of the last, the reader is referred to three excellent publications: *The Structural Study of Myth and Totemism* (1967), edited by Edmund Leach; "Structuralism" (1966), edited by Jacques Ehrmann, *Yale French Studies*, Issue 36-37; and *Introduction to Structuralism* (1970), edited and introduced by Michael Lane. Leach has also written a study (1971) of Lévi-Strauss for the Modern Masters series edited by Frank Kermode. Largely in contrast to these, we have not limited this collection to the critiques of anthropologists, preferring instead to illustrate as far as possible the range of his influence in this country. Thus, the book is intended primarily for a nonprofessional audience, especially college students.

The volume opens, then, with the article already noted. Many people who know of Lévi-Strauss's work make this and essays in *Time* (June 30, 1967) and *Newsweek* (January 23, 1967) their prime sources of information and opinion.

Next are a long essay in which H. Stuart Hughes places the thought of Lévi-Strauss in the intellectual tradition of France, and several general papers on Lévi-Strauss's theories.

There follow a number of reviews, most arranged in the order of publication. Since, as Peter Caws points out, "the event that has brought structuralism most vividly to the attention of the English-speaking world has been the publication of a translation of Lévi-Strauss's *La Pensée sauvage*," we have chosen to emphasize the critical response to that volume. Two of Lévi-Strauss's books published in this country—*Totemism* and *Structural Anthropology*—did not elicit reviews both suitable to our purpose and available to us.

George Steiner discusses the philosophical and historical implications of Lévi-Strauss's work, while Susan Sontag is concerned with the antihistorical approach of Lévi-Strauss and its relationship to what she calls "intellectual homelessness" in modern literature.

Peter Caws's essay deals with some of the outgrowths of Lévi-Strauss's writings and the application of structuralism to other fields.

The last two articles, by Robert L. Zimmerman and Lionel Abel, discuss the implications of Lévi-Strauss's thought for humanism.

A few corrections and minor editorial changes have been made in the articles as previously published.

We have attempted no further interpretation either of Lévi-Strauss or of his critics than appears in this brief preface. We do not even agree between ourselves on the meaning and significance of Lévi-Strauss's thought. One of us, an existentialist humanist, believes that acceptance of his ideas would weaken much that is of value in Western society. The other, searching for alternatives, finds in him a source of intriguing ideas. Nothing could better illustrate certain intellectual aspects of the much-discussed generation gap.

As this preface is being written, reviews and articles on the two latest translations from Lévi-Strauss are beginning to appear in number. Should there be demand for a second edition of this collection, we should want to add several such. Meanwhile, we hope this volume will serve as an introduction to, but not a substitute for, the reading of Lévi-Strauss's works.

We wish to thank authors and publishers alike for their

cooperation and for their permission to reprint materials. We are grateful to Professor Lévi-Strauss, who extended his encouragement and provided the basis of the bibliography that appears at the end.

E. Nelson Hayes
Tanya Hayes

July 1969
Cambridge, Massachusetts

CONTRIBUTORS

LIONEL ABEL was born in New York City and educated at the University of North Carolina. He has been a professional writer and teacher for the last 35 years. His books include *Metatheater* (1963) and *Moderns on Tragedy* (1967), the latter an anthology of statements by writers and philosophers on the tragic. He is currently Professor of English at the State University of New York in Buffalo.

PETER JAMES CAWS was born near London and educated at the University of London (B.Sc. in physics) and at Yale University (Ph.D. in philosophy). He is Professor of Philosophy at Hunter College of the City University of New York and author of *The Philosophy of Science: A Systematic Account* (1965) and *Science and the Theory of Value* (1967), as well as of articles and reviews in quarterlies and professional journals. His next book will deal with the structuralist movement and its philosophical implications.

SANCHE DE GRAMONT is a journalist and the author of several books, including *The Secret War* (1962); *The Age of*

Magnificence (1963), edited and translated from the *Memoirs of the Duc de Saint-Simon; Epitaph for Kings* (1967); and *The French* (1969). He lives in Paris and contributes articles to leading French and American publications.

H. STUART HUGHES was born in New York City, received his A.B. from Amherst College and his A.M. and Ph.D. from Harvard, and in 1967 was awarded an honorary L.H.D. by Amherst. He served in the Army from 1941 to 1945, ending as a Lieutenant Colonel with the OSS in Europe. Since then he has been Chief of the State Department's Division of Research for Europe, Professor and Head of the Department of History at Stanford and, since 1957, Professor of History at Harvard, where he is currently departmental chairman. In 1967 he was Bacon Exchange Professor at the University of Paris (Nanterre). Mr. Hughes is the author of eight books, including *Consciousness and Society* (1958) and *The Obstructed Path* (1968).

FRANCIS HUXLEY is a social anthropologist. Educated at Oxford, he has degrees in zoology and social anthropology. He has worked in museums and in a Canadian mental hospital, and conducted fieldwork that led to two books: *Affable Savages* (1956), on a tribe of Brazilian Indians, and *The Invisibles* (1966), on voodoo in Haiti.

HUGO G. NUTINI holds a B.S. in civil engineering from the Chilean Naval Academy, as well as a B.A. and M.A. in philosophy and a Ph.D. in anthropology from the University of California at Los Angeles. His fieldwork includes nearly a year in Easter Island and six months in Beagle Channel in Alacaluf-Yahgan territory in southern Chile. He is currently Assistant Professor of Anthropology at the University of Pittsburgh, where for four years he has been codirector of the University's field station for the training of graduate students in the Sierra de Puebla, Mexico. He has published numerous articles and has contributed the introduction and an essay on

Lévi-Strauss and Chomsky to *Essays in Structural Anthropology: in Honor of Claude Lévi-Strauss* (1969).

EDMUND LEACH is Provost of King's College and Reader in Social Anthropology at Cambridge University. He is also Chairman of the Association of Social Anthropologists and a Vice-President of the Royal Anthropological Institute. When he was graduated from Cambridge in 1932, his training had been in mathematics and engineering, but after several years of commercial experience in China, he returned to London, where he studied social anthropology under Bronislaw Malinowski and Raymond Firth. He subsequently undertook anthropological fieldwork in Kurdistan, Burma, Borneo, and Ceylon and has published ethnographic reports on these areas. His theoretical position as an anthropologist lies midway between that of the British "functionalists" and the French "structuralists." His 1967 Reith Lectures on the B.B.C. were published under the title *A Runaway World?* (1968).

DAVID MAYBURY-LEWIS is an Englishman who took his B.A. in modern languages at Cambridge and his D.Phil. in social anthropology at Oxford. Since then he has taught at Harvard, where he is currently Professor of Anthropology. He has done extensive fieldwork among Brazilian Indians and for five years directed a program of comparative research in Central Brazil. He is particularly interested in the comparative possibilities of the structural approach in social anthropology. His publications include *The Savage and the Innocent* (1965) and *Akwe-Shavante Society* (1967). He is now working on problems of social change and race relations in Brazil and is preparing a critical analysis of structuralism as it is applied to social organization.

ROBERT F. MURPHY has been on the faculties of the University of California at Berkeley and the University of Illinois. He is currently Professor and Chairman in the Department of Anthropology at Columbia University. His ethnographic research in the Amazon area of Brazil and the Sahara region of West Africa formed the basis of several books and articles, including *Mundurucú Religion* (1958), *Headhunter's Heritage* (1960), and, with B. Quain, *The Trumaí Indians of Central Brazil* (1955).

BOB SCHOLTE was born in Amsterdam, received his B.A. from Yale, M.A. from Stanford, and Ph.D. in anthropology from the University of California at Berkeley, the last in 1969. His fields of specialization are the history and theory of anthropology, anthropological linguistics, Southeast Asian anthropology, and structuralism. He has taught at Stanford University, the University of California at Berkeley and at Santa Cruz, and the University of Pennsylvania, where he is currently Assistant Professor of Communications at the Annenberg School of Communications. His articles and papers have appeared in *American Anthropologist* and other journals.

SUSAN SONTAG, author and critic, was born in New York City. *The Benefactor*, her first novel, was published in 1963. In 1966, *Against Interpretation*, a collection of her critical writings, was issued and subsequently nominated for the National Book Award in the arts and letters category; a second collection, *Styles of Radical Will*, appeared in 1969. *Death Kit*, her second novel, was issued in 1967. Her stories have appeared in *Harper's Bazaar*, *Harper's*, and *Partisan Review*. Her reviews, essays, and articles have appeared in numerous magazines including *Partisan Review*, the *New York Review of Books*, *Film Quarterly*, *Book Week*, *Commentary*, *The Nation*, and the *New York Times*.

GEORGE STEINER was born in Paris and was educated in the French *lycées*, and at the University of Chicago, Harvard, and Oxford (Rhodes Scholar). In 1952–1956 he was on the staff of *The Economist* in London, and in 1956–1958 was a member of the Institute for Advanced Study in Princeton. He is now an Extraordinary Fellow, Churchill College, Cambridge, and a free-lance writer and teacher. He is author of *Tolstoy or Dostoevsky* (1958), *The Death of Tragedy* (1960), *Anno Domini* (1964), and *Language and Silence* (1967). He received the O'Henry Prize in 1969. Since 1964 he has been a Fellow of the Royal Society of Literature.

COLIN M. TURNBULL, born in England, was educated at Westminster School and Oxford University, with additional studies at London University and Banaras Hindu University, India. He studied social anthropology under Professor E. E. Evans-Pritchard, specializing in the African field, with theoretical interests primarily in the social organization of hunters and gatherers. His fieldwork has been mainly among the Mbuti Pygmies (Congo) and the Ik (Northern Uganda). More recently, he has made a preliminary study of certain BaBinga of the Central African Republic. He is currently Associate Curator at the American Museum of Natural History (New York), teaches at New York University and Vassar, and is editor of the Viking Fund Publications in Anthropology.

ROBERT L. ZIMMERMAN is on the faculty of Sarah Lawrence College and also teaches at the New School for Social Research. Formerly, he taught philosophy at Rutgers and during his last year there (1967–1968) was Acting Associate Dean of Livingstone College, a new division of the university. He has published articles in Commentary, The Journal of Aesthetics, Philosophy and Phenomenological Research, and The Journal of Higher Education. He is currently working on a book on Hegel.

CLAUDE LÉVI-STRAUSS:
THE ANTHROPOLOGIST AS HERO

1
THERE ARE NO SUPERIOR SOCIETIES

SANCHE DE GRAMONT

There is an endemic French illness in which the works of serious thinkers mysteriously spread beyond the small circle of initiates for whom they are intended and become the object of a cult. The thinker is afflicted with disciples he never wanted, preaching a gospel he never taught. He is hailed by worshippers who have never read a line of his work. He spends his time denying the paternity of deformed offspring bearing his name. If the movement persists, he must finally imitate Marx, who denied being a Marxist.

Such was the misfortune of Jean-Paul Sartre in postwar France, when existentialism became synonymous with a life of gay abandon in St.-Germain-des-Prés. By some odd metamorphosis, his philosophy became a youth movement embodied by Juliette Greco, who sang morose existentialist songs in dank existentialist cellars, her hair existentially clouding her vision. Sartre disavowed the movement, and having survived it is not the least of his merits.

And such is the current dilemma of Claude Lévi-Strauss, an ethnologist who has spent more than half his 59 years studying the behavior of North and South American Indian tribes. The method he uses to study the social organization of these tribes, which he calls structuralism, has flowered into a movement with many exotic blossoms. It is being applied indiscriminately to areas for which Lévi-Strauss never intended it. From an ethnological method, it has sprouted into a full-fledged philosophical doctrine whose impassioned partisans insist that all human knowledge must be re-examined in its light.

Structuralism, as Lévi-Strauss has used it in his ethnological research, is essentially a way of answering the question, "How do you play this game?" Imagine someone who has never seen a playing card watching a rubber of bridge. By observing the way the cards are played, he should be able to reconstruct, not only the rules (or structure) of bridge, but the composition (or structure) of a deck of cards.

In the same way, the ethnologist observes how marriages are arranged within a tribe and is able to extrapolate certain laws, or structures, that govern the tribe's social organization.

"Structuralism," says Lévi-Strauss, "is the search for unsuspected harmonies. It is the discovery of a system of relations latent in a series of objects."

It is based on the idea that human behavior can be classified scientifically, like a plant or a chemical element. There is nothing arbitrary in nature. Why should there be anything arbitrary in man? There must be laws governing human behavior, just as there are laws governing pollenization or cellular growth. Lévi-Strauss believes you can study a tribe the same way a biologist studies an amoeba.

The variety of experience in the life of a social group seems to defy analysis. Precisely for this reason, Lévi-Strauss chooses to study primitive societies because they are more static than our own. And within these societies, he picks what he calls "crystallized" social activities like myths, kinship laws, and cooking practices. Aside from being unchanging activities of unchanging societies, they are activities at the brink of consciousness—a member of some Brazilian tribe never stops to wonder why he cooks his meat a certain way or believes a myth about a man turning into a jaguar. This is the type of subconscious, taken-for-granted mental process Lévi-Strauss believes lends itself best to scientific investigation.

For instance, he studied gift-giving in Polynesia, of which there were so many forms that most ethnologists had written them off as haphazard. He found that gift-giving could be broken down into four cycles with 35 subcycles. Thus, the structure of Polynesian gift-giving is the sum of all these cycles and subcycles—the law to which every known example conforms. The structure is the hidden order of human behavior.

Lévi-Strauss derived structuralism from a school of linguistics whose principal exponent is Roman Jakobson. Very simply, these linguists study the relations among words, rather than the relation of each word to the object it designates. It is not the meaning of the word that concerns them, but the patterns the words form. The structure of a language is its grammar, and through this kind of analysis, a linguist should be able to discover the grammar of a language he cannot speak, in much the same manner that a cryptographer is able to decipher a code thanks to recurring patterns.

In addition, the modern linguists agree that there is a "ground plan" for all the languages of the world. Every language in every society has the same fundamental properties. Thus, Lévi-Strauss says, "just as the discovery of DNA and the genetic code led biologists tó use a linguistic model to explain a natural phenomenon, I use a linguistic model to explain cultural phenomena other than language. I try to show that the basic structure of language observed by the linguists exists in a great many other activities."

Meaning, in social activities as well as in language, is thus not to be found in the designated activity but in the way it differs from other activities. He is not concerned with the story a myth tells, but in the way the symbols used in one myth become converted into another set of symbols telling the same story. This is the grammar or the code of myths. Once he has unraveled hundreds of South American myths using different symbols and sensory codes (one deals with what is heard, another with what is seen) and found that they can all be reduced to a central idea, the discovery of fire by man, he is also able to reduce the mechanism of the primitive mind to a certain number of recurring types of mental operations. In the same way, the laws governing social organization that he discovers, whether they have to do with gift-giving or marrying off one's daughter, also illustrate the workings of the human spirit.

First, he is able to abolish the distinction made by his predecessors between prelogical and logical thought, by showing that primitive peoples use either-or logical categories just as we do. Next, he infers that social organization and behavior are the result of a limited number of inherent mental categories. Just as there is a ground plan for language, there must be ground plans for other forms of collective behavior.

He sees the ground plan for kinship, for instance, as a problem in the communication of women inside a primitive society, just as an economist considers supply and demand a problem in the communication of goods and services. Instead of studying marriage and kinship in a tribe as a series of personal dramas, each the result of subjective psychological and personal factors, he studies the objective and limited number of ways a woman can pass, thanks to marriage customs, from her own family into another family.

Thus, despite Lévi-Strauss's narrow field of inquiry, there are in structuralism two ambitious implications—that the human sciences can attain the rigor and detachment of the natural sciences and that human behavior is governed by the limitations of man's mental processes. Admirers view his work as the final panel in a triptych entitled "Contemporary Western Thought," the two other panels being occupied by Marx and Freud.

I like to imagine these Three Wise Men of the Occident

bent in contemplation over a South American Indian myth about a boy who steals a pet pig from his father and roasts it in the forest. Freud would conclude that the boy is symbolically killing his father because he desires his mother. Marx would say that this youthful member of the proletariat is seizing control of the methods of production in the class struggle against the landed gentry. Lévi-Strauss would find that, in cooking the pig, the primitive Indian boy had achieved the passage from nature to culture and shown that his thought processes are no different from Einstein's.

For Lévi-Strauss's contribution to the triptych is a theory of how the human mind works. Primitive man, in organizing himself into social groups, passes from a natural to a cultural state. He uses language, learns to cook his food and accepts various laws that ensure the survival of the group. All these activities set him apart from the animal. Structuralism postulates that in achieving this passage from nature to culture, man obeys laws he does not invent. These laws are inherent in human nature, which is everywhere identical, since it is no more than the mechanism of the human brain. The cerebral cortex, like a computer, responds to the outside world according to a limited number of categories. The reason we think human nature is unpredictable is that we have not yet mapped the circuits.

With Lévi-Strauss, the whole humanist tradition goes down the drain. Instead of a free spirit, responsible for its decisions, we have a man responding to programmed circuits called structures. The individual conscience is no longer relevant. The whole body of Western thought, from Plato to Descartes to Sartre, which held that knowledge of the world begins with knowledge of oneself, belongs in the natural-history museum, alongside the witch doctors' headdresses.

Lévi-Strauss is the advance man for an age in which the human sciences will have caught up with the natural sciences. Soon, if he is right, a psychologist will be able to chart a human life as accurately as he now measures the progress of a hungry rat sniffing its way through a labyrinth toward a piece of cheese.

History goes down the drain, too, because it is seen as merely a form of our own society's mythology, a collective delusion irrelevant to the scientific study of man. Lévi-Strauss views man, not as a privileged inhabitant of the universe, but as a passing species, like some form of plant, which will leave only a few faint traces of its passage when it becomes extinct.

The sudden popularity of structuralism has little to do with Lévi-Strauss's own specific research. It is, in part, a fad, the French intellectual's equivalent of the hula hoop. On another level, it is a reaction against centuries of rhetorical philosophers and historians, and an awareness that, today, knowledge of man cannot be divorced from the great scientific advances. Finally, it is a specific attempt to discredit Jean-Paul Sartre as an outdated thinker and relegate existentialism to the philosophical garbage can. "Today," says the critic Bernard Pingaud, "we are no longer existentialist, we are structuralist."

Structuralism has become a skeleton key to all the arts and sciences. There are structuralist novels, symphonies, and paintings, connected by the tenuous link that meaning is irrelevant and that form imposes its own necessities. Samuel Beckett is hailed as a structuralist because his characters are victims of forces beyond their control. The complaint of one of Beckett's characters, "I am made of words, of the words of others," is fast becoming the structuralist motto.

One measure of the movement's extent is a singularly abstruse book called Words and Things, which has sold 40,000 copies to date. The author, Michel Foucault, who attempts to show that thought originates with words rather than the other way around, says he was inspired by Lévi-Strauss.

To show that structuralism is an all-purpose method, the magazine Communications recently published structural analyses of the James Bond novels, the death of Pope John XXIII as reported in the Paris press, and 180 funny stories in the afternoon daily France-Soir. A funny story is broken down according to its structure as follows: (1) Normalization function: A husband tells his wife she should take up knitting. (2) Locutionary engagement: "I haven't time to knit," she says; "I do too much cooking." (3) Disjunctive interlocutory function: "Yes," he replies, "but you can't burn your knitting."

The result of such painstaking classification seems disappointingly tautological. A structural analysis of the French flag would doubtless lead to the discovery that it is made up of three vertical fields of color of identical width which follow one another, according to their normalization function, in the sequence red, white, and blue.

Lévi-Strauss lifts his arms in a gesture of resigned helplessness and complains about the seriousness of the articles in Communications. He is at his desk in the Collège de France, an eminent institution founded in the sixteenth century for a small number of scholars who could, by lecturing there, escape the parochial tutelage of the Sorbonne. He holds the chair of social anthropology and delivers a minimum of twenty lectures a year. His office is decorated with Indian feather headdresses and rattan baskets. Behind his desk there is a large geological map of the United States.

The "father of structuralism" is dapper in a hound's-tooth heather sports jacket and a string tie with a tooled silver clasp. He would make an excellent model for one of the nineteenth-century studies in compared physiology that illustrate his book The Savage Mind—the transformation from fox or hooting owl to human in four or five stages with only slight alterations. A Peruvian condor would become the ethnologist's profile, narrow and aquiline, thatched with white hair.

He is horrified by the fashion for structuralism. He says:

In the sense in which it is understood today by French opinion, I am not a structuralist. I am very much afraid that in France there is a total lack of self-criticism, an excessive sensibility to fashion and a deep intellectual instability. The best way to explain the current infatuation with structuralism is that French intellectuals and the cultured French public need new playthings every 10 or 15 years.

Let's make one thing very clear. I have never guided nor directed any movement or doctrine. I pursue my work in almost total isolation, surrounded only by a team of ethnologists. As for the others, I don't want to name names, but to pronounce the name of structuralism in connection with certain philosophers and literary people, no matter how talented or intelligent they may be, seems to be a case of total confusion. I have the greatest admiration for the intelligence, the culture, and the talent of a man like Foucault, but I don't see the slightest resemblance between what he does and what I do.

Claude Lévi-Strauss's peculiar itinerary, from the deliberate spurning of his own society to unsought notoriety in it, begins in a conventional, cultured, urban, middle-class Jewish environment. His grandfather was rabbi of Versailles. His father and two of his uncles were painters of academic portraits and landscapes.

The impact of other civilizations first struck him at the age of six, when his father rewarded his schoolwork with a Japanese print. He was all the more tempted by other societies because he had little fondness for his own. He has written:

I have little sympathy with the century in which we are living, for the total ascendancy of man over nature and of certain forms of humanity over others. My temperament and tastes carry me toward more modest periods where there was a certain balance between man and nature, the diverse and multiple forms of life.

The young Lévi-Strauss studied philosophy at the Sorbonne for five years, a disappointing experience. He felt his teachers were dealing in meaningless mental gymnastics, and in the aesthetic contemplation of philosophical fine points, such as the consciousness of consciousness.

There was, in counterpoint to his scorn for the scholasticism of the Sorbonne (which did not prevent him from passing his exams with honors), a growing love of nature. After his parents bought a house in the Cévennes Mountains, he would disappear on fifteen-hour walks, forgetting time in the contemplation of a dandelion or in the search for the line of contact between two geological layers of a limestone plateau.

His "three mistresses" were Marxism, psychoanalysis, and geology. From the first he learned that understanding consists in finding common properties among a variety of incidents. Freud taught him that beyond rational categories there existed forms of behavior more valid and more meaningful. In geology he had the example of a science that discovered laws amid the great tumult of nature.

He was already, says an admirer, "a structuralist without knowing it," attracted to types of thought that seek to discover human laws by studying the relations among objects. He took up law to escape an orthodox academic career, but found it a sterile discipline. He gravitated without enthusiasm toward provincial teaching posts. His chance came in 1934, when a senior professor told him about an opening in the sociology department of São Paulo University. If he was interested in ethnology, the professor said, he could visit the Indians in the suburbs on weekends.

As soon as his first teaching contract was up, Lévi-Strauss made for the Brazilian interior, where he spent a year studying the Nambikwara ("pierced ear") tribe in the Mato Grosso, central Brazil's desolate savanna, followed by ten shorter trips, lasting from fifteen days to three months, to visit other more accessible groups.

An account of his trips became the book that has most contributed to his popularity, *Tristes Tropiques*. It is really three books in one. First, it is a return to the eighteenth century genre of the philosophical traveler. He has happened on one of the few societies the white man has left untouched, and he sees it as Rousseau might have. "Their life is a daily joy," he writes in an echo of the "noble savage" theme. "I never saw a people so gay."

Elsewhere, Lévi-Strauss recounts the experience of an anthropologist who noticed that each time he left the tribe he was studying the elders began to weep. They were not weeping because they were sad to see him go, he found, but out of pity for him bcause he was forced to leave the only place on earth where life was worth living. The notion of a primitive happiness and innocence that we have lost forms a romantic counterpoint to his scientific investigation, which is the second level of the book.

For Lévi-Strauss is a Rousseau with a scientific background, an exact observer and a tireless collector of facts. He studies the layouts of villages, the way a chief is chosen, marriage customs, and attitudes toward the dead.

In explanation of his title, he describes the antithesis of the lush, romantic tropics touted in brochures for Caribbean cruises. The tropics he sees are forlorn. Nature here is not plentiful. The inhabitants live on the edge of subsistence. Some tribes have yet to master the techniques of pottery-making and weaving. Worse, these societies are doomed. Civilization—in the form of a telegraph line, rubber planters, missionaries, or a government agency—intrudes and shatters the delicate balance that allowed the society to survive. *Tristes Tropiques* is a melancholy book, an epitaph to condemned societies.

The ethnologist is an incidental victim of these changes, since he has assigned himself the study of vanishing societies. It is with considerable anguish that Lévi-Strauss learns each year of primitive societies that have died out without yielding up the pattern of their social organization. In 1963, for instance, an ethnologist found the remote Bari tribe in the Colombian mountains, thanks to a road that had been opened up by oil prospectors. But in a matter of months, the population of the tribe was decimated by an epidemic benign to Westerners but fatal to a people who had built up no immunity.

The third layer of *Tristes Tropiques* contains the seeds of Lévi-Strauss's future work. He rebels against Western society's smug habit of imposing its standards on the rest of the world. He notes that so-called primitive societies represent perhaps 99 percent of the total experience of humanity. He refutes the traditional notion that these societies are barbaric, or less rational than our own. They are merely different. There are no superior societies.

A tribe that eats roots and spiders and wears no clothes may have solved complex problems of social organization far more satisfactorily than we have. Our parochial refusal to accept cultural diversity, our criticism of those who "don't do as we do," is itself a characteristic tribal attitude.

Human societies all have more or less the same age, but they have developed unevenly. Lévi-Strauss distinguishes between progressive, acquisitive, inventive societies like our own, which he calls "hot" or "mobile" societies, and the societies that lack the gift of synthesis and the possibilities for human exchange, which he calls "cold" or "static" societies.

The cold societies are mechanical in that they do not increase the amount of energy per capita, which is one definition of technical progress. They maintain themselves in their initial state. They have no written tradition and no history in our sense of the term (which is one reason ethnologists find them ideal to study).

They are democratic and nonhierarchical. The society acts unanimously and purges itself of dissent so that there are no disorders or minority groups.

The "hot" society is thermodynamic; it produces and consumes energy, like a steam engine. It develops through conflict and makes technological leaps that are not matched by social progress. If progress is measured by the amount of energy available per capita, Western society is miles ahead. But if the criterion were success in overcoming inhospitable geographic conditions, the Eskimos or Bedouins would rank first. And if progress were based on success in founding harmonius family and social groups, the Australian aborigines would be judged most advanced. Western society is thus not better than others, but simply more cumulative, because it has been less isolated.

Early ethnologists sought proof of the glories of their civilization in the backwardness of primitive peoples. Lévi-Strauss takes the opposite approach. Without a trace of Swiftian irony, he writes a closely reasoned defense of cannibalism in *Tristes Tropiques*. Eating the body of an ancestor or an enemy is intended as a means to acquire his virtue or neutralize his power. To condemn this practice on moral grounds is to believe either in physical resurrection or in a link between body and spirit, convictions identical to those in the name of which ritual cannibalism is practiced. On those grounds, why should we prefer noncannibalism to cannibalism, since we also show disregard for the sanctity of the dead in our own anatomy dissections?

A disinterested observer, says Lévi-Strauss, might distinguish cannibalistic societies—those that believe they can absorb the powers of enemies by eating them—and anthropoemic societies like our own (from the Greek *emein*, "to vomit"), which expel enemies from the body politic by imprisonment or exile. Our penitentiary customs, he points out, would seem to primitive societies as barbaric as their cannibalism seems to us.

There is, however, one tradition of our society for which there is no analogous primitive institution, and that is the written tradition. Without going so far as to suggest a causal relationship, Lévi-Strauss links the origin of writing in the Eastern Mediterranean between the second and third millenniums to one of the constants of Western society, the exploitation of man by man.

Thus, he considers what is usually regarded as the single most important advantage of civilized man—the ability to write—as the harbinger of bondage in Western society. For writing "seems to favor the exploitation rather than the enlightenment of mankind." Writing, which allows man to store a large body of knowledge, "made it possible to assemble workmen by the thousands and set them tasks which taxed them to the limit of their strength. If my hypothesis is correct, the primary function of writing, as a means of communication, is to facilitate the enslavement of other human beings."

Lévi-Strauss was moving toward an intuitive formulation of structualism when the "hot" history of Western society interrupted his research. He was a liaison officer between the French and British Armies on the Maginot line when France fell in 1940. He fled to the United States, and there he met Roman Jakobson, who was already applying structuralism to linguistics. Jakobson did not invent structuralism. He improved a method introduced around 1910 by the Swiss linguist Ferdinand de Saussure, and perpetuated by the Russian school known as "formalists." But Lévi-Strauss, who has collaborated steadily with Jakobson (in 1961 they wrote a structural analysis of Baudelaire's sonnet "The Cats"), was the first to apply structuralism to ethnology.

His first structural work, *Elementary Structures of Kinship*, sought one of the points of primitive man's passage from nature, where he simply responds to biological urges, to culture, where he joins in functioning social groups. Lévi-Strauss wanted to show that primitive man organizes himself, by drawing on what the natural environment provides, in a logical, coherent manner—the very opposite of an irrational, prelogical manner.

He demonstrates that the only social institution enforced to some degree by every existing social group is the prohibition of incest. The reason is not that incest biologically weakens or psychologically damages a species, but that the group derives social benefits from its prohibition. Thanks to the prohibition, each man offers to other men the women he must refuse for himself. The ensuing social benefit is the free circulation of women, similar to the circulation of goods and services in a mercantilist economy.

The bridge from nature to culture is in the priority of the social over the natural, the collective over the individual, and the organizational over the arbitrary. It ensures the integration of the family in the social groups and forges profitable alliances between families. Lévi-Strauss quotes conversations among Indians about the practical disadvantages of incest: "If you marry your sister you will have no brother-in-law. Who will go hunting with you? Who will help you with the planting?"

Since this early work Lévi-Strauss has been writing a series of books that explore the workings of the human mind through tribal myths. The first in the series, Totemism Today, argued that the practice of choosing an animal or a natural object as the symbol of a family or clan was not a ridiculous superstition but part of a larger system of classification, a highly sophisticated mythical universe that he begins to explore in The Savage Mind.

At the root of primitive thought, he says, there is a need for order. The diversity of myths, the fact that the same symbol is used in different ways by different tribes (the Pawnees relate the woodpecker to storms; the Osages, to the sun and stars), led earlier ethnologists to conclude that there could be no order in these infinitely varied and apparently arbitrary data. But this same diversity was a challenge to Lévi-Strauss. He wanted to prove that primitive thought has an inner coherence.

Lévi-Strauss's next volume in his study of myths is called The Raw and the Cooked, but it is not, as some unsuspecting housewives have discovered, a collection of recipes. It is a study of 187 myths from 20 South American tribes, which finds another point of passage from nature to culture in the cooking of meat.

Its conclusion is simple: the myths tell us that meat exists so that man can cook it. The controlled fire used for cooking is a symbol of man's relation to the sun: if the sun were too far from the earth, the earth would rot, and if it were too close, it would burn. Cooking is an agent of passage from nature to culture just as the sun is the mediator between heaven and earth.

But the way Lévi-Strauss solves his mythological puzzle will defeat most readers. His books are possibly the greatest collection of riddles since the Sphinx. In his mythological universe, things are usually the opposite of what they seem. A myth about water turns out to be really about fire. A myth about wild pigs is really about humans who have been punished for their lack of generosity.

He pursues his analysis of myths in a book called *From Honey to Ashes*, where he examines primitive man's relations to the supernatural through Indian myths about honey and tobacco.

Lévi-Strauss's latest book, called *Table Manners*, integrates the mythology of North American Indians into his system. He also shows that "savage thought" contains a philosophy and an ethic. *Table Manners* baffled even its author, who had to reread and rewrite it three times before he decided it was coherent.

Because Lévi-Strauss aspires to the precision of the exact sciences, he is particularly sensitive to the lag of the human sciences. In the past, he believes, anthropologists "behaved like amateur botanists, haphazardly picking random samples," with the result that "we are still at the stage of discovering what a fact is. . . . It is as though cosmic physics had to base itself on the observations of Babylonian astronomers, with the difference that heavenly bodies are still with us, whereas primitive societies are vanishing fast."

An ethnologist cannot, like a physicist or a chemist, repeat his experiments in identical conditions an unlimited number of times. And yet Lévi-Strauss does not think the human sciences need remain in a position of inferiority. He says:

It is true that ethnology is faced with the eventual disappearance of primitive societies, but this is not a threat; on the contrary, it will make us modify our line of vision and recognize our true aims.

In studying primitive societies, the ethnologist's aim was to study a form of humanity as different and remote as possible from his own. But in our own society, there are forms of life, beliefs, types of action, which seem extremely remote to us, and I wonder whether, the more voluminous contemporary societies become, the more they tend to re-create within themselves the diversity they have destroyed elsewhere.

This impresses me particularly in America. For instance, the religious or parareligious sects of the West Coast may seem as mysterious to an East Coast observer as primitive societies. When I read American magazines like *Playboy* and others, which I do with a great deal of care, curiosity, and pleasure, I have the impression of witnessing a sort of ethnological understanding of a society by its own members, who are examining customs which are strange and distant, not because they are thousands of miles away, but because they are the object of a strong prohibition on the part of the society which re-creates the distances.

It is thus perfectly conceivable that ethnology represents a method of approach as eternal as humanity itself. When there is no more ethnology of primitive peoples, there will be an effort to understand man through those of his activities which, for one reason on another, are at the very limit of humanity.

In order to be equipped for this task, Lévi-Strauss believes that

the human sciences will be structuralist or they will not be at all. . . . The ethnologist, faced with thousands of societies and the incredible multiplicity of facts, must do one of two things: Either he can only describe and take inventory of all this diversity, and his work will be very estimable but it will not be scientific. Or else he will have to admit that behind this diversity there lies something deeper, something common to all its aspects. This effort to reduce a multiplicity of expressions to one language, this is structuralism. Maybe someday it will no longer be called that; I don't know and I don't care. But the effort to find a deeper and truer reality behind the multiplicity of apparent realities, that seems to me to be the condition of survival for the human sciences, whatever the undertaking is called.

Thus far, however, Lévi-Strauss has examined only fixed systems, such as marriage customs, within "cold" societies, those that do not have a changing history in our sense of the term. The historical development of man does not interest him, which helps explain both his popularity and the denunciations of his critics. Just as physicists study light either as an undulation or as an emission, says Lévi-Strauss, human phenomena may be explained historically or structurally. Both methods are valid, neither is privileged, but his only concern is with the latter.

With this in mind, an article by François Furet in the review *Preuves* argues that the intellectual establishment has adopted structuralism precisely because it offers an antihistory. French intellectuals, says Furet, are disenchanted with history and the left-wing ideologies that claim to be its agents, for since the end of the Algerian war these ideologies have had little relevance in France. Despite the pronouncements of General de Gaulle in both hemispheres, France no longer has much influence in world affairs. De Gaulle seems, in fact, to want to freeze history by resisting England's vocation as a Continental power and by rekindling nostalgic seventeenth-century thoughts of a French Canada. Perhaps he will be remembered as the first structuralist chief of state. In any case, since history no longer seems to need France, disillusioned intellectuals feel an obscure need for a system of thought that has no need of history.

There is also something reassuring in Lévi-Strauss's insistence that Western civilization is not privileged. We have so many daily reminders of this dismal fact that he has come along with an alternative at a providential moment. We can study primitive peoples, not as amusing throwbacks to the childhood of man, but to learn from their more tranquil ways.

Because Lévi-Strauss has been so ardently taken up by part of the intellectual establishment, he has also become the object of passionate, sometimes obsessive, criticism.

There are, first of all, attempts to discredit him as an ethnologist. Critics point out that Lévi-Strauss, who advises all aspiring ethnologists to spend one year out of every three in the field, has had considerably less field experience himself and has written only one monograph. He is the first to acknowledge this deficiency. "It is because I feel the inadequacy of my own field experience so acutely that I would like my pupils and collaborators to avoid it," he says.

Other critics view him as a man haunted by a grand design, an attempt to reduce all social activity to inherent, mechanical tendencies of the human mind. They say that he freezes and constrains man, divorcing him from life and reality, that instead of an individual capable of modifying his environment, the Lévi-Strauss man is the creature of a formal system whose life is governed by invariable structures.

This charge particularly irks Lévi-Strauss.

To accuse me of formalism [he says as though hardly believing his ears], whereas probably no other ethnologist has been so attentive to the concrete aspects of human life! On the contrary, I try to show that it is impossible even to start interpreting a myth unless one is perfectly informed about the slightest ethnographic details of the society in which it exists. I would say that there is more concrete ethnology in my books than in any other theoretical works in the field.

Some critics become so impassioned that they portray structuralism as the machination of an unbalanced mind to subvert Western thought. Thus, the well-known sociologist Henri Lefèvre writes that one finds in Lévi Strauss "a curious predilection, almost maniacal, almost schizophrenic, for the motionless, the diagram." He goes on to accuse structuralism of being the tool of a capitalist ideology, in that its effort to eliminate historical development is a counterrevolutionary defense of the political status quo.

Lévi-Strauss considers Lefèvre's attacks ridiculous. "I see

absolutely no link between structuralism and any political system," he says. "It is exactly as if an astronomer using a telescope which only modern industry could produce were accused of justifying capitalism with his discoveries.

Lévi-Strauss dismisses the fault-finding of his minor critics handily, but in Jean-Paul Sartre he has a more evenly matched antagonist. The structural ethnologist and the existentialist philosopher have been conducting a running quarrel for seven years. It has taken on a new urgency now that Lévi-Strauss is being crowned as Sartre's successor by the intellectual establishment.

In his *Critique of Dialectical Reason*, published in 1960, Sartre opened hostilities by saying that Lévi-Strauss studied men the way entomologists study ants. Sartre wrote that history is a "rational disorder." For him, historical truth exists, and meaning begins with the individual conscience. Thus, he cannot accept Lévi-Strauss's conception of a single human nature which responds to inherent laws.

In *The Savage Mind*, two years later, Lévi-Strauss replied that Sartre is guilty of "intellectual cannibalism," in that he believes every form of society or thought other than our own can have a meaning only when compared with ours.

To Lévi-Strauss, Sartre describing the French Revolution in terms of the class struggle is himself worthy of an ethnological study, for he is a member of a given society repeating one of that society's myths. Lévi-Strauss contends that there is not one history but a multitude of histories, each of which cannot be more than "the interpretation which philosophers or historians give of their own mythology, and which I would consider as a variant of that mythology."

This does not invalidate history, he says, for

an astronomer knows that the straight line is an abstraction, and that in reality there are only curved lines in the universe, but that is not going to prevent him from using a plumb line when he wants to build a house. We must distinguish the action a man can have inside his own society from the way he tries to explain human phenomena in a general way. Some things which are true on the scale of our own society cease to be true on the scale of thousands of years or on the scale of humanity.

Sartre's latest counterattack appeared in a recent issue of the review *L'Arc* devoted to his work. In it, he placed the discussion on the political level, Lévi-Strauss has always striven to avoid.

Structuralism, he charged, is the *bourgeoisie's* last stand against Marxism, an attempt to set up a closed, inert system where order is privileged at the expense of change. "As it is conceived and practiced by Lévi-Strauss," he said,

structuralism has greatly contributed to the actual discredit of history, insofar as it applies itself only to already constituted systems, such as myths for example. . . . Even "cold" societies have a history . . . but in a structuralist perspective, it is impossible to render this evolution. History appears as a purely passive phenomenon.

Let us end by giving Lévi-Strauss the last word in his dispute with Sartre. He believes that existentialism, not structuralism, is on the defensive. He says:

In existentialism, which was so popular in the postwar years, there was something paradoxical and contradictory which had to come out in the light of day. I mean that existentialism adopted very advanced political positions whereas ideologically it represented on the contrary a conservative and even reactionary endeavor.

Existentialism was an attempt to save philosophy, a sort of morose withdrawal before the great advance of scientific thought, a way of saying: "No, there is still a privileged area, something which was created by man and belongs only to man"—an attempt, in short, to save humanism, whereas the nature of structuralism consists, on the one hand, in frankly accepting the dialogue with science, and, on the other hand, in recognizing that philosophy can no longer be a privileged domain but can survive only in the form of constant dialogue with scientific thought.

2
STRUCTURE AND SOCIETY

H. STUART HUGHES

With Lévi-Strauss, contemporary French thought was back
where it began—in the sphere of social science, international
in scope, and with Frenchmen taking the lead. Like Bloch and
Febvre, Lévi-Strauss was deeply, almost obsessively, concerned
with developing a type of study that would render the "human"
in all its infinite variety. He differed with them, however, in
finding in structure rather than in flow the metaphor best
adapted to convey what he had understood; indeed, he pushed
the notion of structure further than any of his predecessors in
this type of social inquiry. Nor did he limit his work, as Bloch
and Febvre had done, to the analysis of Western societies. He
took up the challenge with which imaginative writers such as
Saint-Exupéry and Malraux had already engaged themselves,

From *The Obstructed Path*, by H. Stuart Hughes (New York,
Harper & Row, 1968), pp. 264–290. Copyright 1968 by H. Stuart
Hughes. Reprinted by permission of the publisher.

of combating French ethnocentricity by an open-minded confrontation with the values of alien people overseas. Like Malraux, Lévi-Strauss tried to understand what it meant for non-Western societies to live "without a history." But he went far beyond the novelists of heroism in the rigor of his method and in the thoroughness with which he shared the life and thought of the "primitives" who were to become the protagonists of his subsequent anthropological studies.

Which is all to say that Lévi-Strauss's intellectual antecedents were inordinately complex and reached back both to his immediate predecessors of the 1930s and to the pre-First World War generation of French social theorists. Among the latter, Durkheim and Bergson naturally loomed the largest. Toward Durkheim, Lévi-Strauss's attitude was of necessity ambivalent. As a young man he had been in "open insurrection" against Durkheim's precepts or any comparable "attempt to put sociology to metaphysical uses." Yet as his professional career went on, he gradually discovered a lingering affinity to the Durkheimian tradition that set him apart from English and American anthropologists.[1] By 1958—the centenary of Durkheim's birth—Lévi-Strauss was ready to dedicate to his predecessor, in the guise of an "inconsistent disciple," the series of essays he had collected under the title *Structural Anthropology*. And he was frank in recognizing his own debt to the kinship and language studies of Marcel Mauss, the most influential of Durkheim's heirs. Toward Bergson, Lévi-Strauss took a more informal tone. In no sense a Bergsonian himself, he nevertheless made a point of recognizing where the philosopher of the *élan vital* could come to the aid of the student of primitive societies. With characteristic urbanity—and a hint of patronizing—Lévi-Strauss congratulated Bergson on being an "armchair philosopher" who in certain respects reasoned "like a savage," since "his own thought, unbeknownst to him, was in sympathy with that of totemic peoples."[2]

---

1 Claude Lévi-Strauss, *Tristes Tropiques* (Paris, 1955), translated (and slightly abridged) by John Russell under the same title, Atheneum paperback edition (New York, 1963), p. 63.

2 *Le Totémisme aujourd'hui* (Paris, 1962), translated by Rodney

A second of Lévi-Strauss's major works, *The Savage Mind*, was dedicated to the memory of Merleau-Ponty, who had died in the year before its publication and had been its author's friend and colleague at the Collège de France. In this book, as throughout Lévi-Strauss's later production, one finds echoes of Merleau-Ponty, notably in the concern for man as "speaking subject." Yet the minds of the two friends—who in age were only a few months apart—worked in radically different fashions. Where Merleau-Ponty preferred to leave his thought open and elusive, Lévi-Strauss strove for closed formulations that had the precision of crystal. Each faced the same methodological problem: where was the study of man to go, once it had absorbed the teachings of Max Weber? Merleau-Ponty's choice was to push Weber's work to its logical consequences by "relativizing" still further the relativist implications in the ideal-type method— that is, by recognizing even more radically than Weber had done the subjective and unverifiable character of the ideal types in question. Hence the floating, unstable intellectual universe of Merleau-Ponty's later thought. For Lévi-Strauss such indeterminacy was intolerable. As convinced as was his friend of the instability of the ideal-type method as currently understood, Lévi-Strauss wanted to redefine and to tighten that method by eliminating its ambiguities.

In so doing, he took up the word "model," which in the meantime had come into currency among American social scientists, equating it with the older term "structure," to which he now gave a more precise significance. For Lévi-Strauss a structure was a model that conformed to several specific requirements:

First, the structure exhibits the characteristics of a system. It is made up of several elements, none of which can undergo a change without effecting changes in all the other elements.

Second, for any given model there should be a possibility of ordering a series of transformations resulting in a group of models of the same type.

Needham as *Totemism*, Beacon paperback edition (Boston, 1963), pp. 98–99.

Third, the above properties make it possible to predict how the model will react if one or more of its elements are submitted to certain modifications.

Finally, the model should be constituted so as to make immediately intelligible all the observed facts.[3]

Thus, the model (or group of models) had an internal consistency that gave an initial guarantee of its validity. But even this progress over Weber was insufficient to satisfy Lévi-Strauss's thirst for certainty. Despite his agnosticism about the values—whether religious or ideological—ordinarily professed in his own society, he refused to remain in a similar state of suspended judgment about the nature of man: the overriding aim of his career as a social scientist was to dig below every theoretical level yet discovered and to come at last to a basic structure of the human mind that would at once cancel out and reconcile the countless explanations of their behavior that men had offered through all ages and all types of savagery or civilization.

A breath-taking quest—as ambitious as that of any twentieth-century investigator—and one that a half-century earlier would have been totally unfeasible. For Lévi-Strauss enjoyed advantages denied to the generation of Weber or of Freud: in the meantime, the study of man had evolved in two new directions that opened up unsuspected vistas of intellectual certainty.

The first was Lévi-Strauss's chosen discipline of anthropology. The latest arrival among the social sciences, anthropology as a clearly delimited field of study was only a quarter-century old when he encountered it in the early 1930s. At that time, its first great generation of field workers was still alive and active. The leaders of this generation, which included Bronislaw Malinowski in Britain and Alfred L. Kroeber in America,

---

3 "La notion de structure en ethnologie" (originally presented in English at a symposium in New York in 1952), *Anthropologie structurale* (Paris, 1958), translated by Claire Jacobson and Brooke Grundfest Schoepf as *Structural Anthropology* (New York, 1963), pp. 279–280.

were of an age to be Lévi-Strauss's fathers, as the generation of Freud and Weber ranked as his intellectual grandfathers. Certain of them he treated with filial respect, others with an equally filial combativity. Much of Lévi-Strauss's work was a polemic against the underlying conviction of Malinowski and the British school that the rites and myths of primitive peoples could be understood in terms of a social function. His admiration, rather, went to such Americans as Kroeber and Franz Boas, in whom he discovered an optimum combination of empirical method and a gift for synthesis.

By the very choice of anthropology as a field of study, Lévi-Strauss was led in a double sense outside France's cultural fortress. The contact with preliterate societies was the more obvious of these outlets; equally important was the fact that the discipline as a whole was dominated by the Anglo-Americans (many of whom, however, had Central or Eastern European origins) and employed English as its international language. Thus, as a cursory sampling of his footnotes revealed, Lévi-Strauss worked at two removes from the familiar idea-world of his countrymen: he dealt with exotic peoples whose customs were for the most part interpreted in a Western language that was not his own.

The fact that the only anthropologist since Sir James Frazer to achieve general public renown was a Frenchman rather than an Englishman or American gave Lévi-Strauss's work an extra dimension. He brought to his labors a characteristic French conviction that cultural phenomena obeyed an immanent law. And more rigorously than his English-speaking colleagues, he insisted on a standard of objectivity in anthropological study that set this discipline apart from the other social sciences. Every social scientist, he recognized, strove to be objective in the sense that he tried to rise above his own value system; yet the anthropologist alone went one step further and questioned the entire method of thinking that permeated Western civilization. The anthropologist in effect jumped backward through time to the moment in pre-Socratic Greece when the canon of logical reasoning had first been established, and then took off from this point to a systematic investigation of how the mind of primitive man worked. Only by divesting himself of the methodological prejudices, scientific or philosophical, that were second nature to Europeans and Americans, could the student of preliterate societies hope to discover the fundamental patterns of human thought that underlay its overwhelming diversity of expression.

In this quest, Lévi-Strauss brought to bear the second—and still more recent—of the new methods of study developed since the time of Freud and Weber, the technique of structural linguistics. Since the original pioneering work of a Swiss scholar, Ferdinand de Saussure, before 1914, linguistics had in a single generation become the most sharply defined of the sciences of man. Having totally separated meaning from sound in their study of language, the structural linguists were free to concentrate their attention on the phoneme, the basic unit of human speech. And once they had done so, they found that the possible combinations of phonemes were finite in number and followed rules that were statistically predictable. Such combinations, since they occurred at the unconscious level and were quite innocent of subsequent policing at the hands of grammarians, had the advantage of being value-free and devoid of meaning. The lesson for anthropology seemed clear:

If . . . the unconscious activity of the mind consists in imposing forms upon content, and if these forms are fundamentally the same for all minds—ancient and modern, primitive and civilized . . . —it is necessary and sufficient to grasp the unconscious structure underlying each institution and each custom, in order to obtain a principle of interpretation valid for other institutions and other customs.[4]

What Lévi-Strauss learned from the structural linguists was to think of his subject in terms of a net of relationships, all of which, if reduced to their essentials, had something in common. In this view, the task of the anthropologist became one of first drawing up an exhaustive inventory of such rela-

4 "Introduction: Histoire et ethnologie" (originally published in *Revue de métaphysique et de morale*, LIV, 1949), *ibid.*, p. 21.

tionships and then establishing their necessary connections. And the area in which Lévi-Strauss himself chose to illustrate his theory seemed at first glance the most difficult of all—the realm of myth, where the human imagination was commonly supposed to wander untrammeled. If in *this* domain, he argued, the mind could be shown as "bound and determined in all its operations, a fortiori, it must be so everywhere."[5] If the systematic study of myth would bear out his basic contention, then he could "buckle together" the untidy loose ends in the study of man and forge a new positivism more potent and more sophisticated than the nineteenth-century positivist teachings that the generation of his intellectual grandfathers had thought they had discredited forever.[6]

Although, as we have seen, Lévi-Strauss was the chronological contemporary of Sartre and Merleau-Ponty, he was launched onto the French intellectual scene later than these two, since he abandoned philosophy for the slow and roundabout path of becoming a field anthropologist. His reasons for so doing epitomized his entire intellectual endeavor: "With philosophy I had a sense of stopping half-way, of stopping at certain types of thought . . . which were those of our Western society, . . . whereas anthropology gave me, rightly or wrongly, an impression of going to the farthest limits of what was possible in the exploration of philosophy's goal."[7]

Like Bergson and Durkheim and Bloch, Lévi-Strauss was of Jewish origin. But no more than for these three was Judaism a living reality to him. (The eminence of this succession of names—as influential a quartet as one can find in the history of twentieth-century French thought—suggests religious agnosticism against a Jewish background as an optimum point of departure for social speculation.) In the case of Lévi-Strauss, the Jewish tradition was attenuated in the extreme: his only

5 "Réponses à quelques questions," *Esprit* (special issue on Lévi-Strauss), XXXI (November 1963): 630.

6 Marc Gaboriau, "Anthropologie structurale et histoire," *ibid.*, p. 595.

7 Claude Lévi-Strauss, "A contre-courant," interview published in *Le nouvel observateur*, No. 115 (January 25, 1967), p. 30.

memories of the ancestral religion derived from the years of the First World War, when, already past his early childhood, he lived with a rabbi grandfather whose formal and desiccated practice of his faith was hardly of a kind to stir the emotions. Ten or fifteen years later, Lévi-Strauss found his philosophical studies equally unappealing: although he did everything expected of him, passing the *agrégation* at an early age and even beginning the normal course of academic advancement by teaching in a *lycée*, he felt that he was simply playing an established set of rhetorical games that bore little relation to "truth." Even the newer forms of philosophical inquiry held no appeal: Lévi-Strauss was suspicious of the phenomenologists' claim to have found a basis for reality in the minute data of experience and of the "indulgent attitude" of existentialism "towards the illusions of subjectivity."[8] Hence, it was with a sense of deliverance that in the autumn of 1934, when he had just turned twenty-eight, he accepted, quite literally on three hours' notice, the chance to go to São Paulo as professor of sociology.

The better part of the following five years Lévi-Strauss spent in Brazil. Although sociology was his designated subject and although he was fascinated by the fast-growing, chaotic metropolis in which he taught, his real purpose in leaving France was to pursue the anthropological interests to which he had already been drawn in amateur and unsystematic fashion. Now he was resolved to make himself a professional: at home base in São Paulo, he read the literature of the field; in vacation time, he ventured even farther into the Brazilian interior to study the Indians at first hand. The last and longest of such expeditions, lasting a full year and unprecedented in its scope and hardship, took him all the way across the center of the continent through endless wastes of scrub growth to the valley of the Amazon. By mid-1939, when he returned to France, Lévi-Strauss had become a seasoned anthropologist.

By the same token, he had become a stranger to France and had fallen out of the customary sequence of university promotion. The tumults of the late 1930s had passed him by: per-

8 *Tristes Tropiques* (English translation), pp. 61–62, 215.

spiring and struggling through the desolation of central Brazil, he had sometimes wondered ruefully whether it was not quixotic to follow so eccentric a course rather than getting ahead in the academic world as a fledgling French intellectual was supposed to do. And these biographical anomalies were reinforced after the outbreak of the war. In early 1941, having finished his military service and feeling threatened (as was only sensible) by the Vichy government's cooperation with German anti-Semitic measures, Lévi-Strauss embarked for the United States, where a group of American anthropologists, to whom his name was already known, were prepared to take care of him. For the remainder of the war years, he taught in New York, at the New School for Social Research and at the Ecole Libre des Hautes Etudes founded by other Frenchmen stranded overseas, notably Jacques Maritain. Here Lévi-Strauss acquired the fluency in English and the familiarity with American anthropology that were later to rank among his most valued assets. But he also remained conscious of his role as a French intellectual: it was as cultural counselor of the French Embassy, a position he held from 1946 to 1947, that he presided over a lecture delivered by Albert Camus at Columbia University.

Back in France at last—and this time for good—Lévi-Strauss brought to completion the anthropological studies he had been working on for more than a decade. In 1948 the publication of his first book, a study of family and social life among the Nambikwara Indians, established him as a leader in his profession. A year later the first of his more speculative works, on the "elementary structures of kinship," brought him to the attention of a wider circle of intellectuals. Finally in 1955—the year of Teilhard de Chardin's death and of the posthumous publication of The Phenomenon of Man—the appearance of Tristes Tropiques made Lévi-Strauss almost overnight a celebrated author in the eyes of the general reading public.

Although it was totally different in style and conception from The Phenomenon of Man, Lévi-Strauss's book derived its popularity from a similar quality of extending the frontiers of a scientific treatise far beyond the usual professional concerns.

Besides giving a systematic account of what he had learned about four different South American Indian peoples among whom he had dwelt, *Tristes Tropiques* was at once an auto-biography and a philosophical reflection on travel in the manner of an eighteenth-century *moraliste*. Its tone (more nuanced than Teilhard's) alternated like his between the dryly factual and the lyric. Its underlying mood, as its title implied, was of restrained elegy. Subtle in phraseology, dense in thought, *Tristes Tropiques* offered the extended meditation of an ultra-civilized Gallic mind on the ways of "savages" whom he had found to be not nearly so unsophisticated as their nakedness and destitution might suggest.

With the publication of his *Structural Anthropology* in 1958, the theoretical outlines of Lévi-Strauss's position had been established; the following year he had received a newly created chair at the Collège de France. It now remained for him to make fully explicit what he had earlier sketched out and to reply to the impatient critics who stood ready to trip him up. This process he began with a small book entitled *Totemism*, the prologue to the most important of his theoretical writings, *The Savage Mind*, published in 1962.

If *Tristes Tropiques* had made Lévi-Strauss famous, *The Savage Mind* made him controversial. As the sharpest expression of his views he had yet set forth, it aroused passionate discussion among social scientists, philosophers, and men of letters. For its combination of ultrarelativism and the new dogmatism of the structural method had something in it to upset or displease almost every French school of social speculation.

The mind of the savage, Lévi-Strauss argued, was neither so simple nor so wayward as it was ordinarily supposed to be. In point of fact, primitive man thought in an exceedingly complicated fashion; his logic was merely of a different order from the logic of abstract science to which Western man had become accustomed. Still more, the savage thirsted for objective knowledge and was adept at observing the concrete; the systems by which he classified plants, animals, and natural phenomena were detailed and sometimes even intellectually elegant. The results of his speculations were preserved in a "science of the concrete"—the "memory bank" of techniques in agriculture, pottery, and the domestication of animals that had made possible the beginnings of settled habitation in neolithic times. After that enormous cultural revolution, mankind had stopped in its tracks—and most cultures had remained there. Even in the West, thousands of years had gone by before the advent of modern science: the scientific speculation of classical antiquity and the Middle Ages was still neolithic in temper. The only way to explain this "level plain" of "stagnation" was to postulate "two distinct modes of scientific thought"—"one roughly adapted to that of perception and the imagination: the other at a remove from it." The former—the "primitive" science of the concrete—had to its credit the achievements secured ten thousand years ago that still remained "at the basis of our own civilization."[9]

Having thus established the credentials of the savage way of thought, Lévi-Strauss went on to point out the vestiges of such thinking in contemporary Europe and America. These vestiges were of the sort that the Freudian school of therapy condemned as magical—that is, the conviction of hidden affinities and sympathies between human actions and the world of nature. But the word "magic"—like everything else in the mental universe of primitive man—held no terrors for Lévi-Strauss. Magic too had its logic: it would be better, he maintained, "instead of contrasting magic and science, to campare them as two parallel modes of acquiring knowledge"; the former, unlike abstract scientific thought, postulated a "complete and all-embracing determinism." And once the principles of such determinism had been fully understood, they were found to work rather like a kaleidoscope: they reshuffled bits and pieces of traditional lore into endless variations of basically similar structural patterns; they displayed both "internal coherence" and a "practically unlimited capacity for extension."[10]

9 *La Pensée sauvage* (Paris, 1962), translated as *The Savage Mind* (Chicago, 1966), pp. 3, 15–16, 42.
10 *Ibid.*, pp. 11–13, 36, 217.

The magical—or totemic—way of thinking was by its nature antihistorical. But it did not deny the category of time: the savage mind simply could not bring itself to believe that anything really changed. Nor did the lack of a sense for history denote some ineradicable inferiority of feeling: an "obstinate fidelity to a past conceived as a timeless model," Lévi-Strauss argued, "betrayed no moral or intellectual deficiency whatsoever." As opposed to the usual "clumsy distinction" between "peoples without history" and those who thought of themselves in historical terms, he preferred to speak of "cold" societies that tried to stay in equilibrium and "hot" ones that were forever on the move.[11] Thus a thoroughgoing ethical relativism lay at the end of Lévi-Strauss's search for the principles of primitive thought: in their acute understanding of the plant and animal world, in their sense of an overarching cosmic harmony, those who dwelt in the "cold" cultures displayed a nobility of temper that the superheated West had long ago forgotten.

Finally, the structures the mind of primitive man revealed could be presumed to be universal. Under the lofty scaffolding of modern science, the mental patterns of the contemporary city dweller in the West were much like those of his neolithic ancestor. The task of the anthropologist was to find those patterns—proceeding on the principle that "either everything, or nothing, makes sense." And when they had been sufficiently understood, Lévi-Strauss concluded, "the entire process of human knowledge" would assume "the character of a closed system."[12]

The completion of The Savage Mind, by Lévi-Strauss's own account, marked a pause in his thought. But the task he had set himself was far from accomplished. He had affirmed the existence of basic mental structures: now he had to prove it. He had declared that myths were capable of structural analysis: to date he had given only a few scattered examples. The purpose of the four-volume series entitled Mythologiques, which

---

11 Ibid., pp. 233–236.
12 Ibid., pp. 173, 269.

he launched in 1964, was to show the structural method in action—to derive from an exhaustive "coding" of mythic material a "picture of the world already inscribed in the architecture" of the human mind.[13]

Drawing his data from the Indians of South America whom he knew at first hand, Lévi-Strauss focused his attention on myths dealing with food, tobacco, and the transformations raw meat and plants underwent in being prepared for human use. The first volume analyzed how the practice of cooking had altered man's relations with nature; the second traced the more complex symbolic significance of smoking and eating honey. In the remote past, the mythic material suggested, men had simply laid out their food on stones to be warmed by the heat of the sun: the sun's rays had united heaven and earth in a harmony in which mankind felt itself to be in no way separate from the world of nature. With the change to cooked food, these relations were profoundly altered: the introduction of cooking was the decisive step in the passage from nature to culture; man was cut off both from the gods and from the animals who ate their food raw. In consequence, his world became problematic and threatening. Only through the mediation of friendly and helpful animals—the tapirs or jaguars or opossums who were the protagonists of the major myths—could a precarious cosmic order be restored.[14]

In his first volume Lévi-Strauss set up a series of opposites that were simple and tangible: the raw as against the cooked, the fresh as against the rotten, the dry as against the humid. In his second volume—the one that dealt with honey and tobacco—the contrasts were more abstract and equivocal: "empty and full, container and contained, internal and external, included and excluded," plus variants in between.[15] This procedure by pairs was the key feature of Lévi-Strauss's coding: it constituted his method of reducing myth to its component

---

13 Le Cru et le cuit (Mythologiques, I) (Paris, 1964), p. 346; English translation, The Raw and the Cooked (New York, 1969).

14 Ibid., pp. 172, 295, 333.

15 Du miel aux cendres (Mythologiques, II) (Paris, 1966), p. 406.

parts, "retaining . . . only a small number of elements suitable for expressing contrasts and forming pairs of opposites." Such codes, he argued, were capable of transformations from one into another. Among them there were no "privileged semantic levels."[16] In a universe of concepts liberated from the "servitude" of "concrete experience," all relationships were equally meaningful—or perhaps equally lacking in significance.[17]

The work of coding and transformation—carried out in meticulous detail—made *Mythologiques* exceedingly difficult to read. It also raised the central problem of meaning in Lévi-Strauss's whole enterprise, which will occupy us shortly: what was one to make of an endeavor that the author himself described as a kind of mythologizing of mythic material?[18] Moreover, all question of meaning aside, certain peripheral features of these volumes were sufficiently extraordinary to suggest both the fascination his work exerted, particularly on the young, and his reputation as an elusive and hermetic thinker.

In *Mythologiques* the mannerism that had always been latent in Lévi-Strauss's prose became explicit and obtrusive. The work was quite unnecessarily precious in tone, and the first volume was organized around a labored (and frequently inappropriate) analogy with musical composition, its chapters including an overture, theme and variations, sonata, symphony, cantata, and fugue. Evidently the author enjoyed playing cat-and-mouse with his readers. As one British critic put it, half admiring and half exasperated:

The prose of Lévi-Strauss is a very special instrument. . . . It has an austere, dry detachment, at times reminiscent of La Bruyère and Gide. It uses a careful alternance of long sentences, usually organized in ascending rhythm, and of abrupt Latinate phrases. While seeming to observe the conventions of neutral, learned presentation, it allows for brusque personal interventions and asides. Momentarily, Lévi-Strauss appears to be taking the reader into his confidence, . . . making him ac-

---

16 *Le Cru et le cuit,* p. 347.

17 *Du miel aux cendres,* p. 407.

18 *Le Cru et le cuit,* p. 14.

complice to some deep, subtle merriment at the expense of the subject or of other men's pretensions in it. Then he withdraws behind a barrier of technical analysis and erudition so exacting that it excludes all but the initiate.[19]

Thus, a writer who ostensibly made no claim to being a literary figure in fact very consciously contrived his work for its effect as literature. And the stance he adopted toward his subject matter was equally ambivalent—stoicism and disengagement alternating with warm human sympathy. If he ruthlessly saw through all meanings and directed his attention to structure alone, he was not ashamed to give voice to his own values when his emotions were stirred: he could write with transparent anger of the ravages of a Western technology that converted South Sea islands into "stationary aircraft-carriers" and threw its "filth . . . in the face of humanity"; he could bemoan the irony of his profession that condemned him to hasten "in search of a vanished reality."[20] He loved his métier; yet it brought him to near-despair as he watched how contact with "advanced" societies dissolved his subject matter before his very eyes. To the young French of the 1960s, such reflections carried the ring of truth: in France too the achievement of technical modernity was being purchased at a painful psychic cost. In sum, the secret of Lévi-Strauss's immense influence lay in his talent for "carrying out a rigorous and strictly scientific work, while at the same time reflecting on this work, examining its method, extracting the philosophic elements from it, and remaining through it all a kind of Rousseau, both misanthropic and a friend of mankind, who sometimes dreams of reconciling East and West by completing the economic liberation inherent in Marxism with a spiritual liberation of Buddhist origin.[21]

The relation to Marx was one central problem that Lévi-

---

19 "Orpheus with His Myths," *The Times Literary Supplement,* LXIV (April 29, 1965): 321. (Reprinted in this volume.)

20 *Tristes Tropiques* (English translation), pp. 39, 45.

21 Jean Lacroix, *Panorama de la philosophie française contemporaine* (Paris, 1966), p. 222.

Strauss's work raised. The relation to Freud was another. Beyond these lay the question of his attitude toward his own contemporaries—more particularly Sartre—and toward the high valuation they placed on historical understanding. Finally, and most troublingly, loomed the problem of meaning, the ground on which compromise between Lévi-Strauss and his adversaries was next to impossible.

Marx he encountered early in life, when as a boy of about seventeen he met a young Belgian Socialist.

A whole world was opened to me. My excitement has never cooled: and rarely do I tackle a problem in sociology or ethnology without having first set my mind in motion by reperusal of a page or two from the 18th Brumaire of Louis Bonaparte or the Critique of Political Economy. Whether Marx accurately foretold this or that historical development is not the point. Marx followed Rousseau in saying—and saying once and for all, so far as I can see—that social science is no more based upon events than physics is based upon sense-perceptions. Our object is to construct a model, examine its properties and the way in which it reacts to laboratory tests, and then apply our observations to the interpretation of empirical happenings.

No more than Merleau-Ponty in his final guise, could Lévi-Strauss be called a Marxist in any simple meaning of the term. It was rather that for him, as for so many of his French contemporaries, Marxism remained a source of inspiration and a point of departure for social-science method.

It was comparable, Lévi-Strauss found, both to geology and to psychoanalysis in that all three tried to reduce an obvious reality to a less apparent one that took care to "evade our detection." In all three cases, the problem was the same— "the relation . . . between reason and sense perception"—as was the goal pursued, which could be defined as a "super-rationalism," an integration of sense perceptions into reasoning in which the former would "lose none of their properties."[22]

Yet if Lévi-Strauss was convinced that Marx had been on

---

22 Tristes Tropiques (English translation), p. 61.

the right track, he was less sure about Freud. One senses that psychoanalytic theory was a point of special difficulty for him: of the various "codes" his predecessors had offered, it was the most recalcitrant to the universal relativizing process at which he aimed. Much of what he wrote in *Mythologiques* about the trauma mankind had undergone in tearing itself loose from the world of nature seemed of a piece with Freud's own musings in *Civilization and Its Discontents*. But this was Freudianism in its speculative and quasi-anthropological manner: toward its clinical claims Lévi-Strauss was more severe. He warned against the possibility that psychoanalytic therapy might result in no more solid a "cure" than a conversion on the part of the patient to the particular and limited mental set of the therapist himself. This was substantially what sorcerers and shamans had always done—and in a tone of scarcely veiled patronizing, Lévi-Strauss remarked that the psychoanalysts of today might learn something from comparing their methods and goals with those of their "great predecessors."[23] Such tolerance for magical procedures, however, did not extend to the work of Jung. Whatever superficial similarities their common interest in the realm of myth might suggest, Lévi-Strauss found Jung's "obscurantism . . . quite abhorrent." Still more, the latter had committed the supreme methodological error of directing his attention to the content of myth rather than to its form.[24]

The emotions, Lévi-Strauss argued, explained nothing; they were "consequences, never causes." These latter could be sought only in a biological investigation of the organism, or in the intellect, which was the "sole way offered to psychology, and to anthropology as well."[25] Lévi-Strauss's own method of coping with the emotions was to intellectualize them. He reduced subjectivity to its "intellectual laws," proposing a "se-

23 "Le sorcier et sa magie" (originally published in *Les temps modernes*, IV, 1949), "L'efficacité symbolique" (originally published in *Revue de l'histoire des religions*, CXXXV, 1949), *Structural Anthropology*, pp. 182–185, 201–204.

24 George Steiner, "A Conversation with Claude Lévi-Strauss," *Encounter*, XXVI (April 1966): 35.

25 *Totemism*, p. 71.

quence of constantly narrower definitions of the unconscious."[26] The result, as the philosopher Paul Ricoeur· complained, was an unconscious that was "rather . . . Kantian than Freudian," an unconscious that dealt in categories and combinations—a formulation of his own thought to which Lévi-Strauss in the end was quite willing to assent.[27]

This process of intellectualization, in terms of method and sympathy, put him closer to Marx than to Freud. While the accusation of hostility to psychoanalysis seems to have bothered him very little, he was quick to reply to the Marxist charge that he was a foe of progress.[28] A lingering affinity for Marxism kept him safely within the camp of France's left-oriented intellectuals and helps explain the surprisingly respectful attention he gave to the work of Jean-Paul Sartre.

Lévi-Strauss regarded the *Critique of Dialectical Reason* as a sufficiently important cultural phenomenon to warrant his devoting to it a special and concluding chapter of his *Savage Mind* and to linking up with it his own reflections on the study of history. Sartre was right, Lévi-Strauss agreed, in distinguishing the dialectical from the analytic method, but he refused to accept the former's sharp separation of the two. Rather than being of a different logical order, the dialectic was a prolongation of analysis onto new and risky territory. Moreover, Sartre had muddled his account by equating dialectical reasoning (in its "true" form) with the historical consciousness of the West, while describing such a procedure among "primitives" as a merely repetitive process that was close to the biological level. Nor was this the end of Sartre's confusions. "In his manner of invoking history," he had mixed up three common but quite distinct meanings of the term—the "history men make unconsciously," the "history of men consciously made by histo-

---

26 Emilio Renzi, "Sulla nozione di inconscio in Lévi-Strauss," *Aut Aut*, No. 88 (July 1965), pp. 57–58.

27 "Structure et herméneutique," *Esprit*, XXXI (November 1963): 600; "Réponses à quelques questions," *ibid.*, p. 633.

28 *Structural Anthropology*, Chapter 16; see also Edmund Leach, "Claude Lévi-Strauss—Anthropologist and Philosopher," *New Left Review*, No. 34 (November–December 1965), pp. 17–19.

rians," and the subsequent interpretations philosophers put on the two previous types of activity.[29]

Most of the time, Lévi-Strauss found, Sartre's work fell within the third definition; he was the architect of a grand historical design in the Hegelian manner. And as such, what Sartre had offered ranked as a "first-class ethnographic document" (again the note of patronizing) that could claim the dignity of myth. Indeed, Lévi-Strauss seemed to suggest, the nobility of Sartre's attitude lay in the intense fashion with which he lived his own myth—the myth of the French Revolution and its thunderous twentieth-century successors. Lévi-Strauss personally had nothing against this way of thinking—as a part-time adherent of the Left he even shared in it—he simply maintained that "in a different register" of their consciousness people like Sartre and himself should recognize that their ideological notion of historical meaning did not constitute eternal truth and that posterity would regard things quite differently.[30] Moreover, they should take care, as Sartre had not done, to distinguish their reflections on history from the second meaning of the word, that is, the history of the historians.

The accusation of antihistoricism lodged against Lévi-Strauss almost invariably referred to the speculative, Hegelian activity that exerted so strong an attraction on postwar French intellectuals. And in such a form he was perfectly willing to accept the charge; he had no use for historicity as the "last refuge of a transcendental humanism."[31] The majestic type of history with a capital "H" was quite foreign to his own concept of social science. But for what the professional historians did he voiced real sympathy. He referred to it as a type of study complementary to anthropology, which organized its data "in relation to conscious expressions of social life," while anthropology proceeded by "examining its unconscious foundations." Nor could even this division be airtight. "To an increasing degree," Lévi-Strauss found, the historian was calling "to his

---

29 *The Savage Mind*, pp. 246, 248, 250–251.

30 *Ibid.*, pp. 249n., 254–255.

31 *Ibid.*, p. 262.

aid the whole apparatus of unconscious elaborations. . . . Any good history book" was "saturated with anthropology"—Lucien Febvre's study of sixteenth-century disbelief offering an illustrious example.[32] Throughout the inaugural lecture he delivered at the Collège de France in 1960, Lévi-Strauss scattered conciliatory remarks in the direction of his historical colleagues. And six years later in his *Mythologiques*, he repeated the reassurance: far from refusing to recognize the claims of history, structural analysis granted it a position of first importance— the position that belonged "by right to the irreducible contingency without which necessity would not even be conceivable."[33]

So much seemed clear: the contingency that historians studied was the indispensable prerequisite to Lévi-Strauss's own efforts to establish the basic categories of human thought and action. In such a methodological program Bloch and Febvre might well have concurred. Or at the very least they would have been willing to give the new procedure a fair hearing. This was the line their successors on the *Annales* took in assessing Lévi-Strauss's work; as long-time proponents of a unified study of man, they were bound to welcome it—if only as a "cathartic" which forced them to question the very language of their craft.[34] Yet with whatever good will historians might greet Lévi-Strauss's attempt to find structure in history, the type of analysis to which he was inviting them to adjust was not always clear. In his methodological statements—as in his *Mythologiques*—he seemed to be proposing a reduction (or coding) of historical material on a mechanistic model; in the bulk of his published work he proceeded in the more conventional anthropological fashion of trying to understand an exotic society in its own terms.[35] The latter was approximately what the school of Bloch and Febvre had been doing all along. The

32 *Structural Anthropology*, pp. 18, 23.

33 *Du miel aux cendres*, p. 408.

34 Roland Barthes, "Les sciences humaines et l'oeuvre de Lévi-Strauss," *Annales: économies—sociétés—civilisations*, XIX (November–December 1964): 1085–1086.

35 Gaboriau, "Anthropologie structurale et histoire," pp. 592–594.

former was a program so alien to the historian's mentality that he had no choice but to watch its development from a respectful distance.

However polite Lévi-Strauss might be to the professional historians—however carefully he distinguished their work from the ideological exploitation of history that he criticized in Sartre— on one point he refused to compromise: he was unwilling to accord history the status of a privileged order of knowledge that constituted the special cultural superiority of the West. To have done so would have been inconsistent with the radical relativism of his approach and with the equal weighting he gave to the values of "cold" societies as against the "hot." In this final sense, there remained an irreconcilable incompatibility between Lévi-Strauss and those who thought in primarily historical terms.

By training and temperament historians were more concerned with the content than with the formal characteristics of their subject. They were similarly inclined to take the values they studied "straight"—rather than trying to convert them into an abstract and universal code. What Lévi-Strauss was after was precisely the opposite: he believed that content in itself had no meaning; it was only the way in which the different elements of the content were combined that gave a meaning.[36] But once meaning had been drained of content, what was left? This was the ultimate question historians and philosophers and social scientists proposed: was there in fact any meaning to Lévi-Strauss's infinitely ingenious constructions?

The basic trouble with this method—quite aside from the closed conceptual universe it presupposed—was that it made no value distinctions among the coded relationships it established. Nor could it even lay claim to an exhaustive process of coding: the elements that went into it, as in the performance of a computer, were limited to the small number that were capable of unambiguous manipulation. The result was perhaps no more than a glorious cerebral game. Or, in terms of formal philosophy, it amounted to a "discourse" at once "fascinating"

---

36 Steiner, "Conversation with Lévi-Strauss," p. 35.

and "disquieting"—an "admirable syntactical arrangement" that said nothing.[37]

Thus, in one guise Lévi-Strauss could be considered the most extreme and consistent of the students of society who in the 1940s and 1950s—throughout the Western world—were inaugurating a new and more sophisticated positivist method. He was convinced that he had fulfilled—or was about to fulfill—the social scientist's eternal dream of integrating method and reality.[38] He had re-established the structure of the mind as basically rational; he accepted the word "determinism"; he was unafraid of materialist explanations. In so doing, Lévi-Strauss accomplished the extraordinary feat of carrying out a universally applicable and intellectualist program in the dominant French tradition while at the same time linking up with the work of other neopositivists outside France who were attracted by the rigor and elegance of his method: he broke out of his countrymen's cultural confinement while remaining authentically and recognizably French.

But there was also Lévi-Strauss's second guise as *moraliste* and *philosophe*, the heir of Montaigne, Montesquieu, and Rousseau. If his first incarnation was of greater interest to the world of science, the second was the source of his prestige among the general public. For it was here that in true eighteenth-century manner he held up the cultural universe of the "primitives" among whom he had dwelt as a mirror in which the French (and Westerners as a whole) could find a critique of their own society. He grieved over the defenseless savages whose way of life stood condemned by material "progress." In a tone of lyric pathos he had written in his travel notebook of the 1930s a passage on the tiny remnant of the once great Nambikwara people, which he was to publish two decades later and which may stand as a sample and symbol of this elegiac aspect of his thought:

---

37 Paul Ricoeur in "Réponses à quelques questions," p. 653.

38 *Totemism*, p. 91. This universalist claim provides the point of attack for Clifford Geertz's expert and ably reasoned critique: "The Cerebral Savage: On the Work of Claude Lévi-Strauss," *Encounter*, XXVII (April 1967): 25–32.

The campfires shine out in the darkened savannah. Around
the hearth which is their only protection from the cold, . . .
beside the baskets filled with the pitiable objects which comprise all their earthly belongings, the Nambikwara lie on the
bare earth. . . . When they lie entwined together, couple by
couple, each looks to his mate for support and comfort and
finds in the other a bulwark, the only one he knows, against
the difficulties of every day and the meditative melancholia
which from time to time overwhelms the Nambikwara. The
visitor who camps among the Indians for the first time cannot
but feel anguish and pity at the sight of a people so totally dis-
provided for; beaten down into the hostile earth . . . by an
implacable cataclysm; naked and shivering beside their gutter-
ing fires. . . . Laughing whispers can still make light of the
Nambikwara's poverty. Their embraces are those of couples
possessed by a longing for a lost oneness. . . . In one and all
there may be glimpsed a great sweetness of nature, a profound
nonchalance, an animal satisfaction as ingenuous as it is charm-
ing, and, beneath all this, something that can be recognized as
one of the most moving and authentic manifestations of human
tenderness.[39]

During his stay with the Nambikwara, Lévi-Strauss had discovered a "society reduced to its simplest expression"—a society
in which "nothing but human beings" remained. It was perhaps
a "vestigial version of what Rousseau had in mind" when he
spoke of a state of nature. As he had proceeded with his field
investigations, Lévi-Strauss's respect for Rousseau had steadily
grown. The author of Emile and The Social Contract, he sur-
mised, had seen the necessity of setting up a model—based on
an exact correspondence to no existing social state—which
would orient future investigations by "enabling us to distinguish the characteristics common to the majority of human
societies." And Lévi-Strauss was "inclined to think" that Rousseau "was right" in believing that the "image nearest" to this
model "was what we now call the neolithic age. For the author
of Tristes Tropiques, as for the philosophe he hailed as his
"master" and "brother," the neolithic was the norm.[40]

---

39 Tristes Tropiques (English translation), p. 285.
40 Ibid., pp. 310, 389–390.

We who dwell in "hot" societies, he constantly implied, could well take lessons from those who have no truck with change. And in an interview he gave after the publication of the second volume of his *Mythologiques*, he made this injunction, and with it his own attitude, explicit at last:

I have little taste for the century in which we live. What seems to me the present tendency is on the one hand man's total mastery over nature and on the other hand the mastery of certain forms of humanity over others. My temperament and my tastes lead me far more toward periods which were less ambitious and perhaps more timid but in which a certain balance could be maintained between man and nature, among the various and multiple forms of life, whether animal or vegetable, and among the different types of culture, of belief, of customs, or of institutions. I do not strive to perpetuate this diversity but rather to preserve its memory.[41]

Thus—despite the contradictions he recognized in such an attitude—Lévi-Strauss found that an anthropologist like himself almost inevitably became a "critic at home" and a "conformist elsewhere."[42] Abroad he resented the inroads of "civilization" on his "primitives." In his own country he saw more starkly than his fellow-citizens what was out of the human scale in modern industrial society. The same range of sympathy came into play in both cases. In this perspective it was perfectly consistent for Lévi-Strauss to preserve an attachment to the ideological Left; it was thoroughly understandable that he should have joined Sartre and the other members of the celebrated "121" in their opposition to the Algerian War.

Yet with Lévi-Strauss—whether in his mood of conservation or with his voice of protest—there was a difference of "register," as he would put it, from other intellectuals of his generation. There was a tone of acceptance, of cosmic resignation in the face of nature reminiscent of Buddhism. "The world began without the human race," he declared in one

---

41 "A contre-courant," p. 31.
42 *Tristes Tropiques* (English translation), p. 384.

of his most quoted utterances, "and it will end without it."[43] Lévi-Strauss was anything but a doctrinaire opponent of progress; his outlook necessarily made him favor the kind of change that would reduce human want and suffering. But he was far more aware than the run of his contemporaries of the enormous price in ugliness and cultural dislocation that progress entailed. His conception of freedom, alternately elegiac and utopian, was authentically of the late twentieth century in that it looked beyond the liberal or radical or Marxist ideology to a time Saint-Simon had glimpsed in his prediction that humanity would finally pass "from the government of men to the administration of things." Lévi-Strauss yearned for that distant era when the imperative of progress would have ceased to operate—or better, when machines would have taken over the task of social improvement—and when the characteristics of the hot and the cold cultures would be gradually fused, until humanity was liberated at last from the "age-old curse which forced it to enslave men in order to make progress possible."[44]

---

43 *Ibid.*, p. 397.
44 Collège de France, *Leçon inaugurale faite le mardi 5 janvier 1960 par M. Claude Lévi-Strauss*, pp. 43–44.

3

LÉVI-STRAUSS IN THE GARDEN OF EDEN: AN EXAMINATION OF SOME RECENT DEVELOPMENTS IN THE ANALYSIS OF MYTH

EDMUND LEACH

The study of myth has always had a central place in anthropological studies, but the views of anthropologists have varied greatly both on matters of definition and of interpretation. In this respect the celebrities of the past 80 years fall into two classes. First, there is a group of writers whom we may call *symbolists*—among whom I would class James G. Frazer, Sigmund Freud, and Ernst Cassirer in his earlier phase—who assume that the elements of myth are to be understood as symbols that are pieced together into a nonrational story much as in a fairy tale or dream. These writers

From *Transactions of the New York Academy of Science*, Ser. II, Vol. XXIII, No. 4 (February 1961), pp. 386–396.

hold that the "purpose" or "meaning" of myth is one of two kinds: (1) myth "explains the inexplicable," for example, the origin of the world, the origin of death; (2) myth is a kind of word magic that purports to alter the harsh facts of reality by manipulating symbolic representations of these facts.

Common to all symbolist writers is the view that a myth can be understood as "a thing in itself" without any direct reference to the social context in which it is told; the meaning can be discovered from a consideration of the words alone.

The second group of writers are the functionalists—among whom I would class Emile Durkheim and his associates, Jane Harrison, B. Malinowski, and Cassirer in his later phase. The key theme here is the assumption of an intimate and direct association between myth and social action; the myth and its associated rite are held to be two aspects of the same unitary whole.

The most explicit formulation of this doctrine was provided by Malinowski (1926) in his well-known essay *Myth in Primitive Psychology*. Myth provides a "charter" or justification for facts in the present-day social situation. For example, in the Trobriand myth of emergence, it is recorded that the brother and sister founder ancestors of each matrilineal subclan emerged from holes in the ground, the positions of which are precisely recorded by tradition. Each ancestral hole is located in territory that is today regarded as the hereditary property of the subclan descendants of the original founder ancestors. Thus a tale that, considered in isolation, has all the appearance of fantasy is seen to "make sense" when related to its social context. Within the framework of Trobriand ideas this myth has the force of a legal precedent in a court of law.

As Lévi-Strauss puts it: "This theory assumes that myth and rite are homologous . . . the myth and the rite reproduce each other, the one at the level of action the other at the level of ideas." (Lévi-Strauss, 1956, p. 289.)

It is a necessary corollary of this functionalist thesis that myth can be studied *only* within its social context. A myth divorced from its associated rite can have no meaning. Myth is never "a thing in itself."

British social anthropologists of my generation·were brought up to believe that, on this issue, Malinowski was right. Detailed modifications of his original theory might be possible, but the essentials of the argument were unassailable.

One consequence of this acceptance of the functionalist thesis has been that the collections of "literary myths" that exist in ethnographic libraries and in the sacred writings of the more sophisticated religions have come to be neglected by the professional anthropologist. Such myths, in the form in which we now have them, are clearly "divorced from their ritual context"; hence, according to the functionalist dogma, they cease to be of interest.

The same line of reasoning eliminates from the field of serious academic discussion the whole of the works of Frazer and other exponents of the Frazerian "comparative method." Many of the comparisons to which Frazer draws our attention are very striking, but since Frazer consistently ignored the context of his evidence, it is a matter of functionalist dogma that we must ignore the apparent implications.

In a number of essays published over the last four years, Lévi-Strauss has quite explicitly repudiated the functionalist thesis (the key document is Lévi-Strauss, 1955) in favor of a revised form of "symbolist" analysis that he calls structural. Lévi-Strauss denies the existence of any causal link by which myth overtly justifies the patterning of social action or vice versa. He concedes that myths and rites that occur in the same cultural environment may very well share a common structure. Hence, if the element of a myth or the elements of an associated rite are treated as the elements in a logical statement, the myth and the rite may appear to "say the same thing." Nevertheless, myth and rite are independent and each can be studied in isolation.

According to Lévi-Strauss, the best method of ascertaining the "meaning" of a myth is to assemble together all the variant forms in which it has been recorded, regardless of their date or source. What we are looking for is the fundamental essence, and this essence, according to Lévi-Strauss, is a matter of logical structure that will persist throughout all the diversities of form by which the myth story has been perpetuated. A comparison of the different versions of a single myth complex will reveal this common structural nexus, and it is this common structure that really gives "meaning" and importance to those who recount the myth.

If we accept this view, then it follows that, despite anything that Malinowski may appear to have demonstrated, the social anthropologist is fully entitled to study myth as "a thing in itself" without regard to detailed consideration of social or ritual context. I do not ask anyone to suspend his critical judgment. Lévi-Strauss's thesis has many weaknesses, and some of them seem a good deal more damaging than the alleged weaknesses of functionalism. Nevertheless, he has made out a case. At the very least he has demonstrated that the functionalist thesis in its more orthodox form is unnecessarily inhibiting. He has reopened what had begun to look like a closed argument. We need not accept Lévi-Strauss's views in every particular, but it is quite clear that the proper understanding of myth is once again a very open question.

As Lévi-Strauss himself recognizes, his new theory is exceedingly difficult to put to the test. In effect, he postulates that the symbolic elements in a myth are analogous to neutral pebbles of diverse colors. One cannot discover what the elements "mean" by any straightforward technique of intuition or verbal interpretation; all that one can do is observe how the pebbles are grouped together into patterns. In principle, this patterning (or structure) of the symbols in relation to each other is a matter of statistics. Lévi-Strauss maintains that a really thorough application of the method would entail the use of punched cards and the services of an electronic computer (Lévi-Strauss, 1955). Since most of us operate under the delusion that some myths appear meaningful in a fairly straightforward way, this kind of intellectual sophistication may arouse suspicion; nevertheless, I suggest that the matter be given serious consideration.

If we accept Lévi-Strauss's view, the heart of the matter

is that myth furnishes a "logical" model by means of which the human mind can evade unwelcome contradictions, such as that human beings cannot enjoy life without suffering death or that rules of incest (which specify that legitimate sex relations can only be between members of opposed kin groups) conflict with a doctrine of unilineal descent. The function of myth is to "mediate" such contradictions, to make them appear less final than they really are and thus more acceptable. This end is not served by isolated myths but by clusters of myths that are similar in some ways but different in others so that, in accumulation, they tend to blur the edges of real (but unwelcome) category distinctions.

Among the examples that Lévi-Strauss has used to illustrate his thesis are the following:

1. He claims that an analysis of certain Pueblo Indian myths shows that the central problem that the myth cluster seeks to resolve is the opposition between life and death. In the myths we find a threefold category distinction: agriculture, hunting, and war. Agriculture is a means to life for man but entails the death of animals. It is thus a mediating middle category.

In another version of the same myth cluster a further threefold category distinction emerges: grass-eating animals, ravens, and predatory animals. Grass-eating animals are vegetarians; they need not kill in order to live. Ravens and predators are meat eaters, but ravens need not kill in order to eat. In accumulation, therefore, argues Lévi-Strauss, this succession of symbol patterns creates a logical model that asserts (or seems to assert) that, after all, life and death are not just the back and front of the same penny, that death is not the necessary consequence of life (Lévi-Strauss, 1955).

2. Lévi-Strauss furnishes other examples. For instance, he claims, rather surprisingly, that the central problem with which the myth of Oedipus is concerned is that of autochthonous creation. In the beginning man was created; but who precisely was created? A man plus a woman of the same kind? If so, then the perpetuation of mankind must have depended upon incest and we are all born in sin. Or was there a double

creation—a man plus a woman of a different kind? In that case what are these two original kinds, and how can we justify a claim to descent from one line of ancestors rather than another?

Perhaps you wonder what all this has to do with the Oedipus myth as you know it, and I do not pretend that the Lévi-Strauss example is easy to follow. Figure 1 may help.

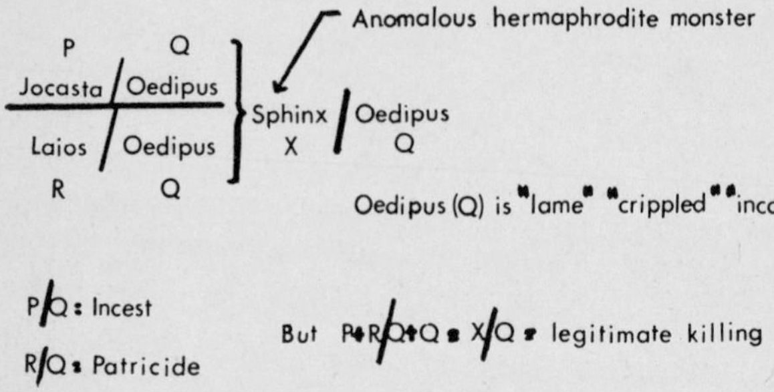

FIGURE 1.

Lévi-Strauss assumes that the myth has a logical form corresponding to the equation: $a:b :: c:d$ (1955, pp. 55–56). The theme of incest (the overemphasis of kinship solidarity), is balanced against the themes of patricide and fratricide (the underemphasis of kinship solidarity), and this corresponds to a similar balance between the highly ambivalent Sphinx and Oedipus, who, in isolation, is incomplete and crippled. The Sphinx is a kind of merging of the two parent figures Jocasta and Laios. Oedipus's legitimate task is to eliminate the Sphinx. He accomplishes this end by sinning doubly—incest with Jocasta and patricide against Laios. Oedipus does not actually kill the Sphinx. The Sphinx, which is primarily female, commits suicide, as does Jocasta. The cause of the suicide is that Oedipus answers the riddle —the answer being, in effect; "the son grows into the father and replaces him" (Lévi-Strauss, 1958, p. 238). On this analysis, the myth centers in a problem of patrilineal descent: the requirement that fathers shall be perpetuated in their sons without the intervention of women, which in simple fact is plainly impossible. However, the impossibility is "resolved" in the myth by mediating the antithesis between male and female parents into the ambivalent person of the Sphinx. Lévi-Strauss is somewhat free with his editing of the mythology, and I have been decidedly free with my editing of Lévi-Strauss. For further enlightenment, I must ask you to read him in the original.

For my part I find the whole analysis extremely interesting. I feel that Lévi-Strauss has a case. We ought to investigate the hypothesis with all the means at our disposal—with or without resort to mathematical computers.

With all this in mind, I decided to take another look at the creation as recorded in Genesis. How well do the various theories about myth that I have mentioned stand up when put to the test against this basic myth of our own society?

The first point that struck me was that the different types of theories that I have mentioned throw the emphasis on different aspects of the story, or rather stories, for, as is well known, there are two distinct creation stories in Genesis.

The symbolists favor the story concerning the Garden of Eden. Frazer and Freud and most medieval artists are in agreement that the core of the story is the matter of Eve and the serpent and the forbidden fruit. From this point of view, the myth seems to provide a rather elementary example of the use of phallic symbolism. Frazer, however, made the further penetrating observation that the Tree of Knowledge of Good and Evil, from which Eve's apple comes, is ambiguously stated to be the Tree of Death that stands opposed to another special tree, the Tree of Life. Moreover, while Adam and Eve were forbidden to eat of the Tree of Death they were not, in the first instance, forbidden to eat of the Tree of Life (Genesis 2, v. 17).

A functionalist approach would be quite different. The story of the seven-day creation provides a mythical charter for the seven-day week. Also, in a more roundabout way, the creation story provides a charter for the Jewish rules of taboo as recorded in Leviticus, chapter 11.

The creation story specifies all living things as belonging to a very limited number of precisely defined categories: fowls of the air, fish, cattle, beasts, and creeping things. Similarly, the plants are categorized as grass, herb-yielding seed (cereals), and fruit trees. It is further specified that the animals are intended to eat the grass while the cereals and the fruit and the meat of the animals themselves are intended for man's exclusive benefit (Genesis 1, vv. 29 and 30). As Mary Douglas has pointed out (Douglas, 1959), the creatures classified as "abominations" in Leviticus 11 are those that break out of these tidy categories: water creatures with no fins, flying creatures with four legs, animals and birds that eat meat or fish, and certain animals that are indiscriminate in their eating habits such as dogs and pigs.[1]

This functionalist treatment of the material leads to an orthodox thesis about the close association of ideas concerning taboo, sacredness, and abnormality (Radcliffe-Brown, 1952, chap. VII).

Having said all this, one notices that it is only the first part of the creation story that seems to serve as a "charter" in Malinowski's sense. The second part—the Garden of Eden story that appeals so strongly to the symbolists—has no obvious implications for the functionalist. Thus, neither the symbolist nor the functionalist approach can be considered adequate. Each tells us something but neither offers an answer to the total question: What is Genesis 1 to 4 all about?

However, if we now apply a Lévi-Strauss style of analysis,

---

1 The thesis that tabooed animals are always "anomalous" in respect to the categories of the creation story holds good in nearly every case but not all. Thus, it is not obvious to me why a camel should be an anomaly. The treatment of "creeping things" in Leviticus 11, vv. 29 to 43, is particularly illuminating in the light of the argument given below. The text starts out by attempting to distinguish as abominable certain special "anomalous creeping things," namely, the weasel, the mouse, the tortoise, the ferret, the chameleon, the lizard, the snail, and the mole, but this leads logically to the conclusion that creeping things are anomalous ab initio, so that at v. 41 we are told that all creeping things without exception are abominations.

everything takes on a completely new shape; moreover, it is a shape that recurs in both parts of the story and is repeated again in a third form in the Cain and Abel story that follows. The complex diagram (Figure 2) has been designed to display this structure. At every step we find the assertion of a category opposition followed by the introduction of a "mediating" category. The seven-day creation story (upper section of the diagram) may be analyzed as follows:

Genesis 1, vv. 1 to 5 (not on diagram). Light divided from darkness. Initial introduction of concept of category opposition, heaven versus earth.

Genesis 1, vv. 6 to 8 (column 1 of diagram). Fresh water above (fertile rain) opposed to (salt) water below (sea). Mediated by firmament (sky).

Genesis 1, vv. 9 and 10 (column 2 of diagram): Sea opposed to dry land.

Genesis 1, vv. 11 and 12 (column 3 of diagram): Mediated by grass, herb-yielding seed, and fruit trees. These grow on dry land but need water. Very significantly, they are classed as things "whose seed is in itself" (thereby contrasted with such creatures as animals and birds, which are divided into males and females).

The creation of the world as a static (that is, dead) entity is now complete, and this whole phase of creation is opposed to the creation of moving (that is, living) things.

Genesis 1, vv. 13 to 18 (column 4 of diagram): The mobile sun and moon are placed in the firmament of column 1. Light and darkness, opposed at the beginning of the story, are now presented as alternations. By implication the life-death opposition is also an alternation.

Genesis 1, vv. 20 to 23 (column 5 of diagram): Fish and birds are living things corresponding to the category opposition of column 2 but they also mediate the oppositions between sky and land and between salt water and fresh water.

Genesis 1, vv. 24 and 25 (column 6 of diagram, left half): Cattle, beasts, and creeping things (that is, domestic animals, wild animals, and anomalous animals) correspond to the static

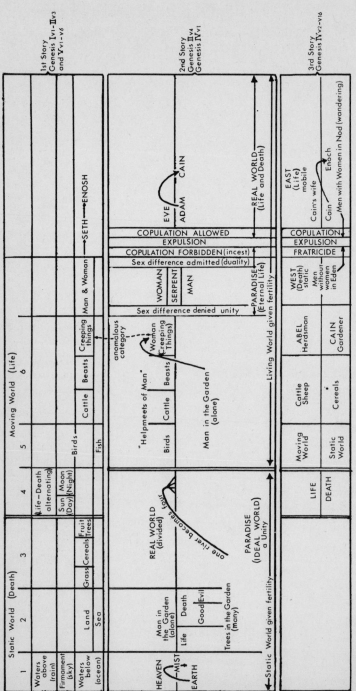

FIGURE 2.

triad of column 3 but are not allocated accordingly. Only grass is allocated to the animals; the rest is reserved for man (vv. 29 and 30).

Genesis 1, vv. 26 and 27 (column 6 of diagram, right half): The final act of creation is the simultaneous creation of man and woman: "Male and female created he them."

The whole system of living creatures is instructed to "be fruitful and multiply," but the problems of life versus death and incest versus procreation are not faced.

The Garden of Eden story that now follows attacks from the start these very problems that have been evaded in the first version. We start again with a category opposition of heaven versus earth, but this is mediated by a fertilizing mist that is drawn up out of the dry infertile earth (Genesis 2, vv. 4 to 6). The same theme recurs throughout the story. Living Adam is formed from "the dust of the ground" (v. 7); so are the living animals (v. 19). The dry lands of the real world are fertilized by a river that comes out of the ground of Eden. In Eden (Paradise) it is a unitary river; in the real world it is divided (vv. 10 to 14). Finally, fertile Eve is formed from the rib of infertile Adam (vv. 22 and 23).

The opposition of Heaven and Earth (column 1) is followed by the opposition of Man and the Garden, and in the Garden are trees that include a Tree of Life and a Tree of Death (column 2: Genesis 2, vv. 8 and 9). Notice that the Tree of Death is called the "Tree of Knowledge of Good and Evil," which might also be called the "knowledge of sexual differ-ence," or the "knowledge of logical categories." The theme is repeated: isolated unitary categories such as man alone, life alone, one river, occur only in ideal Paradise; in the real world things are multiple and divided; man needs a partner, woman; life has a partner, death.

The other living things are now created because of the lone-liness of Man in Eden. The categories are cattle (domestic animals), birds, and beasts (wild animals). These are unsatis-factory as helpmeets of Man, so Eve is drawn from Adam's rib: "they are of one flesh" (columns 5 and 6: Genesis 2, vv. 18 to 24). Comparison of the two stories at this stage shows that Eve in Eden is, from a structural point of view, the same category as "the creeping things" of the first story. Creeping things were anomalous in the category opposition "cattle versus beasts"; Eve is anomalous in the category opposition "man versus animal"; and finally "the serpent" (a creeping thing) is anomalous in the category opposition "man versus woman." The parallels with the Oedipus-Sphinx story are here extremely close, as may be seen from Figures 1 and 3. The Bible does not

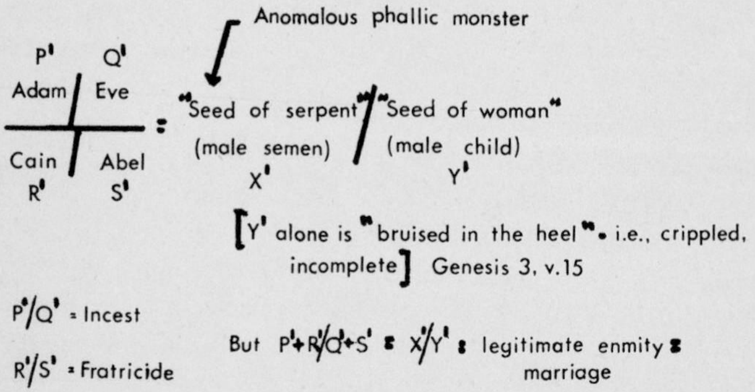

FIGURE 3.

specify the serpent's sex. Medieval artists made it female, Freud might have argued for a male; the structural argument suggests hermaphrodite qualities.

Adam and Eve eat the apple and become aware of sexual difference, and death becomes inevitable (Genesis 3, vv. 3 to 8)—also, of course, pregnancy and life become possible. Significantly, Eve does not become pregnant until after they have been expelled from Paradise (Genesis 4, v. 1). The curse that is imposed on the serpent deserves especial note (Genesis 3, vv. 14 and 15). There is to be enmity between the serpent and the woman and between "the seed of the serpent" and the "seed of the woman"—the latter being specified as male; "*he* shall bruise thy head; and thou shalt bruise *his* heel."

One is inevitably reminded of Lévi-Strauss's point that autochthonous heroes are very commonly lame (Lévi-Strauss, 1955). Indeed, the whole formula parallels that of Oedipus.

If "the seed of the serpent" be here read as "the semen of the father," while "the seed of the woman" be read as the son of the father by his impregnated wife, the curse refers to the opposition between man and woman and the hostility between father and son. It might even be taken as a "charter" for circumcision.

Finally, although very briefly, let us notice that the Cain and Abel story repeats the same story. The opposition between Cain the gardener and Abel the herdsman is the same opposition as that between the first three days of the creation and the last three days, the static world versus the living. Cain must eliminate his brother and substitute a wife in order that a sterile homosexual world shall become a fertile heterosexual world (Genesis 4, v. 17). Some extra elements come in here. The dead world of Eden-paradise is said to lie to the west; the living world (significantly called Nod, "wandering") lies to the east (Genesis 4, v. 16); moreover, although Cain is cursed for the sin of fratricide in terms nearly identical to those imposed on Adam for the sin of incest (compare Genesis 3, vv. 17 to 19 with Genesis 4, v. 11 and 12), he is also declared a sacred person whose life is protected (v. 15).[2] Cain is the ancestor of "wanderers" in general—pastoralists, traveling musicians, traveling metal-workers (Genesis 4, vv. 19 to 24)—groups with special skills but not servile outcasts.

I do not claim that this kind of "structural" analysis is the one and only legitimate procedure for the interpretation of myth. It seems to me that whether any particular individual finds this kind of thing interesting or stimulating must depend on personal temperament; some may think it is too like a conjuring trick. For my part, I do find it interesting. All I have done here is to show that the component elements in some

---

2 Cain's peculiar status as a divinely protected person has been examined from a functionalist point of view by Schapera (1955). Here I am concerned only with the strict structural parallelism between the expulsion of Adam from Paradise followed by the pregnancy of Eve (Genesis 4, v. 1) and the expulsion of Cain from paradise followed by the pregnancy of Cain's wife (Genesis 4, vv. 16 and 17).

very familiar stories are in fact ordered in a pattern of which many have not been previously aware. However, the pattern *is* there; I did not invent it, I have merely demonstrated that it exists. No one will ever again be able to read the early chapters of Genesis without taking this pattern into account. Whether the analysis has any "value" for anthropologists or for anyone else I am not sure, but at least it surely throws new light on the mysterious workings of what Durkheim used to call the "collective conscience."

REFERENCES

DOUGLAS, M.
1959 Leviticus XI. Lecture delivered at University College. London, England. Unpublished.

LÉVI-STRAUSS, C.
1955 The structural study of myth. *In* Myth: A symposium. T. A. Sebeok, Ed. Bibliographical and Special Series of the American Folklore Society 5. Indiana Univ. Press. Bloomington, Ind.

LÉVI-STRAUSS, C.
1956 Structure et dialectique. *In* For Roman Jacobson: Essays on the Occasion of his Sixtieth Birthday: 289–294. Mouton. The Hague, Netherlands.

LÉVI-STRAUSS, C.
1958 Anthropologie Structurale. Libraire Plon. Paris, France.

MALINOWSKI, B.
1926 Myth in Primitive Psychology. Kegan Paul. London, England.

RADCLIFFE-BROWN, A. R.
1952 Structure and Function in Primitive Society. Chap. VII. Cohen and West. London, England.

SCHAPERA, L.
1955 The Sin of Cain. Journal of the Royal Anthropological Institute 85.

4
WHICH MAY NEVER
HAVE EXISTED

FRANCIS HUXLEY

A World on the Wane—this is the title of the British edition of *Tristes Tropiques*, and a gloomy phrase it is. The American edition keeps the original title, which is less extreme but also puzzling. Why are the tropics sad? What world is on the wane?

The opening sentence of the book is strange as well. "Travel and travelling are two things I loathe—and yet here I am, all set to tell the story of my expeditions." No travel book can afford to be quite so frank, and indeed it is not really a travel book. Nor is it an autobiography. If one is to set off on the right foot, the words to look for in the above sentence are "and yet," because worlds of meaning are to come out of them. In the beginning it is difficult to see this: Lévi-Strauss, in

From *The Kenyon Review*, Vol. XXIV, No. 1 (Winter 1962), pp. 150–156. Copyright 1962 by Kenyon College, Gambier, Ohio.

telling us the story of his expeditions and as much of his life as is useful, seems to be like some willful knight on a chessboard, jumping in dog's legs from place to place and topic to topic. From his opening diatribe on travel and travel books—an invigorating performance—he moves to an account of his education, of his first trip, the war, a view of the Antilles, Brazil and—but only in the French edition—a giant leap to India. What is his object? The answer comes later, in the words of Jean-Jacques Rousseau: "To know closely a state which no longer exists, which may never have existed, which probably will never exist . . . ."

He is, of course, an anthropologist. Now according to him an anthropologist is, psychologically speaking, a mutilated man: in a curious revolt against his own society he travels to others to see if they have that which is missing in his own. Should he find what he is looking for, he may by no means keep it, if he is to continue as an anthropologist, for as such he must deny his roots. Therefore, he travels. Travel then becomes a kind of fungus on his material that must be scraped clean before he can work on it. It is, besides, a tantalizing experience, perpetually giving promise of some splendor or revelation—round the corner the landscape will surely people itself with meaning—though a traveler's journals are most often packed with weary details and irritations; with accounts of strange meals, insect bites, broken paddles, and all the perfectly usual discomforts that lie just under the seductive surface of the exotic. Not that, in any case, the exotic is the real subject of anthropology.

If one were a novelist, the exotic might be a legitimate subject. Anthropologists, however, must treat it with care. They are no doubt first drawn to their profession by an urge to have done with the commonplace and to see right into the origin of things. Ever since the discovery of the New World, one of the great romantic longings has been to see Man in his unspoiled condition, placing his splendid meanings wholeheartedly and accurately on the world around him. But how is one to write of such a state of affairs when even the *mise en scène* is not yet understood? Malinowski, the father of anthropo-

logical fieldwork, may have modeled his style on that of Conrad and perhaps wished he might write about the same things:
about the moral nature of man when confronting his enemies
or some great natural turmoil, or even of the effects of the
exotic on his own romantic weakness. Conrad could do it because the moral actions he wrote about were European in style
and more or less simple in nature. Malinowski, in shifting the
context onto his Trobrianders, had first to make sense of all
their customs and activities before he could even consider the
morality of any particular action.

In any case, a man cannot long retain an ambition to be a
novelist in anthropology. There comes a time when he realizes
that there is a sudden discontinuity between the facts he is
dealing with and the ideas which are to make sense out of
them, and that he prefers the ideas to the facts. Anything like
a novelist's response to a situation then disappears, leaving behind it telltale fragments: Lévi-Strauss's great descriptive ability,
for instance, and his way of piecing things together in such a
way that the answer appears just as the last piece is put into
place, are evidence of this, as is his need to write a travel book
despite his loathing for travelers' tales.

His description of the anthropologist as an amputated man
thus makes sense, and so does his title. The world that is on
the wane is that which gives a sense of undisturbed totality, is
that Golden Age where sorrows are somehow dissolved by festiv-
ities and human beings can converse with the forces that sur-
round them. This totality is immensely attractive to an outsider,
whether he be anthropologist, missionary, or tourist. The anthropologist, who seeks sensation despite himself, is eager to
see a society that functions so perfectly, and yet owes a duty
to himself not to fall victim to its morality. For if he does, he
will never see what it is all about, nor will he be able to expose
the fact that a fatal flaw is at the center, and the self-sufficiency
an illusion.

To follow a mind intent upon such an undertaking as far as
it will go is a disconcerting experience. It is as disconcerting
as his chapter on a sunset. Nowhere else, surely, has a sunset
been anatomized so carefully, with such proud and fastidious

precision. As a piece of bravura on an everyday spectacle it certainly comes neither from a novelist's nor a painter's hand, for all its wealth of detail. It is in a genre all its own, finding a gloomy triumph in the splendors of closely observed and reasoned description. At once metaphysical and concrete, he has what is perhaps an architect's eye: an eye for the construction of things, as they await the great event that ought to make sense of them.

We can see something of this in the account of his education. First came logical exercises in the Sorbonne, where problems were to be solved by a skillful if unrewarding dialectic. Second came the discovery of geology—the same subject that nourished Darwin's genius—which gave him an eye for country that two other great influences, Marx and Freud, translated into different spheres. Lastly came the Anglo-American school of anthropology, starting with Lowie, that marvelous observer, "who had been so committed as to keep intact the full meaning of his experience." And, all around him, the great French tradition, from Rousseau to Mauss and Durkheim.

Out of this has come one of the great minds of modern social anthropology. Why Lévi-Strauss chose anthropology is in a sense the subject of this book. The simple answer which he gives is that by it "my life and character were reconciled." Now, such a reconciliation is always a fascinating process, because where there is a vocation there is the closest relationship between what a mind is and what it does; between those, too, and what it chooses to work on. The "tristes tropiques" of the title shows itself, in this light, to be a complicated zone, in which the destruction of the New World, the failure of the exotic, the inability of experience to justify itself and the search for "that which probably will never exist" join hands with an increasing number of other problems. These tropics are sad, too, quite literally: between sunsets and journeys he tells us how Indian cultures change and disappear before the white man, of the earth eroded by bad agriculture, of the peasant Brazilian with his oxcarts and pitiable fiestas. It must also be confessed that this sadness comes partly from a far-seeing pessimism, as witness the wonderful comparison he makes between two equally appalling places: the lugubrious town of Porto Esperança, stuck in the swamps, and the sterile acres of Fire Island, with its homosexual couples. The same kind of sociological absurdity unites these two places, and it is this that he discovers to the reader.

This, then, is how those two words "and yet" are put to work. Two apparently quite different themes are contrasted, and out of their counterpoint a paradox is created and a meaning evolved. Take, for instance, the assortment of facts about the remnants of the Caduveo Indians, near Porto Esperança, out of which he manages to produce a sudden and astonishing view into that state "which may never have existed." These Indians are a kind of Brazilian Spartans who were once supported by the labor of an enslaved population and who lived noble lives of warfare, tournaments, and ceremonial. The early Spaniards called them Don and Dona because of their arrogance, which was caused by a horror of natural functions: thus they plucked out all their body hair, eyelashes included, and disguised their flesh by painting curious designs over it; they also held childbearing in disgust, and raided neighboring tribes for children whom they brought up carefully, in order to keep up their numbers.

Of all things about the Caduveo, the painting on their faces and bodies is the most obvious and enigmatic. Many of the motifs that appear—arabesques, curlicues, angled lines—are to be found elsewhere in South America, but that is hardly important. What is strange is the way they have been put to-together. Many of the patterns, at first, look quite asymmetrical, till a closer examination shows that in fact the pattern is repeated but in reverse and on the bias, like a court card. The image of a court card, as Lévi-Strauss says, is very apposite for the Caduveo, since it too stands for a world of high artificiality, while its skewed design indicates that it is meant to be looked at from both sides simultaneously. However, the fact that the Caduveo cannot retreat from their ideal of artificiality and the nonnatural means that their lives are centered upon the hierarchical principle: not for them the experience of reciprocity, whether in marriage, resulting in reproduction, or between different members of the tribe, since the principle of regarding no one as your equal is at work even here. Yet how can natural impulses entirely be kept down? The Caduveo do practice the division of life into two, and mirror this division on their faces, but since the division is kept unfruitful, and only one of the terms is honored, the pattern is skewed. Thus, concludes Lévi-Strauss,

The mysterious charm and (as it seems at first) the gratuitous complication of Caduveo art may well be a phantasm created by a society whose object was to give symbolical form to the institutions which it might have had in reality, had interest and superstition not stood in the way. Great indeed is the fascination of this culture, whose dream life was pictured on the faces of its queens, as if, in making themselves up, they figured a Golden Age that they would never know in reality. And yet, as they stand before us, it is as much the mysteries of that Golden Age as their own bodies that are unveiled.

"And yet"—a splendid conclusion! For the Golden Age is what we must deal with, since it is the dream of perfect social relationships, even though the dream, being unfulfilled, is forever on the wane. Can it ever come true? Certainly it never has so far, perhaps because the elements of the dream have never been properly examined, obscured as they are by the dream's effect of mystery. However, the examination of this dream is Lévi-Strauss's main concern, and he carries it out, despite his interest in mythology and Freud, consistently in sociological terms. This may seem a backhanded compliment, but it points in fact to one of his greatest achievements. After all, anthropology does deal with society, and all things to do with human beings form miniature societies on their own— look, for instance, at the fascinating relationship between kinship structure and linguistics, which he has described in an essay published elsewhere. And so firm is his hold on the sociological universe that he is not deceived into skating over contradictions by any sense of mystery, even when it is as evasive and apparently fundamental as mana. On the contrary, what is basic for him is precisely the fact of self-contradiction, the very sign and product of symbolic thought, while mana and mystery have no more than a semantic function—much like that of the figure zero, which has no meaning but gives meaning to what it is joined to—in allowing such thought to continue without coming to a stop in its own self-contradictions.

The consequences of this unfriendly definition of the great poetic secret are perhaps hard to bear. We can see them, at a safe distance, in his analysis of the Bororo Indians. This tribe has a moiety and clan system, both exogamous, and each moiety is responsible for carrying out innumerable duties and rites for the benefit of the other. The obligations of reciprocity appear endless: surely here is that anthropological classic, a dualist society, with a perfect balance between duties and pleasures, between men and women, even between the living and the dead, all of them bound into a fraternal relationship. But here we notice the anomaly. The Bororo village, which is a diagram of their society, is circular, the two moieties living in opposite halves. In the middle, however, is the Men's House, the center of religious activity. The women are excluded from it and live on the periphery, they having prior rights in housing and descent. They can, however, witness various ceremonies, such as funerals, when men impersonate the spirits of the dead who come visiting from two spirit villages nearby, and who seem to be responsible for the existence of yet another moiety system that does not at all correspond to the main one.

Can there be two moiety systems in a dualist society? Why are they then not coincident? If we are to take the Bororos' account of things literally, and the dualism were honest, they should be. But underlying the reciprocities between man and man there is quite a different relationship between man and woman, expressed not through the moiety system but in the opposition of the center to the periphery. It is also apparent in that inescapably unequal relationship between the living and the dead which cannot be properly expressed through the dualism of the second moiety system, which is skewed round apparently in an effort to disguise this. And, last of disillusionments, the clan system, which appears exogamous, in fact hides—according to Lévi-Strauss—a stringent endogamous ruling in its heart, and serves three quite separate groups of clans that compose the village. Here indeed is a place for mana to work, to hide the fundamental inequalities that the ceremonies of brotherhood try to overcome, but do so only by falling into further contradictions. Indeed, justice on the Bororos' terms is impossible, not only because men and women are different, but because men do die "and die never to return: and all forms of social order draw us nearer to death, in so much as they take something away from us and give nothing back in return."

No wonder the tropics are sad, if even the dream of a perfect social order is a denial of life. The relationships within a society are always complex, for there cannot be ideals of unity if there are no institutions that keep people separate: the one is the condition of the other. Anthropology then seems to be a purely destructive science, intent on showing up the flaws in every society and demonstrating the absurdity of the human predicament both for its observers and for its actors. Certainly it has once seemed so to Lévi-Strauss, who gives us the plot of a remarkable play he wrote in the jungle, as an analogy of this position. It deals with the clash between Augustus, the representative of social order who is about to be deified and then comes to realize the horrible consequences of an apotheosis, and Cinna, a poet who has exiled himself for years in exotic deserts in order to escape from society, till he finds that the exotic is as tedious and ordinary as Rome itself. This somewhat macabre plot deserves to be read in full, though it has no proper end: the resolution of such a state of affairs, indeed, requires an effort on a different plane. In his last chapters, a profound and moving apology for his vocation, Lévi-Strauss does in fact resolve it, with the help of Rousseau.

Rousseau is perhaps the last person we should expect in such a place. Did he not advocate a return to the Golden Age and the life of the Noble Savage? But this, Lévi-Strauss points out, is an unhappy misreading of his position. The Natural Man for Rousseau was not something separate from Social Man, for society was, he knew, inherent in mankind. What he questioned was the belief that the evils of society are inherent. Our task, says Lévi-Strauss,

is to rediscover the "natural Man" in his relation to the social state outside which our human condition cannot be imagined: the anthropologist must draw up, therefore, the programme of experiments which "are necessary if we are to understand natural Man"; and he must "determine the best way of making these experiments within Society itself."

The solution is exciting, though not easy, leading to that final stage where Augustus and Cinna can meet without wanting to destroy each other and where, in Lévi-Strauss's words, the problem of metaphysics is reconciled with the problem of human behavior. The *Social Contract* here turns into the Great Vehicle, the final and consummate surprise of this remarkable book.

5

SOME CONSIDERATIONS ON THE NATURE OF SOCIAL STRUCTURE AND MODEL BUILDING: A CRITIQUE OF CLAUDE LÉVI-STRAUSS AND EDMUND LEACH

HUGO G. NUTINI

That branch of anthropology, or rather that anthropological approach, that is known today as social anthropology has a long and intricate genealogy that goes back to the eighteenth-century French philosophers Montesquieu and Rousseau, to the encyclopedists, and so forth. The approach to the study of society initiated by these men was kept alive in the nineteenth century by people of such diverse interests as "sociologists," philosophers,

Reproduced by permission of the American Anthropological Association from the *American Anthropologist*, Vol. 67 (1965), pp. 707–731.

"economists," and "scientists," such as Spencer, Comte, Saint-Simon, and Adam Smith. This intellectual tradition culminated in the so-called French sociological school which began in the late nineteenth century with Emile Durkheim as its most important and original exponent.

Implicit in this approach is the holistic idea that societies are not random associations of persons but well-ordered systems with built-in dynamic mechanisms, very much like the combustion engine of a motor car. However, modern anthropologists speak of societies not as being systems but as "having structures." Thus, the term "social structure" is used by most social anthropologists, and occasionally by many who do not call themselves such (they prefer to use "social organization"), with reference to a set of problems that have to do mainly with the description, analysis, and ultimate explanation of social life.

The concept of social structure is strongly associated with Professor A. R. Radcliffe-Brown, who is generally regarded as the most important exponent in England of the theories advocated by the French sociological school. His theoretical approach has dominated the thought of most social anthropologists and has been the chief source of inspiration for much of the work done in England, and to a lesser degree in America, for the past 35 or 40 years.

Although the French sociological school, as exemplified by its three major exponents, Durkheim, Lévy-Bruhl, and Mauss, has been and continues to be the main inspiration of social anthropologists in England and America, it did not produce a major social anthropologist of its own (in the sense of combining in the same person a theoretician and fieldworker) until the appearance of Claude Lévi-Strauss. In his book, Les Structures élémentaires de la parenté, and in several subsequent articles (1951, 1952, 1953, 1956, 1960a, 1960b, 1962a), Lévi-Strauss has put forth a substantially different and improved approach to the study of social structure that makes him one of the few great contributors to this branch of anthropology. Thus, I maintain that Lévi-Strauss's approach to the study of kinship and his general conception of social structure represent the first genuine and important contribution to the development of social anthropological theory since Rivers, Kroeber, Lowie, Radcliffe-Brown, and Malinowski.

In the following pages I shall be concerned largely with Lévi-Strauss's conception of what "social structure" is, as put forth primarily in his article entitled "Social Structure" (1953), an excellent and important work. But however great my admiration for Lévi-Strauss's contributions, I disagree with several aspects of his analysis of social structure and its relationship to a body of empirical data. I hope that the ensuing discussion will shed some light on the explanatory dimensions of social anthropology. Let us begin by stating Lévi-Strauss's position.

I

Social structure, for Lévi-Strauss, is definitely not a province of inquiry or a field of study but an explanatory method that can be applied to any kind of social studies. In his own words, "the object of social-structure studies is to understand social relations with the help of models" (1953:532). For Lévi-Strauss, "the term 'social structure' has nothing to do with empirical reality, but with models which are built up after it" (1953:525). This assertion is the result of the categorical distinction that he makes between the concepts of *social structure* and *social relations*. For Lévi-Strauss, social relations are the raw data of social experience of which the model or models comprising the social structure are built. Social structure, on the other hand, belongs to a different epistemological category; it can never "be reduced to the ensemble of the social relations to be described in a given society" (1953:525).

In the application of structural analysis, Lévi-Strauss goes on to say, we must be careful to distinguish between observation and experimentation and between the conscious and unconscious character of the models involved. The observation of social facts (social relations) and the construction of models after these facts are not the same as to "experiment on the models." By experimentation Lévi-Strauss means simply the controlled comparison of models of the same or of a different kind. Although they are different levels of the same process, these two levels should always be kept separate, with the level of observation always taking precedence over experimentation. Thus, in any type of structural analysis, the first step is to gather and observe the facts without any theoretical bias and to describe them in relation to themselves and in relation to the whole. There should be a direct relationship between the levels of observation and experimentation, or between "the concreteness of ethnographic detail" and the models constructed after it, for in the final analysis the best model is that which accounts for all of the observed facts.

There are conscious and unconscious structural models. Lévi-Strauss is not altogether clear on this point, but it is evident that the distinction between conscious and unconscious models is a matter of degree and not one of categorical differences. Furthermore, they are defined with reference to society and not to the anthropologist who studies society. Conscious models he calls those "homemade" models according to which the society views itself. These are what are usually termed norms, and more often than not they stand in the "collective consciousness" as a screen, hiding a deeper and more transcendental structure. Unconscious models, on the other hand, are those that are not directly or consciously perceived by the society, because they lie at a great depth. It is generally more profitable for the anthropolgist to work with models that he has elicited and constructed out of these deeper-lying phenomena—that is, with unconscious models—than with conscious models or norms, since by definition the latter "are not intended to explain the phenomena but to perpetuate them" (Lévi-Strauss 1953:527). This need not always be the case, as some homemade models are more accurate than any that could be built by the anthropologist. Thus, for two reasons, anthropologists cannot afford to dismiss conscious models when analyzing the structure of a society: even if they are inaccurate, they give an insight into the nature of the deeper structure, and the very errors are part of the social facts under study. Lévi-Strauss concludes that we must at no time forget that "cultural norms are not of themselves structures." Here he seems to be saying that there are only unconscious models, since he equates conscious models with norms.

We finally come to what I think is Lévi-Strauss's most important contribution to the theory of social structure, namely, the distinction between what he calls "mechanical models" and "statistical models." Here again, we must credit Durkheim with having first envisaged the distinction between these two types of models, as exemplified respectively in his books *Division of Labor* and *Suicide*. However, this does not diminish the importance of Lévi-Strauss's formulation of the problem, as he was the first anthropologist to state explicitly the consequences and implications of making such a distinction. Since Durkheim, every anthropologist of note dealing with this area (for example, Radcliffe-Brown, Malinowski, Evans-Pritchard, Fortes) has been aware, explicitly or implicitly, of the problems entailed by this distinction, although not always in the same frame of reference. Thus, I find it difficult to understand why, with the exception of Leach (1954) and Nadel (1957), theoretical anthropologists have paid so little attention to Lévi-Strauss's formulation of this problem and his solution to it, or why they have failed to follow his insightful suggestions. They seem to have been more stimulated by his contributions to the solution of specific problems such as the nature of affinity or cross-cousin marriage than by what he has to say about models and model building.

According to the scale between the model and the phenomena (social relations), there are two basic types of models in social structure, "mechanical models" and "statistical models." Models on the same scale as the phenomena are called "mechanical"; those on a different scale are called "statistical." Lévi-Strauss never explains what he means by "on the same scale as," nor is it entirely clear in the context of the article, but we may safely assume that it refers only to the differential quantitative elements involved in the construction of the models. Furthermore, he does not define the two types of models analytically, but instead characterizes them ostensibly by means of examples. Thus, we are told that "the laws of marriage provide the best illustration of this difference. In primitive societies these laws can be expressed in models calling for factual grouping of the individuals according to kin or clan; these are mechanical models." On the other hand, "no such distribution exists in our own society, where types of marriage are determined by the size of the primary and secondary groups to which prospective mates belong, social fluidity, amount of information, and the like. A satisfactory (though yet untried) attempt to formulate the invariants of our marriage system would therefore have to determine average values—thresholds; it would be a statistical model" (Lévi-Strauss 1953:528). While there is no doubt as to the differing natures of these basic types of structural models, Lévi-Strauss's brevity of exposition and lack of formal definition arouse a feeling of uncertainty as to the inherent characteristics of the models by themselves.

In studies of social structure it is important to keep two things constantly in mind. First, there may be intermediate forms between mechanical and statistical models, such as "the case in societies which have a mechanical model to determine prohibited marriages and rely on a statistical model for those which are permissible" (Lévi-Strauss 1953:528). Second, in order to explain a given set of social facts, it may be necessary to construct both mechanical and statistical models, depending on the internal relationship of these facts and their relationship to other social facts. For example, "a society which recommends cross-cousin marriage but where this ideal marriage type occurs only with limited frequency needs, in order that the system may be properly explained, both a mechanical and a statistical model" (Lévi-Strauss 1953:528).

In conclusion, Lévi-Strauss maintains that the value of structural studies lies in the comparable nature of the structures as models, so that the work of the structuralist is to "recognize and isolate levels of reality which have strategic value from his point of view, namely, which admit of representation as models, whatever their kind" (1953:528). This declaration should make clear the dual character and ultimate aim of structural studies. On the one hand, "they aim at isolating strategic levels, and this can be achieved only by 'carving out' a certain family of phenomena." On the other hand, "the essential value of these studies is to construct models the formal properties of which can be compared with, and explained by, the same properties as in models corresponding to other strategic levels" (Lévi-Strauss 1953:529).

An assessment and criticism of Lévi-Strauss's theory of social structure would be incomplete without a discussion of Edmund Leach's position on the same topic. Under the influence of Lévi-Strauss, Leach has expressed very similar views on the nature of social structure. It would be useful to outline Leach's position briefly before dealing with Lévi-Strauss, and to criticize both at the same time.

As early as 1945 ("Jinghpaw Kinship Terminology"), Leach was concerned with the nature of social structure. In more recent years (1951, 1957, 1958), under the stimulating influence of Lévi-Strauss, which he explicitly acknowledges, he has more or less independently formulated a conception of social structure that is essentially the same as Lévi-Strauss's. In the same manner as Lévi-Strauss, Leach "bifurcates" (and I shall have more to say about this concept presently) the "social universe" into different epistemological categories: the raw data of social experience, and the models that are constructed from it. This he does by denying the empirical reality of the models. As he puts it, "the structures which the anthropologist describes" are no more real than "models which exist only as logical constructions in his mind"; in a different context, they "provide us with an idealized model which states the 'correct' status relations between groups . . . and . . . social persons" (1954:5, 9). In a milder form, he says that "kinship systems have no 'reality' at all except in relation to land and property" (1961:305). But here again, as with Lévi-Strauss, Leach seems dogmatic in this assertion, inasmuch as he never explains the substantive meaning of denying the empirical reality of the models, or the implications that follow such a stand. The distinction between the raw data of social experience and the models built after it is a useful one, but both Leach and Lévi-Strauss have obliterated its usefulness and have exposed themselves to serious objections by not analyzing the full implications of making such a categorical distinction between experience and its positional models.

Leach is particularly anxious to avoid reification, that is, the treatment of social structure, which he considers a mental construct, as a "thing"; he rightly charges Radcliffe-Brown, Fortes, Evans-Pritchard, and even Durkheim himself with having done this, although they started from different premises. Leach himself arrives at the postulation of mechanical and statistical models in the same fashion as Lévi-Strauss. Mechanical models he calls "jural rules," while statistical models are termed "statistical norms," but despite the differences in terminology the concepts stand for approximately the same referents. However, it is important to note that Leach goes beyond Lévi-Strauss in two ways. First, unlike Lévi-Strauss, who at least implies that mechanical and statistical models, as explanatory constructs, are of roughly equal heuristic value and that they complement each other, Leach maintains that "jural rules and statistical norms should be treated as separate frames of reference, but that the former should always be considered secondary to the latter" (Leach 1961:9). My reaction to the second part of his statement coincides with that of Oliver, who says in his review of *Pul Eliya* that the subordination of jural rules to statistical norms "cannot be proved by findings from any one—or any 100—societies" (Oliver 1962:622). Second, following Durkheim, Leach elaborates on the inherent nature of mechanical and statistical models and rightly points out the important fact that mechanical models or jural rules are qualitative rules of behavior that are supported by sanctions and have (or should have) coercive power, whereas statistical models or norms are only statistical averages of individual behavior that have no coercive power (1961:297-298), although he maintains that jural rules as such are mere fictions.

I have briefly outlined Lévi-Strauss's and Leach's views on the nature of social structure, and I contend that they have presented anthropologists with the first genuine and original contribution to the theory and study of social structure since Radcliffe-Brown. Moreover, I believe that their views should be carefully studied if we wish to advance our discipline to the status of a science. I agree with their orientation and with most of their concrete ideas regarding the nature of social structure, but I must register a certain disagreement by criticizing them on two counts. One is fundamental and the others are semantical, since a more systematic exposition and clarification of terms could do away with them. My fundamental criticism of Lévi-Strauss and Leach has to do with the empirical reality of models. Their categorical distinction between social relations and social structure leads them to deny the empirical reality of social structure, or rather of the models that compose it. I am not prepared to accept this position, at least in its entirety. I shall try to prove the undesirability and perhaps the untenability of such a position in dealing with social phenomena. My second set of criticisms of Lévi-Strauss and Leach is less fundamental but no less important, in that a series of great importance to anthropology revolves around their conception of social structure. My criticisms have to do mainly with the nature of model building in anthropology, the heuristic value of such models, their interaction and time precedence, and their methodological implications. I think that both Lévi-Strauss and Leach have sometimes been hasty in formulating their theories on social structure. I am inclined to believe that the reasons for this are, on the one hand, Lévi-Strauss's passion for synthetic exposition, and, on the other, Leach's tendency to use the shock method in order to propound his ideas. Here I will try to clarify obscure points of exposition, to bring to their logical conclusions the views expressed by these authors, and at the same time to point out the divergences between them when there is seeming agreement. In one or two instances, I shall depart from their viewpoint and express my own view.

II

Lévi-Strauss has performed a great service to anthropology in rescuing the notion of social structure from the narrow and provincial conception of Radcliffe-Brown and his followers—with its rather microscopic view and somewhat faulty methodological approach—and in transforming it into a broader and more fruitful province of inquiry. He maintains that the first step in the scientific procedure is the structural study of a subject matter—be it a set of social facts, linguistic facts, or whatever —or, as he puts it, the construction of models that tells us more than the mere description of the facts involved. Following the physical scientist (he does not seem to visualize any other point of departure), he is well aware that the raw data of social experience are not amenable to manipulation, either for comparative purposes or for the analysis of their internal constitution; hence, his great emphasis on model building. Like the physicist who is not concerned with simply describing, say, the composition of the hydrogen molecule, Lévi-Strauss is not concerned with the mere description of a given set of social facts. His main objective is to construct a model or models abstract enough for purposes of comparison, which would not only describe the given set of social relations, but at the same time explain them, that is, give us additional information as to their internal relationship, position of subordination and superordination, and so forth.[1] Thus, all his efforts to delineate problems of method, define terms, and make systematic dichotomies such as differentiating the levels of observation and experimentation, the conscious and unconscious character of the anthropologist's working material, are exclusively directed toward construction of easily manipulable models that comply with the aforementioned requisites.

The distinction between conscious and unconscious models is not clear, as I have pointed out, for there is no indication in the context of the article, or elsewhere in Lévi-Strauss's work, as to why and how it is important to keep this distinction in mind at a theoretical level. Neither are its advantages or heuristic value at the observational level made clear. It is simple enough to construe it as a warning to anthropologists not to take the rationalizations of their subjects at face value in their

---

1 This not the place for a philosophical discussion of the meaning of "description" and "explanation" in dealing with social phenomena, but for readers who wish to go into these problems I suggest Robert Brown's book, *Explanation in Social Science* (1963).

model building, since this might lead to a great deal of confusion, but Lévi-Strauss has more in mind in postulating the distinction. In order to understand his position fully, we must turn to a short article entitled "Les Structures sociales dans le Brésil central et oriental" (1952).

In this article Lévi-Strauss aims to demonstrate, and for clarity of exposition I quote him *in extenso*, that

the description of the indigenous institutions given by field-workers—including myself—no doubt coincides with the image that the Indians have of their own society, but that this image is nothing more than a theory, or rather a transfiguration of the reality, which is of a completely different nature. From this fact, which up to now had been only faintly perceived for the Apinaye, two important consequences follow: the dualistic organization of central and eastern Brazil is not only adventitious but often illusory. Above all, we are brought to conceive of social structures as objects independent from the awareness that men have of them (whose existence they nevertheless regulate), and as capable of being different from the image that they have of them as physical reality differs from the sensible representations that we have of it, and from the hypothesis that we may formulate about it [my translation; Lévi-Strauss 1952:302].

The Sherente, Bororo, Canella, Apinaye, and other tribes of central and eastern Brazil, as described by Nimuendaju, Albisetti, Lévi-Strauss himself, and others, are organized into patrilineal or matrilineal exogamous moieties subdivided into an even number of clans and subclans. In addition, there are several men's and women's "associations" and age grades associated with this dual organization. The clans, subclans, and, to a certain degree, the age grades and associations have largely a ceremonial and ritual function, while the sole function of the moiety system is to regulate marriage. Let us take the case of the Bororo, whose physical village arrangement gives us a mirror image of their conscious social structure. Briefly, the Bororo are organized into two exogamous matrimoieties subdivided into four clans each. The circular Bororo village is divided into halves by an east-west axis; each half is occupied by one of two moieties, and the huts of the clans composing the moieties are arranged in a circle.

Since Nimuendaju's time, this interpretation of the social organization of the central and eastern Brazilian Indians has been more or less universally accepted and described as the classic type of dualistic structure. But, according to Lévi-Strauss, a closer and more thorough examination of the data, especially for the Sherente and Bororo, reveals a deeper and more fundamental structure. Careful analysis of kinship terminologies, marriage rules, reciprocity in exchange, and in general the application of his now classic distinction between "restricted exchange" and "generalized exchange," together with additional data, leads Lévi-Strauss to postulate a radically different social structure. Again, to give the example of the Bororo, each of the four clans composing the two moieties is divided into three segments, which he entitles upper, middle, and lower. In turn, these three segments or subclans have strict marriage prescriptions such that marriage always takes place between persons belonging to the same named subclans (upper, middle, lower) in opposite moieties. Thus, it is clear that the classic Bororo system of exogamous moieties divided into clans loses its functional importance as a result of being underlain by a more fundamental tripartite endogamous structure.

Lévi-Strauss goes on to say that each of these tribes has systematized its real institutions in a simpler manner than that explicitly formulated. At the same time, the different social units found in these societies, such as clans, subclans, age grades, and associations, are not functional units as they are in the case of the Australians, for example, but rather partial and incomplete expressions of a deeper structure. He believes that this represents an effort on the part of the society to relegate to the background the tripartite endogamous structure and to place in the foreground the dual structure of exogamous moieties. He concludes the article by warning fieldworkers to

get used to envisaging their research under two different aspects. They are always in danger of confusing the natives' theories on their social organization and the real functioning of the society. . . . The sociological representations of the natives are not merely a part or a reflection of their organization, but they can, as in the case of more advanced societies, contradict it entirely, or ignore certain elements [my translation; Lévi-Strauss 1952:310].

We now have a specific and well-documented example that leaves no doubt as to what Lévi-Strauss means by conscious and unconscious models. On the one hand, the superficial dual organization of exogamous moieties subdivided into clans, with little or no functional importance, represents a conscious model; on the other hand, the deeper and more fundamental structure consisting of three endogamous sections or groups, each divided into exogamous units, represents an unconscious model. I have already taken for granted the practical importance, at the observational level, of distinguishing between these two types of models. But we may ask at this point, what is the substantive meaning and importance, at the theoretical and experimental level, of making such a distinction? Let us take the theoretical question first. In the present case, does the distinction help us to solve the problem posed by Lévi-Strauss himself when he asks "why do societies with a high degree of endogamy have such a pressing desire to mystify themselves, and to conceive of themselves as regulated by exogamous institutions of a classic type, of which they have no direct knowledge?" [my translation; 1952:310]. In more general terms, why do societies try to hide their fundamental structure by screen-type models, figuratively speaking, with little or no functional validity? The answer must be an emphatic no, the distinction does not help to solve the problem. Lévi-Strauss himself evades answering by stating that the answer is part and parcel of general anthropology and that he has solved the problem elsewhere. But, as far as I have been able to determine by reading all of Lévi-Strauss's books and the majority of his articles, nowhere does he answer the question within the context of distinguishing conscious from unconscious models. If we cannot answer this all-important question, the distinction loses most of its importance and functional validity, in much the same way that the dual organization of the Bororo loses its functional validity when we determine its underlying endogamous tripartite structure.

Passing now to the level where observation and experimentation meet, can we validate the distinction between conscious and unconscious models insofar as it may help us elucidate problems of interaction, or to bridge any of the usual gaps between theory and a body of concrete data? In other words, has the distinction any functional and operational validity in relating the raw data of social experience to its positional models? Here again, the answer is no. Going back to the example of the central and eastern Brazilian Indians, Lévi-Strauss implies that fieldworkers, including himself, had been deceived by their informants into taking the dual organization as the real structure of the society, until a thorough analysis of the available and additional data revealed the deeper and more important structure. But had Nimuendaju, for example, or any other early observer spent enough time with these tribes to take marriage censuses and extensive genealogical charts showing who married whom and the moiety, clan, and subclan membership of the contracting parties, he would surely have arrived at the tripartite endogamous structure underlying the apparently real dual system. In this case, the brilliant analysis that Lévi-Strauss made in order to arrive at the same solution and that was confirmed later by more reliable data would have been unnecessary. As Lévi-Strauss correctly points out, self-mystification is not peculiar to the central and eastern Brazilian Indian societies; many other societies also do it. It may not be as spectacular as in the Bororo case, but it is of the same order and is similar in nature.

Lest it be thought that I misinterpret Lévi-Strauss's views, as is often the case with his critics, let me repeat again that I take for granted the well-established ethnographic fact that there are conscious and unconscious phenomena. But what is the functional and operational validity of making a distinction between conscious and unconscious models if it does not, on the one hand, help us to determine why societies mystify themselves by constructing screen-type models to hide a more transcendental structure, or, on the other hand, make us aware of an underlying structure because of the distinction rather than despite it, when all the factors involved (additional and more complete data, complementary approaches, etc.) are brought to bear upon a given situation? None, must be the answer, for what is the purpose of making a distinction that has no operational, or functional validity? It would be the same as to continue maintaining that the dual organization of Bororo society represents its real structure once the underlying structure has been delineated, or maintaining that the molecule is the basic particle of matter once the atom has been discovered. What I am objecting to in Lévi-Strauss's presentation of the problem is the treatment of the conscious screens as models. Although they are part of a model or models and thus worth studying for the light they shed on the total structure of the phenomena, as Lévi-Strauss himself makes clear, these conscious phenomena—structures or whatever one wishes to call them—are not themselves models.

As a ground rule of real heuristic value, the distinction between conscious and unconscious phenomena and the models that anthropologists (or, for that matter, the subjects of our investigation themselves) build upon them is highly commendable; it is valuable not only at the observational level but at the level of experimentation as well. But it is not warranted to construe this distinction into a theoretical doctrine about the nature of the subject matter of social structure, for conscious paradigms are not models at all, if we take for granted that a model must be an explanatory construct. I believe I have made it clear that conscious models are not explanatory, that is, they do not entail causality; Lévi-Strauss himself seems to recognize this when he equates conscious models with "norms," which "are not of themselves structures"—that is, models.[2]

---

2 It is interesting that such a careful scholar as Lévi-Strauss could contradict himself on so crucial a point. We must regard this as a logical slip, unless we assume that he writes "norms are not of themselves structures," he is using *structure* in a different sense. There is no doubt that in the preceding section of his article he equates structure with model, and in many of his writings he uses the terms interchangeably.

In conclusion, while I regard the distinction between conscious and unconscious models as a valuable heuristic rule at the observational level and to some degree at the experimental level as well, the use of conscious models as theoretical ones must be rejected as unwarranted.

III

Lévi-Strauss's most distinctive and important contribution to the theory of social structure was his dichotomizing of models into mechanical and statistical. He was the first to discern clearly their importance in structural studies, and his article "Social Structure" (1953) must be regarded as an effort to bring to the attention of anthropologists the far-reaching consequences of their differing natures. Unfortunately, few anthropologists seem to have been awakened from their "dogmatic slumber" by Lévi-Strauss's remarks. Among the few who have heeded his suggestions is Leach, who sometimes has even gone beyond him. Leach has repeatedly and strongly criticized his British colleagues for their reifications, narrowness, "empirical idealizations," and sometimes, by implication, for their uncritical acceptance of Radcliffe-Brown's unqualified empiricism. In this context, Leach's *Pul Eliya* (1961a) may be interpreted as a strong reaction against his British colleagues for their almost exclusive concern (Fortes may perhaps be considered an exception) with mechanical models at the expense of statistical models in their structural studies.

Lévi-Strauss, I repeat, performed a great service to anthropology by rescuing social-structural studies from Radcliffe-Brown's narrow conception, which in a sense leads to a blind alley. Radcliffe-Brown's extreme reluctance to distinguish between the levels of observation and experimentation leads him to postulate that social structure, or rather the models that comprise it, not only lie at the same level as the raw data of experience but are an integral part of it. In other words, he regards the structure of a given set of social facts as the general ensemble of its parts. But Lévi-Strauss insightfully perceived that the mere ensemble of social relations does not constitute a structure and that the model or models that make up a given structure must be at a higher level; they are not only more abstract than the set of social relations but of a different nature. Nadel, who seems also to have been stimulated by Lévi-Strauss on this point, states the position in this way:

Like myself, he [Lévi-Strauss] thus stipulates a further "order," over and above the one implicit in the relationships, and inter-relating the latter. Let us note that this is not merely a two-level hierarchy of, say, first-order relations (linking and arranging persons) and second-order relations (doing the same with relationships). We are dealing here with differences in kind; the orderliness of a plurality of relationships differs radically from the ordering of a plurality of individuals through relationships [1957:12].[3]

However, the idea that the structure of a given phenomenon is to be sought at the empirical level is so ingrained in many social anthropologists that this is one of the aspects of Lévi-Strauss's conception of social structure that they find most difficult to accept, and it is the point on which Lévi-Strauss has been most misunderstood.[4]

Lévi-Strauss has also been misunderstood with regard to the nature of mechanical and statistical models themselves, and I think this stems from the fact that he is not altogether clear in his exposition. Nadel (1957:147), for example, misinterprets him when he equates only statistical models with social structure, assigning to mechanical models a different epistemological

---

3 It is interesting to contrast Nadel's position at the time of his death, with the position he entertained at the 1952 meeting of the Wenner-Gren Foundation four years earlier (Tax 1953: 112–118). Lévi-Strauss undoubtedly convinced him that models are not merely abstractions of the empirical data of social experience, but that they represent different kinds of entities. In other aspects of structural theory, however, he remained an empiricist in the Rad-cliffe-Brownian tradition.

4 For example, Maybury-Lewis in his article "The Analysis of Dual Organizations: A Methodological Critique" (1960) completely misses the point of what Lévi-Strauss understands by a model. The reader is directed to Lévi-Strauss's devastating reply, in an article entitled "On Manipulated Sociological Models" (1960c).

status seemingly outside the realm of social structure. He rightly points out, however, as does Leach, that the latter are "efficacious," while the former are not. Thus, it seems imperative that Lévi-Strauss's concept of mechanical and statistical models must be clarified and in some instances modified, if we are to continue using them meaningfully and profitably. It is also in this restricted but important area of structural theory that a comparison and discussion of Lévi-Strauss's and Leach's views is most profitable. I shall begin by stating what seems to me essentially correct in Lévi-Strauss's and Leach's positions, by themselves and vis-à-vis each other, and I shall justify my contentions with examples whenever possible.

1. The first point to be considered is the basic and substantive difference between mechanical and statistical models. Leach is quite clear in this matter when he equates mechanical models with jural rules and statistical models with norms; mechanical models are ideal paradigms of what people *should* do, while statistical models represent what they actually do. Leach's clear conception of the differences between mechanical and statistical models is good insofar as it helps us to keep in mind the distinction between ideal and actual behavior, but at the same time it leads him into considerable difficulty. Lévi-Strauss, on the other hand, may have visualized the danger of making any clear-cut distinction between mechanical and statistical models, and thus he never offers explicit definitions. Only obliquely, and by restricting himself to the most formal characteristics of the models, does he point out their real differences. Only after considering Lévi-Strauss's published work in a general context can we come to the conclusion that mechanical and statistical models, in some aspects at least, stand for or are based on ideal and actual behavior respectively.

2. Leach's clear-cut distinction between mechanical models or jural rules and statistical models or norms leads him to differ from Lévi-Strauss on what seems to me a crucial point. Leach often maintains (he is not always consistent on this difficult point) that jural rules are ideal paradigms; they are ideal not only in subject matter—that is, they express what people should do—but in form as well—that is, they are constructs not only

at a higher level of abstraction but of a different nature from what they are supposed to explain. Statistical norms, on the contrary, are nothing more than the ensemble of empirical facts of what people actually do in a given social situation. For Leach, therefore, only mechanical models are supraempirical; statistical models are not, since their relationship to the empirical social facts is not one of superordination. If we define model as an explanatory construct at a higher level of superordination and of a different kind from the social facts it purports to explain, then Leach's statistical norms are not models at all. They must then be considered at most as a descriptive abstraction of a given set of social facts, not amenable to manipulation as mechanical models or any other types of supraempirical models are.

This is no doubt the most serious shortcoming of Leach's theory of social structure. Unwittingly and unnecessarily, he gets into difficulty in *Pul Eliya* by his excessive concern with the empirical recurrence of social facts; this, paradoxically, causes him to sin in the same way as the anthropologists he is avowedly criticizing, although at the opposite extreme. The difficulty is increased by his hastiness of exposition and his failure to carry the substantive meaning of his premises to their logical conclusions. This extreme and poorly thought out position "commits him," in Oliver's words (1942:621), "to producing a book (*Pul Eliya*) very much like *Suicide*, in its laudatory empiricism as well as in its inevitable shortcomings." In this respect at least, Leach is much like Radcliffe-Brown in remaining a prisoner of the empirical facts. No wonder, then, that he asserts that jural rules and statistical norms should be treated as different frames of reference and that the former should be considered secondary to the latter! In Leach's terms, it is justifiable on purely theoretical grounds to maintain that jural rules and statistical norms should be treated as separate frames of reference; indeed they must be, since they represent two different epistemological entities. But the second part of the thesis is wrong in both theory and practice. Indeed, it is meaningless. To assert, on practical and historical grounds, that jural rules (ideal behavior) are secondary to statistical norms (actual behavior) either chronologically or in importance is as nonsensical as to ask whether the chicken or the egg came first. On purely theoretical grounds, it is even more nonsensical to compare or arrange in positions of subordination two different types of social phenomena: ideal behavior construed into mechanical models, and actual behavior or norms that are not models at all. Furthermore, we can realize now that for Leach "having nothing to do with empirical reality" means simply that actual behavior or norms never correspond exactly with ideal behavior or jural rules. They do not refer to the categorical distinction between the raw data of experience and its positional models.

As I write this, I have the uneasy feeling that either I may have misunderstood Leach's conception of what a model is, based primarily on what he says in *Pul Eliya*, or that not only his statistical norms but his jural rules as well are not models at all—at least not in Lévi-Strauss's sense, which I have accepted as generally correct. Leach is not always clear (although for the purpose of exposition I have granted that he is) when he talks about jural rules as being ideal either in the sense that they represent an abstraction of what people should do or in the sense of being supraempirical explanatory constructs. If he means the former, jural rules are not models; if he means the latter, they are. If I were considering his excellent and pioneering article "Jinghpaw Kinship Terminology" (1945), there would be no doubt that he was referring to models as supraempirical constructs. But this is not the case in his later work such as *Pul Eliya* (1961), and even *Political Systems of Highland Burma* (1954), in which he becomes sidetracked by other issues; these are important contributions, but rather than representing an improvement or modification of earlier views, they tend to obscure them. In the light of *Pul Eliya*, his latest pronouncement, I have not been able to make up my mind entirely. The handling of empirical data in the central chapters leaves no doubt that he is concerned with neither mechanical nor statistical models as explanatory constructs. But in the introduction and conclusion, he makes certain statements that can be interpreted to mean that he regards at least jural rules as models. I believe that Leach's latest writings warrant the preceding remarks, but what bothers me most is his cavalier attitude in not carrying to their logical conclusions the assumptions involved in his premises. I hope that I am wrong in my interpretation of his conception of both jural and statistical rules, and that the trouble can be reduced to the kind of semantic difficulty that is bound to arise in the exposition of such an elusive subject. If not, Leach's latest views on social structure represent a backward step.

By contrast, Lévi-Strauss does not go into the nature of mechanical and statistical models as means of organizing data or, as Leach does, into the more practical aspects of model building and application. Instead, he concerns himself exclusively with model building as supraempirical explanatory constructs. Thus, Lévi-Strauss usually is operating at the experimental level, whereas one is not always certain when Leach is operating at the experimental level and when at the descriptive level. This, I strongly believe, is responsible for his unclear exposition of the issues involved in his treatment of jural rules and statistical norms. However, it must be strongly emphasized that although Lévi-Strauss is almost exclusively concerned with models as constructs, this does not imply that he is totally unconcerned with the practical application of models or that the level of observation and description is any less important than the level of experimentation. He has clearly demonstrated in several articles the usefulness and applicability of his conception of models, and he explicitly states that the best model is that which accounts most accurately for all the known facts. I am in favor of Lévi-Strauss's manner of exposition of and attack on the problems involved, for once one has clearly established the relationship between the models and the empirical data that they purport to explain, then one is free to deal with them as formal constructs, that is, to determine the degree to which they can be manipulated, their amenability to treatment by mathematical methods, and so on.

3. In his discussion of mechanical and statistical models as explanatory constructs, Lévi-Strauss does not state their analytical properties, and it is only by means of examples that he

points to their general nature. However, in the context of his published work it can be established that mechanical and statistical models as theoretical constructs and as heuristic devices have the following properties by themselves and vis-à-vis each other: (a) they are both supraempirical; that is, although based on or constructed from empirical facts, they are not themselves part of the facts; (b) their values as models lies in the fact that they can be studied and compared independently of their component parts; (c) social structure, or for that matter any structure, is composed of or can be explained by mechanical models, statistical models, or both at the same time, depending upon the ordered arrangements and internal relationships of the elements involved; (d) although never explicitly stated, it is suggested that mechanical models, at least as heuristic constructs, correspond closely to Leach's jural rules, that is, they explain ideal behavior, while statistical models correspond to societal norms or actual behavior;[5] (e) given the proper contextual matrix, statistical models can be translated into mechanical models, and vice versa. I have already touched in some detail on (a), (b), and (d), and they are explicit enough to obviate any further comments. But the other two, especially (e), still need clarification and modification. In the following paragraphs I shall be concerned primarily with the heuristic and theoretical value of mechanical and statistical models in relation to each other, and vis-à-vis a body of empirical data.

When Lévi-Strauss says that, given the proper conditions, it should be possible to translate statistical models into mechanical models and vice versa, he seems to be maintaining that both types of models are heuristically and theoretically equal. But at other times, such as when he criticizes Murdock for trying to construct mechanical models with the help of a statistical method (1953:544), he seems to imply that this trans-

---

5 For example, when Lévi-Strauss says that "A society which recommends cross-cousin marriage but where this ideal marriage type occurs only with limited frequency needs, in order that the system may be properly explained, both a mechanical and a statistical model" (1953:528), it is clear that mechanical models stand for ideal behavior, and statistical ones for actual behavior.

lation is not possible and, further, that mechanical models are heuristically superior. Be this as it may, I do not think that Lévi-Strauss is clear on this point. For my part, I believe that statistical models, as heuristic devices, are inferior to mechanical models, because they are not on the same scale with the phenomena that they purport to explain; that is, the margin of error is much greater when working with statistical models. Furthermore, there can be no translation of mechanical into statistical models or vice versa, if by "translation" we mean a one-to-one correspondence of elements when we shift our conceptual viewpoint. Thus, mechanical and statistical models must be treated as separate frames of reference, but this does not mean that statistical models are not useful in "arriving" at mechanical models.

Lévi-Strauss seems to forget that if he conceives of mechanical models as constructs purporting to explain the formal and explicit rules of a society, and statistical models as purporting to explain the frequency of events (as I think he does), then he is committed to maintaining that statistical models cannot be translated into mechanical models or vice versa. It is impossible to translate even the models of ideal behavior, or what people should do, into the models of what people actually do. Statistical models tell us only that such-and-such is the state of affairs at a given moment, whereas mechanical models provide knowledge not only of this state of affairs but at the same time of the reason for it. Mechanical models, therefore, explain not only the "how" of social phenomena but the "why" as well, hence their heuristic superiority over statistical models. As a corollary, it follows that while we can never translate one type of model into the other, from a statistical model we can "arrive" at the construction of a mechanical model if we can determine independently the "why," that is, the efficient cause of the phenomena. Thus, while we cannot speak of mechanical and statistical models as being translatable into each other, it is perfectly valid, in social-structural studies, to express their relationship as being complementary in nature.

Let us look at the problem from a different point of view and determine what it means to explain a given social phenomenon in terms of either mechanical or statistical models. First, we must assume that we are not dealing with absolute situations but with approximate ones, in that there are no societies or parts of societies in which actual (statistical) behavior coincides exactly with ideal (mechanical) behavior. In other words, no societies can be explained entirely in terms of mechanical models, nor are there societies or parts of societies that have no ideal standards that can be explained entirely in terms of statistical models. Second, we must realize that the models themselves, be they mechanical or statistical, are only a partial explanation of any social phenomenon (although an extremely important one), for neither in the most mechanical of societies are there no contraventions of the ideal standards, nor in the most statistical of societies are there no ideal standards regulating behavior. Thus, when we say that a set of empirical social facts is explained by a mechanical model, we mean that the behavior of the social facts tends to an ideal limit; conversely, when a set of social facts is explained by a statistical model, the behavior of the facts tends to a statistical limit, that is, to the maximum differentiation in behavior. The question then arises, at what point in this approximation of actual behavior toward the ideal limit are we warranted in constructing mechanical models to explain social phenomena, and at what point in the approximation toward maximum differentiation are we warranted in explaining the phenomena in terms of statistical models? The answer is difficult; and it is not a theoretical answer but a practical matter that varies according to the situation. However, some important rules that apply to all situations must be kept always in mind in model building:

The models should explain the phenomena in the simplest possible manner; the carved-out segments of a social phenomena that a model purports to explain must be viewed, in relation to the global situation, as occupying a definite position of interaction with other parts of the whole; a model designed to explain a given social segment must never contradict other models designed to explain other segments of the global situation; work with mechanical models whenever possible for they are heuristically superior and simpler than statistical models.[6]

I believe that by following these rules, we can arrive at a satisfactory solution of the dilemma. In order to make things clearer, I shall give an example. Let us take two societies, X and Y, that practice polygyny. In society X the ideal type of marriage prescribed by the culture is the polygynous type in which a man is married to two women, but owing to the equal ratio between men and women, economic considerations, and other well-established variables, only 10 percent of the total number of marriages are polygynous. On the other hand, in society Y the ideal cultural standard is monogamy, but owing to the unequal ratio between men and women, economic considerations, and other controllable variables, 10 percent of the total number of marriages are polygynous. We have, then, two societies with the same percentage of polygynous unions, but within cultural matrices prescribing different ideal standards.[7] The question then becomes: what type of model or models are we warranted in constructing in order to explain the marriage structure of these societies? We must conclude, with

---

6 Many anthropologists concerned with problems of ideal and actual behavior, which are so closely related to model building, have tried to express this relationship on a metrical basis. Thus, they say that we can speak of polygyny as an ideal standard in a given society when, say, at least 10 percent of the population practice it, or that the levirate exists as an ideal rule when such-and-such percentage of the population practice it, and that these metrical standards are the same for all societies. This, of course, is false. It is perfectly correct to set up a metrical criterion for a given social phenomenon once we have analyzed its position vis-à-vis the total society, but we cannot apply this metrical criterion to other societies in which the position of the phenomenon within the total society may be quite different.

7 These are not merely hypothetical cases. The anthropological literature is full of polygynous societies of type X in which from 5 to 15 percent of the total number of marriages are polygynous; societies of type Y, while not common, can also be found in the literature. This is exactly the case with San Bernardino Contla in which 10 percent of all marriages are polygynous, yet the ideal standard is monogamy.

Lévi-Strauss, that both situations require mechanical and statistical models to be correctly explained. But the real question is: in what "proportion" and in what order of subordination?

At the outset, allow me to maintain that most anthropologists would say, "We must construct a mechanical model of polygyny for each of the societies." This is the obvious answer, of course, but in this case it is completely wrong because we cannot construct a mechanical model of polygyny for a society in which monogamy is the ideal standard. The correct solution to the problem is as follows: First, we must construct a mechanical model of polygyny for society X and a mechanical model of monogamy for society Y. Second, we subordinate a statistical model of monogamy to the mechanical model of polygyny in society X and a statistical model of polygyny to the mechanical model of monogamy in society Y. This is what I did in my own work in the municipio of San Bernardino Contla, where the situation required a mechanical model of monogamy and a subordinate statistical model of polygyny (constructed by recording the frequency of polygynous unions in reference to locality, lineage, and clan; by the type of family structures they entailed; etc.) in order to account for the total marriage structure. On the other hand, in societies of type X the mechanical model would account for only a fraction of the total number of marriages, and the statistical model for the great majority. Yet I would still maintain that the statistical model should be subordinated to the mechanical model, for, given the proper cultural conditions, the overlapping of ideal and actual behavior would tend to the ideal limit. What I am saying here is not only the result of the application of the aforementioned rules, but it is especially due to the all-important fact that mechanical models are always heuristically superior to statistical models and that they stand for or are constructed out of ideal behavior, while statistical models stand for or are constructed out of actual behavior.

A note of explanation is needed here. The reader must not interpret this to mean that we can construct mechanical models only out of or based on ideal behavior, or statistical models out of or based on actual behavior. This is not what I am saying, for all models, be they mechancial or statistical, can be constructed out of any set of empirical data as long as they explain the facts in question. What I am maintaining is that mechanical models constructed out of ideal behavior, and statistical models based on actual behavior are the best; they are the "most explanatory" models that we can build in dealing with social phenomena. In other words, what I am trying to convey is only that mechanical and statistical models, as explanatory constructs, must always be regarded vis-à-vis their proper epistemological referents if they are to explain a given set of social facts in the best possible manner. I could have constructed a mechanical model of polygyny in San Bernardino Contla, but it would have been heuristically inferior to the statistical model that I actually built, both by itself and in relation to the total marriage structure of the municipio. In the light of these remarks, it may very well be that the charges of reification, idealization, and mystification that Leach levels at his British colleagues is simply a case of inefficient and negligent model building.

Finally, a few words about the extreme situations. In cases when the juxtaposition of ideal and actual behavior tends considerably toward the ideal limit (high degree of overlapping), such as in societies with strict prescriptive marriage rules, or toward the maximum differentiation, such as marriage regulation in our own society, the problem is much simpler in that social phenomena can be explained with a rather high degree of accuracy by either mechanical or statistical models, respectively. This is possible because the few contraventions of ideal behavior in the former case and the little adherence to a certain pattern in the latter may either be disregarded as metrically unimportant or explained in contraposition to the models.

4. I come now to an issue that, although not explicitly mentioned in the preceding discussion, is at the heart of anthropological theory and has a great bearing on the conception of models and their relation to empirical data. This is the nature of "custom." Although Lévi-Strauss says little about this concept, its importance is implicit in his writings. Leach, on the other hand, does say something explicit, and therefore I shall

deal largely with him. However, in these brief remarks I shall not try to explain the nature of custom, for this is not the place to do it; nor will I try to illuminate the concept by specific analysis. I shall simply try to determine the nature of custom that we must assume in order to arrive at the formulation of the type of models discussed in the preceding pages. If, in this process, some light is shed on the general concept of custom, so much the better.

In the discussion of 1, 2, and 3, one of my principal aims has been to show that we must clearly separate behavior (ideal, actual) from its positional models (mechanical, statistical), that not everyone who concerns himself with ideal behavior can be said to be working with mechanical models (witness the case of Radcliffe-Brown), and that not everyone who concerns himself with actual behavior can be said to be working with statistical models (witness the case of Leach). With this in mind, let us turn to the problem of customs as stated by Leach (1961a:296–301).

Leach begins by stating that the ethnographer is primarily concerned with recording "custom," that is, the formalized standard of behavior, and the members of society are viewed as blind prisoners of these rules. The social anthropologists, on the other hand, "stresses that custom is synthetic and quite distinct from the behavior of individuals" (1961a:296). Then he discusses the two principal approaches in the treatment of custom, which vary "according to the empiricist and idealist bias of the writer's underlying philosophy."

On the one hand, the "idealist" anthropologists, such as Radcliffe-Brown and most of his followers, view custom as "providing a body of moral rules worked out in behavioristic form; the discrepancies between individual behavior and customary behavior are due simply to the inability of the average man to live up to moral demands of society" (Leach 1961a: 297). This conception of custom, Leach goes on to say, makes them postulate concepts such as "social solidarity," "social equilibrium," and so on, which are nothing more than convenient descriptive abstractions, not based on or elicited from empirical reality. For the "empirical" anthropologists, prin-

cipally exemplified by Malinowski, custom is not a superimposed and coercive rule or ideal standard, but the actual state
of affairs at a given moment; it is what people actually do. In
Leach's own words, "despite the underlying assumptions that
every custom serves a utilitarian purpose and the emphatic
assertion that the individual is not a "slave of custom," no clear
distinction ever emerges between customary behavior on the
one hand and individual behavior on the other. Custom is
what men do, normal men, average men" (1961:298).

   Let us put Leach's remarks within the context of my discussion of models and their relation to social phenomena.
Leach clearly equates custom with ideal behavior in one instance,
and with actual behavior in the other. Thus, it appears that,
at the strict level of observation and description, custom is not
a constant; it varies with our shift in emphasis from ideal behavior to actual behavior, and vice versa. I agree that this is a
correct conclusion. But can we say the same at the experimental
level? Can we assert that we must assume the equation of ideal
behavior with custom in dealing with mechanical models, and
the equation of actual behavior with custom in dealing with
statistical models? I have two reasons for thinking that we cannot: first, theoretical models or constructs are true only in their
correct relationship to the empirical facts, and not because of
the nature of the facts themselves; and second, as I made
clear in 3, mechanical and statistical models as explanatory
constructs are conceived as limiting parameters enabling us
to explain social facts by contraposition, without the aid of
any other postulated empirical abstraction (custom). Thus, we
can see that the notion of custom is irrelevant at the experimental level, as it would be a tautology to equate it either with
the ideal limit or with the point of maximum differentiation.

   Going back to the level of observation and description, I
agree with Leach that it is useful to equate custom with ideal
behavior at certain times and with actual behavior at other
times. But does it make any sense to say, with Malinowski,
that custom is what men actually do, or with Radcliffe-Brown
that custom is the principle governing behavior, when we can
logically conceive that customs, as ideal rules, may well have

arisen from actual behavior or that actual behavior may have arisen from ideal rules? In other words, isn't it meaningless to speak of historical posteriority or anteriority? Again, I think this would be one of those questions having to do with whether the chicken or the egg came first. Leach was no doubt aware of the problems posed by the concept of custom when he charged Malinowski with failing to answer the question as to "how the social fact of normal behavior can emerge from a sum of seemingly arbitrary individual choices" (1961a:298).

In conclusion, I must point out that I have not explained anything about the concept of custom, but rather have explained it away. I am convinced that the concept of custom has no heuristic value either at the experimental or observational level and that anthropologists dealing with social structures should be well advised to ignore it. We must start with the given fact that societies always have ideal rules, which may differ greatly in degree but which nevertheless determine whether the situation warrants the construction of mechanical or statistical models for its explanation. If we introduce the concept of custom, in either of its two principal forms, we complicate matters by bringing in historical and other considerations that only obscure the problem without adding anything substantial to its solution. I am not denying that the concept of custom, in either of its two principal forms, is useful in other contexts. But it is tautological and therefore confusing in situations such as social-structural studies, which have so many variables that are hard to control.

Before leaving this section, let me recapitulate the salient points: (a) Following Lévi-Strauss, I have chosen to call models only those supraempirical explanatory constructs of the type whose analytical properties are clearly discerned by Nadel (1957:12). (b) Following both Lévi-Strauss and Leach, I maintain that mechanical models stand for or are constructed out of ideal behavior, and statistical models stand for or are constructed out of actual behavior, and that they are the best type of models. But ideal behavior (or rather the ideal standards or rules that govern it) may lie in the "collective consciousness," hence the need to keep constantly in mind the conscious and unconscious character of social phenomena. (c) At the descriptive or observational level, I agree with Leach: by all means deal with statistical norms, as well as with "ideal paradigms." Indeed, we must deal with both, since they complement each other, but we must also keep in mind that they are not yet models, that is, supraempirical constructs, according to the definition. But at the experimentation level, we should whenever possible construct mechanical models, for they are superior heuristic devices. (d) In explaining a society or a part of a society in isolation, that is, at the experimental level, mechanical and statistical models complement each other, when they do not by themselves explain the phenomena in question. In comparative situations, on the other hand, we must always compare mechanical models, for I do not think it possible to compare statistical models, or what people actually do. Even if we could, the models themselves would be of lesser heuristic value, and not as amenable to manipulation by the mathematical method, or by any other.

Finally, let me note that the structural approach described here—essentially Lévi-Strauss's and to a lesser degree Leach's—is more flexible and does not demand the unifying notion of "function" as in the case of Radcliffe-Brown's holistic approach and, in a sense, the approach of the so-called French Sociological School. Holism is very appealing, but its inconveniences outweigh its neatness and descriptive amenabilty.

IV

In the preceding two sections I have tried to clarify and expand the notions of mechanical and statistical analysis (as conceived by Lévi-Strauss and Leach) as explanatory constructs and descriptive devices and, to a certain degree, their relationship to the raw data of social experience. The subject is extremely elusive, and, in a sense, these two sections may be regarded as an exercise in avoiding the "fallacy of misplaced concreteness." Our imagination is so incurably concrete and pictorial that, as soon as we depart from mathematic and logical representations, we tend to express theories and abstract reasoning in language that asserts much more than we mean to assert. I have spoken of mechanical models as being "based on" or "constructed out" of ideal behavior, and statistical models "based on" or "constructed out" of actual behavior. This suggests that I am dealing with the transitive relation of "part" to "whole" ("collection"), when I am really dealing with the intransitive relation of "member" to "class." Similarly, I have maintained that mechanical and statistical models complement each other in explaining social phenomena, thus suggesting that there is a necessary "internal relatedness" holding the resultant system together, when I am really saying that the validity of the system is contingent upon external variables. So tricky is the verbalization of abstract concepts in concrete language, that I have even employed the same language and the same concepts used by the anthropologists that I am criticizing, with reference to the relation of models to the empirical data that they are supposed to explain, when I wanted to avoid this at all costs. Allow me, then, to turn to my "fundamental" criticism of Lévi-Strauss and Leach.

In stating their positions, I asserted that their categorical distinction between the levels of observation and experimentation leads them to deny the empirical reality of the positional models built in order to explain a body of social phenomena. I maintained that, while the distinction is useful, their dogmatic all-or-nothing attitude, which is not supported by clarifying or analytical arguments, obliterated the usefulness of the distinction and exposed them to serious criticism for not considering the substantive and epistemological implications of taking such a stand. I made this my "fundamental" criticism, in the sense of its encompassing and underlying importance. Since it is the most "philosophical" of the problems discussed, and the one that underlies everything else discussed in Sections II and III, I left it to be discussed by itself in the last section of this article. In stating the problem, I have slightly exaggerated Lévi-Strauss's and Leach's positions by the strength of the language used and by the omission of a few relevant factors, as one does when one wishes to make a point. However, I think it has been clear that I did not want to imply as much as my actual phrasing would suggest. In this way, in speaking of the relationship between models and empirical data, I used many of the same expressions used by Lévi-Strauss and Leach, such as "having nothing to do with empirical reality," "having no reality," and "logical constructions." I have even invented a few expressions of my own, such as "supra-empirical" and "different epistemological referents," which indicate that there is substantial area of agreement with their views. Thus, I must first establish how much agreement and disagreement there is between Lévi-Strauss's and Leach's positions, and my modified version.

I am in agreement with Lévi-Strauss and Leach (insofar as the latter follows Lévi-Strauss) on the following points: (a) Models must be explanatory, and not merely descriptive devices; they must answer, to some degree, questions about the nature of the "why" and "how" of the phenomena. (b) Models are supraempirical; they are not found at the same level as the empirical phenomena that they purport to explain. (c) At the descriptive level, we may speak of constructs or paradigms of a higher degree of abstraction, but these do not yet amount to models. (d) While models are supraempirical, they are always based on empirical data, and the "truest" model is that which best explains the facts under consideration. My disagreements are of two kinds, explicit and conjectural. I have no explicit disagreements with Lévi-Strauss. However, I believe I demonstrated that, while Leach seems to be speaking of models as supraempirical constructs, he is in fact not doing so when he refers to statistical norms, nor perhaps when he speaks of jural rules. My conjectural disagreements stem from the fact that neither Lévi-Strauss nor Leach explains the meaning of the terms "real" or "reality," as they use them in expressing the epistemological status of the models vis-à-vis empirical phenomena. If there is so little disagreement as to the nature of the relationship between model and empirical phenomena, the reader may ask why I go to the extreme of asserting that Lévi-Strauss's and Leach's bifurcation of the social universe into two distinct epistemological entities is a fundamental criticism, when I do basically the same thing myself. The answer may best be given by establishing what is meant by "real" and "reality."

At the outset, I must note that we are dealing here not with a philosophical question but with a genuine scientific question. That is, we must disregard as irrelevant any strictly philosophical solution tending to explain the concept of "reality" as participation in some higher form or as opposed to the concept of appearance. The problem under consideration has to do strictly with the relationship between two equally real "philosophical" entities. We may ask ourselves, then, what it means scientifically to say that models "have no reality," or "have nothing to do with empirical reality."

I have established that models are supraempirical; that is, we are dealing not with entities that merely represent two different levels of abstraction of the same phenomena but with different kinds of entities. Nor are we dealing with models conceived merely as the logical structure (principles, formulas), in order to explain the raw data of experience or, if you wish, social reality. Leach's statement to the effect that models are "logical constructions" in the anthropologist's mind would lead us to believe this, but I agree with Nadel when he says, "I consider social structure, of whatever degree of refinement, to be still the social reality itself, or an aspect of it, not the logic behind it" (1957:150).[8] This position in no way contradicts the conception of models as supraempirical, for its only implication is to make models and what they are supposed to explain equally "real," which was my original assumption. If we are dealing with a scientific question concerning the relationship between two kinds of entities that does not refer entirely to the logic behind one to explain the other, does it make any sense to say that one is "real" and the other is not? Indeed it does not. Here again, we have not so much explained a

---

8 Our agreement is at an end, however, when he adds, ". . . and I consider structural analysis to be no more than a descriptive method, however sophisticated, not a piece of explanation" (1957: 151). It is anachronistic of him to delineate clearly the nature of models and their relation to empirical phenomena and yet regard them as merely descriptive devices.

concept, the meaning of "reality," as explained it away. In other words, I regard Leach's use of the term "reality" (and to a certain degree Lévi-Strauss's) used in referring to the model–empirical phenomena relationship as misleading and unfortunate, for it may easily lead to many wrong conclusions. No questions as to degrees of "reality" need to be asked when dealing with models designed to explain a body of empirical data, as both are equally "real." However, we may unwittingly be led to maintain that models are less "real" than the concrete phenomena that may explain, because of the association that one inevitably makes in working with abstractions: the higher the abstraction, the less real it becomes. This, of course, is a purely psychological association that does not have any external validity. Furthermore, I think Lévi-Strauss and Leach phrased the relationship between models and empirical phenomena in terms of the exaggerated concept of "reality" because of their insistence on always keeping the levels of observation and experimentation separate (concept reality, reality). Conversely, if this position is carried to the extreme of dichotomizing the social universe into two different epistemological entities, it can be as dangerous, or perhaps even more so, as confusing the levels of experimentation and observation. This is why I have stated my position in extreme terms that were not meant to imply as much as they may occasionally have seemed to.

At this point, another question arises. While it is permissible to speak of models and empirical data as equally real from an epistemological point of view, if they are two different kinds of entities, how can one explain the other? In other words, how can they be interrelated? This question pertains to the general methodology of science, and we cannot undertake to explain it here. Furthermore, the interrelationship should be taken for granted, as physical scientists do in their hypotheses and model building. I am speaking now, of course, of the bifurcation of nature that, according to most philosophers of science, is inevitable in the physical sciences.

While we cannot avoid bifurcation in the physical sciences, this is not so in the social sciences. In fact, there is fairly good evidence that we shall never be faced with the problems that the physical scientist, or rather the philosopher of science, has to face. I cannot go into the details that underlie this assertion, but I can enumerate my reasons for believing that bifurcation is not possible in the social sciences: (a) While it is both permissible and empirically well established to substitute constructions out of known entities for inferences to unknown entities in the physical sciences, this is not possible in the social universe where the order must be reversed. (b) Although I stated that a model is not merely a more abstract version of the empirical phenomena that it purports to explain (that is, they are entities of a different kind), we must never forget that, while the sensed is given and the postulated inferred in the physical sciences, this is not true in the social sciences; there we deal always with sensed and never with postulated space, time, or physical entities. (c) Constructing a physical model is not the same as constructing a social model; in the former we are dealing with postulated space and time, while in the latter we are dealing with sense-delivered space and time.

In summary, we must agree with Lévi-Strauss in regarding models and empirical phenomena as essentially different things in structural studies, but this does not amount to bifurcation of the social universe; we are never dealing with postulated entities, be they space, time, or social relations. Therefore, we should never have to contend with the problems faced by the philosopher of science in trying to relate two seemingly unrelatable entities. At the same time, we should not be surprised, as many of Lévi-Strauss's critics seem to be, that a model can explain a certain set of social facts.

Throughout this article, my aim has been to clarify and perhaps bring to their logical conclusions some of the implicit and explicit assumptions of Lévi-Strauss, and to a lesser degree of Leach, regarding social structure. These revolve largely around the concept of model and its relation to empirical phenomena. I have advanced some ideas of my own, but in general I have confined myself to the role of commentator and interpreter. My hope is that this discussion will in some measure stimulate anthropologists to further exploration of some of the issues raised here. If this article induces only one anthropologist to do this, its purpose will have been accomplished.

REFERENCES

BROWN, ROBERT
1963 Explanation in social science. Chicago, Aldine Publishing Company.
DURKHEIM, EMILE
1947 The division of labour in society. Glencoe, Ill., The Free Press.
1951 Suicide: a study in sociology. Glencoe, Ill., The Free Press.
LEACH, EDMUND R.
1945 Jinghpaw kinship terminology. Journal of the Royal Anthropological Institute 75:59–72.
1951 The structural implications of matrilateral cross-cousin marriage. Journal of the Royal Anthropological Institute 81:23–55.
1954 Political systems of highland Burma. Cambridge, Harvard University Press.
1957 On asymmetrical marriage systems. American Anthropologist 59:343–344.
1958 Concerning Trobriand clans and the kinship category 'Tabu.' Cambridge, Cambridge Papers in Social Anthropology 1:120–145.
1961 Rethinking anthropology. In Rethinking anthropology, London, London School of Economics Monographs on Social Anthropology 22:1–28.
1961a Pul Eliya, a village in Ceylon: a study of land tenure and kinship. Cambridge, Cambridge University Press.
LÉVI-STRAUSS, CLAUDE
1936 Contributions à l'étude de l'organisation sociale des indiens Bororo. Journal de la Société des Américanistes 28:269–304.
1944 On dual organization in South America. America Indígena 44:37–47, Mexico City.
1945 L'analyse structurale en linguistique et en anthropologie. Word, Journal of the Linguistic Circle of New York 1 (2):1–12.
1948 Les structures élémentaires de la parenté. Paris, Presses Universitaires de France.
1951 Language and the analysis of social laws. American Anthropologist 53:155–163.
1952 Les structures sociales dans le Brésil central et oriental. In Proceedings of the 29th Congress of Americanists 3:302–310, Chicago, University of Chicago Press.

1953 Social structure. *In* Anthropology Today, pp. 524–553, Alfred L. Kroeber (Ed.), Chicago, University of Chicago Press.
1956 Les organisations dualistes existent-elles? 'S-Gravenhage, Bijdragen tot de Taal-, Land- en Volkenkunde 112 (2):99–128.
1960a Le dualisme dans l'organisation sociale et les représentations religieuses. Paris, Annuaire de l'Ecole Pratique des Hautes Etudes 5e Section, Sciences religieuses), année 1958–1959.
1960b On manipulated sociological models. 'S-Gravenhage, Bijdragen tot de Taal-, Land- en Volkenkunde 112 (1):45–54.
1962a Les limites de la notion de structure en ethnologie. *In* Sens et usages du terme structure, Roger Bastide (Ed.), Paris, Janua Linguarum 18:40–45.
1962b Le totémisme aujourd'hui. Paris, Presses Universitaires de France.

MAYBURY-LEWIS, DAVID
1960 The analysis of dual organization: a methodological critique. 'S-Gravenhage, Bijdragen tot de Taal-, Land- en Volkenkunde 118 (1):2–44.

NADEL, SIEGFRIED F.
1957 The theory of social structure. Chicago, The Free Press of Glencoe.

OLIVER, DOUGLAS
1942 Review of Pul Eliya, a village in Ceylon: a study in land tenure and kinship. E. R. Leach. American Anthropologist 64:621–622.

TAX, SOL (ED.)
1953 An appraisal of Anthropology Today. Chicago, University of Chicago Press.

6
EPISTEMIC PARADIGMS: SOME PROBLEMS IN CROSS-CULTURAL RESEARCH ON SOCIAL ANTHROPOLOGICAL HISTORY AND THEORY[1]

BOB SCHOLTE

In *The Structure of Scientific Revolution* Thomas S. Kuhn uses the term "paradigms" to suggest examples and models of scientific law, theory, application, and instrumentation shared by men committed to similar rules and standards of scientific

Reproduced by permission of the American Anthropological Association from the *American Anthropologist*, Vol. 68 (1966), pp. 1192–1201.

1 A preliminary version of this paper was originally presented at the annual meeting of the History of Science Society on December 29, 1965. The author wishes to acknowledge the financial assistance of the Social Science Research Council and the Wenner-Gren Foundation, which in part made the writing of this essay possible.

practice. He points out that from these paradigms "spring particular coherent traditions of scientific research," traditions that, explictly or implicitly, perpetuate a series of "interrelated theoretical and methodological beliefs that permit selection, evaluation and criticism" (Kuhn 1962:10, 17).

But the appearance of paradigms not only allows for a certain historical persistence in given scientific practices and an internal consistency of scientific theories, but may, and frequently does, create a theoretical provincialism and professional incestuousness detrimental to the progress of a discipline as a whole. The theoretical and sociological narrowing of perspective and debate is especially evident in the case of a critical confrontation between competing and rival paradigms. Sociologically, the choice between alternative paradigms may "prove to be a choice between incompatible modes of community life" (Kuhn 1962: 93); theoretically, it may consist of a choice between quasi-metaphysical dogmas and normative imperatives. At this point, either communication between scholars of differing persuasions may become impossible, and hence preclude a productive resolution of alternatives, or a dialogue may be instigated that will seek to resolve and re-evaluate the nature and function of the rival paradigms. This latter alternative is possible only if the adversaries are cognizant of the theoretical assumptions and methodological standards of each other's paradigms. This productive alternative is precluded, however, if one or both adversaries persist in misunderstanding one another, that is, in molding the precepts of the other's paradigms to suit the purposes of their own assumptions.

Contemporary social anthropological theory is, I believe, confronted by such a case of rival paradigms. This confrontation is a dramatic one because until quite recently neither side had shown a clear willingness to face one another empathetically and productively. Rather, each tended to persist in socio-cultural isolation (one school being primarily, but not entirely, Anglo-American; the other largely, but not exclusively, continental European) and in normative theoretical self-justification (sometimes surpassing the quasi-theological admonitions we have come to expect from political figures). In this short and tentative paper I should like to sketch briefly the basic world view of each of the paradigms, focusing primarily on the paradigm of the European school since it has fewer spokesmen on this continent. I should like to conclude with some indication of the present situation in this confrontation and to suggest a possible means by which a more productive and less antagonistic atmosphere might be created.

The paradigms of one school, the French, are, broadly speaking, selective and social-scientific versions of rationalist philosophy, while the paradigms of the other, the Anglo-American, are largely statements of empiricist philosophical premises. Hence, despite internal differences in the two schools, each tends to perpetuate and adhere to a set of interrelated presuppositions, methods, and characteristic problems. The protagonists of the French anthropological tradition generally assume the primacy of the human mind, their investigations proceed along formal and structural lines, and their questions are posed in synchronic-relational and logically deductive terms. The adherents of the Anglo-American tradition, in its widest sense, assume the primacy of the behavioral act, their methods are essentially quantitative and descriptive, and their problems are phrased in diachronic-causal and empirically inductive terms.

The French anthropologist Claude Lévi-Strauss, the major representative of contemporary continental theoretical anthropology, might be characterized as a philosophical rationalist; that is, he assumes that logic and reality follow the same dialectical process and that both ideas and actions derive from fundamental categories of the human mind (cf. Murphy 1963). The emergence of mind coincides with that of language; together they constitute an intellectual and qualitative mutation in time and, even more important, represent a priori and generic givens from which all further historical events and human creations may be deduced. Lévi-Strauss characterizes this universal esprit humain as follows: like language, the human mind differentiates empirical reality into constituent units; these units are organized into systems of reciprocal relations, and these systems enunciate rules to govern their possible combinations. Further, the qualities of mind and language are not only universal (all men have the intellectual capacity to make and use symbols, and all languages exhibit universal features) but unconscious as well (men do not "know" the universal rules of language, but any particular language nevertheless constitutes a concrete universal). The assumption that structures of the human mind are unconscious and generic, universal and invariable, is of critical importance. It allows Lévi-Strauss to interpret conscious and variable human events and particular and historical cultural institutions as conscious expressions of a more fundamental unconscious reality. And if we recall the attributes of the human mind itself, these unconscious structures are not merely the same for all men and for all materials to which their function is applied, they are also few in number. Hence, the world of mind and language is infinitely diverse with respect to its content, but always limited in its laws.

In Lévi-Strauss's work, the subject matter and method of social anthropology are also derived from the nature and primacy of mind and language. Since social life is both logically and temporally a posteriori to the a priori capacity to symbolize, Lévi-Strauss tends to regard cultures as codes to allow significant communication or exchange, and all social processes as grammars governing particular rules of reciprocity; for example, kinship systems are alliances between groups to ensure the exchange of women, and economic systems to allow the exchange of material goods. Given this interest in the syntax rather than the content of culture, anthropological method should be formal and structural rather than descriptive and empirical. As in mathematical logic, what matters are not the things but the relations between them. In essence, anthropological analysis consists of isolating comparable and formal properties from empirical data and of stating their necessary relations in the form of dialectical transformations. Lévi-Strauss describes his procedure as follows: first, "define the phenomena under study as a relation between two or more terms, real or supposed"; second, "construct a table of possible permutations between these terms"; finally, "make this table the general object of analysis which, at this level only, can yield necessary connections" (Lévi-Strauss 1962a:16).

Lévi-Strauss's method also inclines him to pose anthropological problems in synchronic-relational terms and permits him to explain empirical events by logical deduction from the social-scientific models constructed by his method. Ethnology seeks to interpret "each act as the unfolding in time of certain non-temporal truths" (Lévi-Strauss 1955:61), i.e., those of the logic of mind and language. This does not mean that anthropology is disinterested in historical facts, but it does imply that diachronic events are mere reflections of a more fundamental synchronic and unconscious level of reality. The permanent structure of the human spirit, rather than its history, ultimately explains human behavior; conversely, "the possibility of understanding [historical] change assumes that one has been able to attain to the essence of that which changes" (Sebag 1964:82). The ultimate explanatory value of invariable synchronic structures of the human mind also demands that anthropological problems be phrased in structural or mechanical terms rather than in causal or statistical ones. Thus, ethnology uses "reversible and noncumulative" mechanical time, while historical time is "oriented and nonreversible or statistical" (Lévi-Strauss 1952: 529–530). Like quantum mechanics, anthropological explanations are "morphologically deterministic," while historical explanations "are governed by statistical laws" (Jakobson, quoted in Tax 1953:311).

If empirical and historical events are conscious expressions of a more fundamental unconscious reality, it follows that data are not of themselves intelligible but require a supraempirical model for their explanation. It may be recalled that Lévi-Strauss's method ensures a model composed of analytically comparable and logically abstracted terms based on initial empirical givens. But to *explain* these empirical givens, the model must be manipulated; that is, the various possible relations between terms and their dialectical transformations must be ascertained, "the empirical phenomena considered at the beginning being one possible combination among others" (Lévi-Strauss 1962a:16). For Lévi-Strauss, "to experiment is to create that which wasn't [and] to integrate what is with the network of its possible transformations." In other words, scientific construction means the "primacy of method over substance or, more precisely, of conceptualization over that which is conceptualized" (Sebag 1964:206, 277). Although Lévi-Strauss would readily admit that the final aim of scientific practice is to return to the data, the usefulness of models lies precisely in the fact that they "tell us something more and differently from the [initial] data" (Lévi-Strauss 1960:51). He claims that the final empirical experiments,

guided and suggested by deductive reasoning will not be the same as the unsophisticated ones with which the whole process had started. These will remain as alien as ever to deeper analysis. The ultimate proof of the molecular structure of matter is provided by the electronic microscope, which enables us to see actual molecules. This achievement does not alter the fact that henceforth the molecule will not become any more visible to the naked eye. Similarly, it is hopeless to expect a structural analysis to change our way of perceiving concrete social relations. It will only explain them better. If the structure can be seen, it will not be at an earlier, empirical level, but at a deeper one, previously neglected; that of those unconscious categories which we may hope to reach, by bringing together domains which, at first sight, appear disconnected to the observer [Lévi-Strauss 1960:53].

And it is at this unconscious level that the relations between domains can be shown to conform to the dialectical logic that governs the whole of social and mental life. Returning to its first premises, structural anthropology becomes, in the final analysis, a scientific verification of the rationalist philosopher's intuitive notion of dialectics by pointing to the empirical and social manifestations of this notion in ethnographic fact.

Although many of the presuppositions, methods, and terms used by the French anthropological school admittedly require a far more detailed treatment than the one given here,[2] it

2 My very brief analysis has been especially neglectful of the important notion of dialectics in the structural anthropology of Lévi-Strauss. For a highly informative work on the subject, the reader might consult Lucien Sebag's *Marxisme et structuralisme* (1964).

should be clear that its paradigms are in nearly all cases in-
commensurable with those of the Anglo-American school. In
the first place, the empiricist tradition tends to see mind and
language not as a priori givens but as a posteriori activities,
united with the rest of sociocultural life in their observable role
in the behavioral act (cf. Hymes 1964). The very notion of
mind as advocated by the French school is alien to the Anglo-
American tradition. Even Leach, one of the most sympathetic
critics of Lévi-Strauss, derides the latter's notion of esprit:
"spirit (esprit) is presumably Hegel's objektive Geist, a concept
which doubtless seems quite straight forward to continental
minds but is quite incomprehensible to mine. In plain English
such metaphysical discourse hardly makes sense" (Leach 1965:
779). Leach neatly summarizes the general Anglo-American
suspicion of Hegel, metaphysics, and the notion of Geist. (Nor
is the Englishman's appeal to "commonsense" or "plain"
language philosophically surprising.) The sociological correlate
of his scepticism is, of course, the critique of Durkheim's conscience collective and the latter's alleged equation between God
and society.

Unfortunately, Lévi-Strauss's valuable critique of materialist
anthropology, which his notion of mind implies, is often over-
shadowed by the animosity his style of argumentation arouses.
I do not think that Lévi-Strauss in fact reifies society; rather,
as noted above, "society is, by itself and as a whole, a very large
machine for establishing communication between human beings" (Lévi-Strauss, quoted in Tax 1953:323). This cybernetic
orientation is of necessity intellectualistic. As Bateson has
pointed out, "this world of communication is a Berkeleyan
world, but the good bishop was guilty of understatement . . . ;
in thought and in experience there are no things, but only
messages and the like" (Bateson 1960:480–481). With regard to
the qualities of mind, Lévi-Strauss's understanding of dialectics
is, interestingly enough, only rarely considered by Anglo-American authors (Leach and Needham being notable exceptions);

Lévi-Strauss himself has also written extensively on the importance
of the dialectic, e.g., in the final chapter ("Histoire et dialectique")
of La Pensée sauvage (1962b).

if they do, it is customarily met with derision (cf. Scholte 1966).[3]

With regard to method, empiricist anthropology tends to favor quantitative and descriptive procedures over formal and structural ones. Nadel, for instance, considers structure to be a property of empirical data and conveniently accommodates structural analysis to his own paradigms: it is "no more than a descriptive method, however sophisticated, not a piece of explanation" (Nadel 1957:151–152). For Nadel, explanation is presumably a question of quantitative statistical evidence; that is, to explain is to anticipate. For Lévi-Strauss, on the other hand, the criterion of social-scientific verification is not empirical prediction but analytical intelligibility (cf. also above). Even Hymes, in my estimation one of the few scholars to try to understand Lévi-Strauss in his own terms, complains of the lack of descriptive and empirical evidence: "I have tried but failed to understand how the generalization and universality of which Lévi-Strauss speaks is to be obtained, as he argues, without any counting of cases" (Hymes 1964:46). But for Lévi-Strauss the counting of cases is irrelevant; the existence of "concrete universals" allows for the careful analysis of only a few typical cases and does not demand the establishment of a broad inductive basis for generalization (Lévi-Strauss here echoes Durkheim's famous "when a law has been proven by a well-performed experiment, this law is valid universally" [Durkheim 1912:593]). In Lévi-Strauss's judgment, the social anthropologist faces here a difficult and crucial choice: "either to study many cases in a superficial and in the end ineffective way; or to limit oneself to a thorough study of a small number of cases, thus proving that, in the end, one well-done experiment is sufficient to make a demonstration" (Lévi-Strauss 1952:531).

To turn briefly to the problem of terms and their implications, Murdock's comment on one of Lévi-Strauss's papers expresses a general reaction of empiricist anthropologists: "much

---

3 The persistent neglect of the dialectic implicit in Lévi-Strauss's structural anthropology may prove an interesting problem in the sociology of knowledge. (A similar suggestion for a study in the history of sociology may be found in Gouldner 1962.)

of the difficulty that some readers have had with Dr. Lévi-Strauss's paper revolves around . . . the use of certain terms and forms of expression which may initially rub an American the wrong way" (Murdock, quoted in Tax 1953:108). He further describes Lévi-Strauss as one who "treats social structure as a series of abstract forms, for all the world like a high-school mathematics teacher's blackboard demonstration of a theorem in geometry, rejecting even processless history along with all psychology and even culture, and reducing man himself to an automaton actuated by stresses flowing from structural principles" (Murdock 1955:363). Even if Murdock cannot be credited with great depth of understanding when it comes to Lévi-Strauss, he does point out some of the major "paradigmatic" misgivings of the Anglo-American school. Most American anthropologists find Lévi-Strauss's emphasis on synchronic sociological rules antithetical to their own interest in diachronic and psychodynamic relations. As Schneider has pointed out, American anthropologists are concerned with concrete social groups that endure over time, or with the individual's action within the framework of a particular situation or structure. This understandably leads to various misunderstandings, for example, the usage of the term "choice" in structural anthropology. According to Schneider, "the word 'choice' in English takes at its focus the individual's action . . . , and [the] structure is treated as given." The structuralist is, of course, concerned primarily with "systematic models" composed of logico-mathematical choices among logicostructural alternatives. He is concerned *not* with models "within which actors choose among alternative courses of action," but with the rules and regulations that structure a given system (Schneider 1965:67).

One of the main contentions between the two rival sets of paradigms revolves around the issue of inductive empiricism versus deductive rationalism. One commentator says: "Lévi Strauss's 'clever dialectics' are among the most imaginative and stimulating in the literature, yet their validity has not been scientifically demonstrated." Once tests have been devised, he continues, "I suspect that Lévi-Strauss's work will be very much outdated" (Colby 1963:275). Leach is even more skeptical in his review of Lévi-Strauss's latest work on mythology: it is "incredibly clever, but is it more? In other words, does this work really tell us something about South American myth or something about the complexities and ingenuities of la pensée Lévi-Straussienne?" (Leach 1965:776). What all these comments amount to is that unless Anglo-American anthropologists see their own criteria of verification met in the work of Lévi-Strauss, they have a predilection toward accusing him of molding the data to suit his own theories. This, to a greater or lesser extent, leads to dismissing all of Lévi-Strauss's structural anthropology as—to quote one of the least empathetic or profound critics—"somewhat mystical and seemingly predicated on a sort of circular reasoning," a product of a mind given to the "delusions produced by reification" and "unwarranted speculation" (Coult 1963:268, 269, 273). But as has been shown throughout this paper, one cannot criticize Lévi-Strauss in terms of criteria to which his work *is not meant to conform*. Admittedly one may question his assumptions regarding proper social-scentific verification, but this seems to me a problem for the philosophy of science generally—not one to interfere with the proper *understanding* of Lévi-Strauss's intentions. And I think it will be granted that understanding ought to precede evaluation, not vice versa, as is too often the case.

Again, the brevity of this paper precludes a greater elaboration here of the basic issues involved in this confrontation between differing paradigms. Although this paper has stressed the incompatibilities between the two orientations, I should like to point out briefly that mutual interests and potential agreements are also in evidence.[4] Thus, despite the controversies that rage within the field of kinship studies, "it is to struc-

---

4 The ensuing examples are admittedly highly selective. They are certainly *not* to be interpreted as any indication of an Anglo-American movement to follow the lead of continental structural anthropology. As this paper has sought to show, differences in understanding basic scientific premises and in the interpretation of ethnographic data remain immanently real, even among those most sympathetic to Lévi-Strauss. But these few examples *are* to be understood as an indication of some general common interests among adherents of rival paradigms. The relevant literature and the details of this exchange will be further clarified in a forthcoming essay (Scholte 1966).

tural linguistics, logic, and mathematics . . . that [Anglo-American] investigators are now turning for new analytic and comparative models" (Davenport 1963:218). Clearly this trend is in keeping with Lévi-Strauss's methodological interests. The work of Needham (1962) and Leach (1961a) has further clarified Lévi-Strauss's position in this area, and their fellow English-speaking anthropologists, although often critical (e.g., Homans and Schneider 1955), have at least begun to clarify their own premises and to compare them intelligently with those of structuralists (see especially Schneider's excellent article, 1965). In the area of folklore and mythology there has been a surprising and hopeful interest in the work of Lévi-Strauss. For example, Leach, despite his ambivalent review (1964) of Lévi-Strauss's *Mythologiques: Le Cru et le cuit*, has recently developed a theory of taboo based on "Lévi-Strauss's version of the Hegelian-Marxist dialectic in which the sacred elements of myth are shown to be factors that mediate contradictions" (Leach 1964:34; see also 1961b). In America, the work on folklore by Sebeok represents a methodological perspective similar, although by no means identical, to that of Lévi-Strauss, for example, in its use of qualitative and deductive analysis and its appeal to Saussure and structural linguistics (Sebeok and Ingemann 1956). More recently, Kongas and Maranda (1962) have applied some of Lévi-Strauss's most important concepts to the analysis of American folklore (an attempt severely criticized by Dundes [1964]). Fischer, in a review article, has also aided in bringing Lévi-Strauss's structural analysis of myth to the attention of American scholars (Fischer 1963).

There are indications that Lévi-Strauss is equally interested in a rapprochement between Anglo-American and continental social anthropology. In fact, in all his writings, Lévi-Strauss stresses his indebtedness to Anglo-American anthropology; but he also adds that "it is to a historical situation, not an intellectual tradition, that I am paying homage" (Lévi-Strauss 1955:64). In addition to the historical interest, however, Lévi-Strauss has also expressed positive sentiments of a more systematic nature. In a recent article he comments with approval

on contemporary developments in the "behavioral sciences"—
a term he considers "peculiar to the history of ideas in America" but of great value generally. The term implies, according
to Lévi-Strauss, "the notion of an exact treatment of human
phenomena." These sciences treat of problems similar to those
of structural anthropology, for example, "the theory of communication among individuals and groups, based on the use
of mathematical models." Similar again to Lévi-Strauss's interests, "the research involved . . . presupposes close collaboration between certain social and human sciences—linguistics,
ethnology, psychology, logic, philosophy—and certain of the
exact and natural sciences, such as mathematics, human anatomy and physiology, and zoology" (Lévi-Strauss 1964:547).[5]

By way of conclusion allow me to suggest briefly that even
if a historical perspective has not been an integral part of this
paper, I believe that the resolution of the problem of productive communication between rival paradigms lies largely in the
domain of history—especially in the intellectual-historical perspective generated by a comparative and sociological study of
alternative philosophies of social science. Such proposed studies
must above all conform to the canons of "historicism" and
only potentially to those of "presentism" (Stocking 1965:211).
Debates between rival paradigms often tend to reverse that
order; in a normative and judgmental confrontation history has
all too frequently become a "dramatic struggle between children of light and children of darkness." But—as Stocking also

---

5 The inclusion of zoology requires an additional comment. Lévi-
Strauss is certainly not thinking here of recent developments in the
fashionable area of primatology. For Lévi-Strauss, "the structure of
the molecule provides a much better model for understanding what
human culture is than does the behavior of the chimpanzee"
(Lévi-Strauss, quoted in Tax 1953:61). Rather, he is thinking of
the philosophical and logical principles involved in zoological
classification. This is evidenced by his admiration for George G.
Simpson's *Principles of Animal Taxonomy*. According to Lévi-
Strauss, Simpson has clearly pointed out the primacy of the notion
of order—however defined from one epistemic concern to another
—in both the development of scientific thought and the logic of
the human mind generally (Lévi-Strauss 1963:140).

points out—in a truly historical study one seeks to "understand the past for the sake of the past"; and he adds an especially relevant remark for social anthropology today: "by suspending judgment as to present utility, we make that judgment ultimately possible" (Stocking 1965:212, 217).

In addition, a truly historical perspective may alleviate another main shortcoming of the protagonists of the rival schools: the naive assumption that major theoretical and epistemological issues can be resolved and understood *merely* in terms of the internal chronological development of social anthropology. But in all actuality, crucial assumptions and methods in anthropology are usually the result of numerous environmental factors, both systematic and historical. For instance, the proper understanding and subsequent evaluation of Lévi-Strauss's work must be founded on the philosophical and intellectual-historical awareness that his structural anthropology is in large part an eclectic version of some of the insights of men such as Rousseau, Kant, Hegel, Marx, Durkheim, Freud, and innumerable others. In general, even if men and ideas such as these may not *determine* specific issues in contemporary social anthropology, in large part they and their descendants do give those issues their historical relevance and philosophical justification. This is of course a topic entirely beyond the scope of this paper. But at least I wish to call attention to the problem; I sincerely believe that paradigmatic rivals cannot hope to debate social anthropological issues productively and intelligently unless they *first* comprehend and account for the broader intellectual-historical context in which their own and rivals' paradigms are grounded and through which they develop. Here, I think, an immense contribution can and must be made by the historians of social science.

REFERENCES

BATESON, GREGORY
  1960 Minimal requirements for a theory of schizophrenia. American Medical Association Archives of General Psychiatry 2:477–491.

COLBY, B. N.
1963 Comment on Fischer: The sociopsychological analysis of folktales. Current Anthropology 4:275.

COULT, ALLAN D.
1963 Causality and cross-sex prohibitions. American Anthropologist 65:266–277.

DAVENPORT, WILLIAM
1963 Social organization. *In* Biennial review of anthropology. B. J. Siegel, ed. Stanford, Stanford University Press.

DUNDES, ALAN
1964 The morphology of North American folklore. Helsinki, Suomen Tideakatemie.

DURKHEIM, EMILE
1912 Les formes élémentaires de la vie religieuse. Paris, F. Alcan.

FISCHER, JOHN L.
1963 The sociopsychological analysis of folktales. Current Anthropology 4:235–295.

GOULDNER, ALVIN W.
1962 Introduction. *In* Socialism. E. Durkheim. New York, Collier Books.

HOMANS, GEORGE C., AND DAVID M. SCHNEIDER
1955 Marriage, authority and final causes: a study of unilateral cross-cousin marriage. Glencoe, Ill., Free Press.

HYMES, DELL H.
1964 Directions in (ethno-) linguistic theory. American Anthropologist 66, no. 3, pt. 2:6–56.

KONGAS, ELLI-KAIJA, AND PIERRE MARANDA
1962 Structural models in folklore. Midwest Folklore 12, no. 3. Bloomington, Ind., Indiana University Press.

KUHN, THOMAS S.
1962 The structure of scientific revolution. Chicago, University of Chicago Press.

LEACH, EDMUND R.
1961a Rethinking anthropology. London, Athlone Press.
1961b Lévi-Strauss in the Garden of Eden: an examination of some recent developments in the analysis of myth. Transactions of the New York Academy of Sciences, Series 2, 23(4):386–396.
1964 Anthropological aspects of language: animal categories and verbal abuse. *In* New directions in the study of language. Eric H. Lenneberg, ed. Cambridge, Mass., M.I.T. Press, pp. 23–63.
1965 Review of Claude Lévi-Strauss's Mythologiques: Le cru et le cuit. American Anthropologist 67:776–780.

LÉVI-STRAUSS, CLAUDE
1952 Social structure. In Anthropology today. A. L. Kroeber, ed. Chicago, University of Chicago Press, pp. 524–553.
1955 Tristes tropiques. Paris, Plon.
1960 On manipulated sociological models. Bijdragen tot de Taal-, Land- en Volkenkunde 116:45–54.
1962a Totemism. Boston, Beacon Press.
1962b La Pensée sauvage. Paris, Plon.
1963 Review of G. G. Simpson's Principles of animal taxonomy. L'Homme 3:140.
1964 Criteria of science in the social and human disciplines. International Social Science Journal 16:534–552.

MURDOCK, GEORGE P.
1955 Changing emphases in social structure. Southwestern Journal of Anthropology 11:361–370.

MURPHY, ROBERT F.
1963 On Zen Marxism: affiliation and alliance. Man 21:17–19.

NADEL, S. F.
1957 The theory of social structure. Glencoe, Ill., Free Press.

NEEDHAM, RODNEY
1962 Structure and sentiment: a test case in social anthropology. Chicago, University of Chicago Press.

SCHNEIDER, DAVID M.
1965 Some muddles in the models: or, how the system really works. In The relevance of models for social anthropology. A.S.A. Monograph 1. London, Tavistock, pp. 25–85.

SCHOLTE, BOB
1966 Annotated bibliography of Anglo-American publications on Claude Lévi-Strauss. Information sur les sciences sociales. MS.

SEBAG, LUCIEN
1964 Marxisme et structuralisme. Paris, Payot.

SEBEOK, THOMAS A., AND FRANCIS J. INGEMANN
1956 Studies in Cheremis: the supernatural. New York, Viking Fund Publications in Anthropology No. 22.

STOCKING, GEORGE W., JR.
1965 On the limits of "presentism" and "historicism" in the historiography of the behavioral sciences. Journal of the History of the Behavioral Sciences 1:211–218.

TAX, SOL, ED.
1953 An appraisal of Anthropology Today. Chicago, University of Chicago Press.

7

BRAIN-TWISTER

EDMUND LEACH

The problem is: Just where do we fit in? Are we better or worse or indeed in any way different from our prehistoric ancestors or our primitive contemporaries? We are animals and, therefore, a part of Nature, but we are also self-conscious human beings who can somehow or other conceive of ourselves as outside observers, looking on. And then again the process we call "thinking" is quite clearly something that goes on inside our heads, a function of electrochemical processes in the brain, yet it is also a response to signals that we receive from outside through our senses. How can I believe that I can think *about* Nature, when quite clearly thinking is a phenomenon in which I and Nature interact?

Claude Lévi-Strauss is a prolific writer, but his commen-

From *The New York Review of Books*, Vol. IX, No. 6 (October 12, 1967), pp. 6, 8, 10. Reprinted with permission. Copyright © 1967 The New York Review.

tators are even more so, and as each new volume appears, the whole business becomes more and more a private dialogue for the initiated. It is esoteric stuff, and although this review is addressed to a more general reader, it can scarcely avoid some touches of gobbledegook.

The Savage Mind is a translation, in plain cover, of La Pensée sauvage, which started out in a baffling jacket illustrated with a picture of wild pansies—"there is pansies, that's for thoughts." The translation is anonymous, but it is common knowledge that it has proved a publisher's nightmare. At least three distinguished hands had their share in the final product. Professor Geertz has declared the result to be "execrable"; Dr. Rodney Needham, on the other hand, reports that "a word-by-word collation of the first chapter with the French text yields only a few inconsequential slips." Perhaps both are right. A passage such as "When therefore I describe savage thought as a system of concepts embedded in images, I do not come anywhere near the robinsonnades of a constitutive constituent dialectic: all constitutive reason presupposes a constituted reason" (p. 264) can hardly be said to make much sense though it is a literally exact transformation of the corresponding passage at p. 349 of the French original. Perhaps you have to be an initiate even to understand the French. All the same, I do feel that the translators have fuzzed things up quite unnecessarily in places. Take the title, for example. The obvious translation of La Pensée sauvage is "savage thought"—as in the quotation above—whereas The Savage Mind recalls Lévi-Strauss's much used, but decidedly ambiguous, l'esprit humain, which might suggest that the book is about metaphysics, whereas, in fact, it is about logic.

The fundamental theme of this book is that we are at fault if we follow Lévy-Bruhl (and by derivation Sartre) in thinking that there is a historical contrast between the "prelogical" mentality of Primitives and the "logical" mentality of Modern Man. Primitive people are no more mystical in their approach to reality than we are. The distinction rather is between a logic that is constructed out of observed contrasts in the sensory qualities of concrete objects—for example, the difference between raw and cooked, wet and dry, male and female—and a logic that depends upon the formal contrasts of entirely abstract entities—for example, $+$ and $-$ of $\log e^x$ and e^x. The latter kind of logic, which even in our own society is used only by highly specialized experts, is a different way of talking about the same kind of thing. Primitive thought differs from scientific thought much as the use of an abacus differs from mental arithmetic, but the fact that, in our present age, we are coming to depend on things outside ourselves— such as computers—to help us with our problems of communication and calculation makes this an appropriate moment to examine the way in which primitive peoples likewise are able to make sense of the events of daily life by reference to codes composed of things outside themselves—such as the attributes of animal species. Lévi-Strauss's investigation is complicated, ingenious, and, in my view anyway, persuasive, although the uninitiated will certainly find it easier going if they take a preliminary bite at the cherry by first tackling Le Totémisme aujourd'hui.

What excites the anthropologist is the way in which Lévi-Strauss sees that quite disparate kinds of ethnographic fact, culled from entirely different geographic regions, are ordered according to the same kind of logical principles. Thus, Indian caste systems consist of endogamous groups that are distinguished by cultural criteria (occupations), whereas Australian aboriginal societies consist of exogamous groups that are distinguished by natural criteria (totems), yet considered as total systems, that is, as structured arrangements of categories, these entirely different patterns of culture are strictly comparable. Lévi-Strauss's demonstration that this is the case has the appearance of a highly sophisticated conjuring trick, and his problem throughout is how to convince the reader that the logic of primitive thought, which he exhibits, is a genuine characteristic of the way the human brain operates—an aspect of l'esprit humain—rather than just an exemplification of the ingenuity of Claude Lévi-Strauss.

Noninitiate readers who are intrigued but not wholly persuaded will either have to take the argument on trust or tackle the detailed evidence that Lévi-Strauss is providing in his huge study of the mythology of the tribal peoples of South America. This is planned as a four-volume work, of which two volumes have so far appeared: *Le Cru et le cuit* and *Du miel aux cendres*. It is an extraordinary performance. In *Le Cru et le cuit* Lévi-Strauss claims to demonstrate, by reference to 187 different myths, that in this region of the world there is felt to be a logical similarity between polarities of cooking, the polarities of sound, and the polarities of human self-consciousness of the form:

the transformation Raw—Cooked:
the transformation Fresh—Putrid::
Silence: Noise:: Culture: Nature

In the new book, which includes references to an additional 166 myths, the themes of honey and tobacco are seen as the "penumbra of cooking" (*les entours de la cuisine*), and their contrasts are said to correspond, in the logic of mythology, to contrasts "internal to the category of noise," such as the opposition: continuous sound *versus* discontinuous sound or modulated sound *versus* unmodulated sound. The argument is that objects and sensory characteristics of things "out there" are manipulated by the brain, through the thought system incorporated in myth, just as if they were symbols in a mathematical equation. As an illustration of just how complicated this mathematics is said to be, I provide a quotation from the end of the book:

When used as a ritual rattle (*hochet*) the calabash is an instrument of sacred music, utilized in conjunction with tobacco which the myths conceive under the form of [an item of] culture included within nature; but when used to hold water and food, the calabash is an instrument of profane cooking, a container destined to receive natural products, and thus appropriate as an illustration of the inclusion of nature within culture. And it is the same for the hollow tree which, as a drum, is an instrument of music whose summoning role is primarily social, and which when holding honey, has to do with nature if it is a question of fresh honey being enclosed within its interior, and with culture if it is a question of honey being put to ferment within the trunk of a tree which is not hollow by nature but hollowed artificially to make it into a trough [pp. 406–407].

If Lévi-Strauss is justified in believing that primitive people "think like that," then quite clearly the Frazer–Lévy-Bruhl–Sartre notion that primitive thought is characterized by naïveté, childishness, superstition, and so on, is wholly misplaced. Lévi-Strauss's primitives are just as sophisticated as we are; it is simply that they use a different system of numeration.

But is he justified? The ethnographic worry is that Lévi-Strauss may have selected his evidence so as to fit his theory, that if he had used other evidence the thesis might fall to pieces; for it must be understood that, despite the formidable list of 353 myths, there is a lot of other rather similar stuff that *might* have been used. Of course, there are two volumes still to come, but it worries me that at least one important source has so far been largely neglected, namely, von den Steinen's materials on Bakairi myth.[1] These data are unusually detailed, and since the Bakairi live next door to the Bororo, whom Lévi-Strauss utilizes as his basic "type" of Amazonian Indian, one would have thought that this evidence must be highly relevant.

But that is by the way. I have put in that cautionary paragraph for the benefit of my anthropological colleagues, some of whom seem to think that I am such a devoted Lévi-Straussian that I can no longer exercise any scholarly detachment on the subject at all. In fact, I think the case does stand up; the fault, if there is one, is that Lévi-Strauss tries to make his mathematics of manipulated sensory objects too systematic. He fails to allow for the fact that, whereas the symbols used by mathematicians are emotionally neutral—ix is not more *exciting* than x just because i is an imaginary number—the concrete symbols used in primitive thought are heavily loaded

1 Karl von den Steinen, *Die Bakairi Sprache,* Leipzig, 1892, and *Unter den Naturvölkern Zentral-Brasiliens,* Berlin, 1894, Chapter XIII.

with taboo valuations. Consequently, psychological factors such as "evasion" and "repression" tend to confuse the logical symmetries. This does not mean that Lévi-Strauss's calculus must be "invalid," but it may be much less precise than he seems to suggest. Or to put the same point another way: because he takes his cue from Jakobson-style linguistic theory and the mechancis of digital computers, Lévi-Strauss tends to imply— as is clearly shown in the long quotation cited above—that the whole structure of primitive thought is binary. Now there is not the slightest doubt that the human brain does have a tendency to operate with binary counters in all sorts of situations —but it can operate in other ways as well. A fully satisfactory mechanical model of the human mind would certainly contain many analog features that do not occur in digital computers. For example, most human beings make a distinction between *b* sounds and *p* sounds, also between *green* color and *yellow* color, and also between the value *good* and the value *bad*. These distinctions are of the either/or (binary) kind, but they cannot be mechanical in any simple sense because different human beings can cut up the cake of experience in quite different ways. But quite apart from that, we can also make distinctions of intensity—louder-softer, brighter-darker, betterworse, and these are not binary discriminations at all. So far, the Lévi-Straussian scheme of analysis cannot take such factors into account.

Oh dear! Once again I seem to be talking polemic for the initiates! Novices who tackle *The Savage Mind* as their introduction to the mind of Lévi-Strauss will, if they are patient, get an enormous brain-twisting enjoyment out of the first eight chapters, which provide a basic introduction to the logic of "the science of the concrete." They will not be in a position to judge whether Lévi-Strauss is correct in claiming that this logic is a universal human characteristic, but they will certainly begin to see some of their own familiar behavior in a new light. May I commend in particular the extensive references to be found in the Index under: "Dogs, names given to"? The basic point here is that, with us, dogs, as pets, are a part of human society but not quite human, and this is expressed when we give them names that are like human names but nearly always slightly different from real human names. Well, perhaps! But then Lévi-Strauss goes on to argue that the names we give to racehorses are of quite a different kind (as certainly they are) because racehorses "do not form part of human society either as subjects or objects. Rather they constitute the desocialized condition of existence of a private society; that which lives off racecourses or frequents them." The train of thought is to me quite fascinating, but what sort of "truth" is involved? Even if we grant that the names given to racehorses form a class that can be readily distinguished, is this juxtaposition of the type of name and the type of social context anything more than a debating trick? The question needs to be asked. Whether it can be fairly answered I am not sure. Each reader needs to consider the evidence and think it out for himself.

What will doubtless puzzle the novice reader—more particularly when he comes to *Du miel aux cendres*—is how on earth Lévi-Strauss comes upon his basic oppositions in the first place. How could it ever occur to anyone that an opposition between roast pork and boiled cabbage might reflect a fundamental characteristic of human thinking, or that honey and tobacco (of all things) might come to have a significance as fundamental as that which opposes rain and drought? The answer, I think, is that Lévi-Strauss starts at the other end. He first asks himself: How is it and why is it that men, who are a part of Nature, manage to see themselves as "other than" Nature even though, in order to subsist, they must constantly maintain "relations with" Nature? He then observes, simply as a fact of archaeology rather than of ethnography, that ever since the most remote antiquity men have employed fire to transform their food from a natural raw state to an artificial cooked state. Why is this? Men do not have to cook their food; they do so for symbolic reasons to show they are men and not beasts. So fire and cooking are basic symbols by which Culture is disinguished from Nature. But what about the honey and tobacco? In the case of cooked food the fire serves to convert the inedible natural product into an edible cultural product;

in the case of honey the fire is used only to drive away the bees, that is, to separate the food, which can be eaten raw, from its natural surroundings; in the case of tobacco, it is the conversion of food by fire into a nonsubstance—smoke—which makes it a food. So here already we have a set of counters of different shapes and sizes each with a front and a back that can be fitted together into patterns, and that could be used to represent the exchanges and transformations that take place in human relations, as when a boy becomes an adult, or the sister of A becomes the wife of B. With some such framework of possibilities in his mind, plus the basic proposition that mythology is concerned to make statements about the relations between Man and Nature and between man and man, Lévi-Strauss looks at his evidence and the pieces of the puzzle begin to fit together.

Because the game is unfamiliar, the whole business at first seems very astonishing; there must be a catch in it somewhere. On the other hand, if Lévi-Strauss's basic assumptions are valid —as I myself think they are—it could hardly be otherwise! Even if his argument eventually has to be repudiated in certain details, we simply must accept certain fundamental parts of it. Any knowledge that the individual has about the external world is derived from structured messages that are received through the senses . . . patterned sound through the ears, patterned light through the eyes, patterned smell through the nose, and so on. But since we are aware of a single total experience—not a sound world plus a sight world plus a smell world—it must be because the coding of the various sensory signal systems can be made consistent—so that hearing and sight and smell and taste and touch, etc., seem all to be giving the same message. The problem then is simply to devise a means of breaking the code. Lévi-Strauss thinks he has solved this problem; even those who have doubts should be fascinated by the ingenuity of the exercise.

The ninth chapter of The Savage Mind is of a different kind from the rest. It is a direct critical attack on the presuppositions of Sartre's Critique de la raison dialectique, and it is, for me anyway, extremely difficult to pin down just what all the pother is about. What Lévi-Strauss seems to be saying is that Sartre attaches much too much importance to the distinction between history—as a record of actual events which occurred in a recorded historical sequence—and myth, which simply reports that certain events occurred, as in a dream, without special emphasis on chronological sequence. History records structural transformations diachronically over the centuries; ethnography records structural transformations synchronically across the continents. In either case, the scientist as observer is able to record the possible permutations and combinations of an interrelated system of ideas and behaviors. The intelligibility of the diachronic transformations is no greater and no less than the intelligibility of the synchronic transformations.

The argument is close-woven and full of splendidly distracting rhetorical flourishes—at one point, Sartre's views are rated "a sort of intellectual cannibalism much more revolting to the anthropologist than real cannibalism"! The synchrony of ethnographic variation corresponds to a characteristic of savage thought itself, which Lévi-Strauss compares to the effect of a hall of mirrors in which "a multitude of images forms simultaneously, none exactly like any other, so that no single one furnishes more than a partial knowledge . . . but the group is characterized by invariant properties expressing a truth." The truth is a totality, the sum of many overlapping partial images. History, on the other hand, sacrifices totality in the interest of continuity. "In so far as history aspires to meaning, it is doomed to select regions, periods, groups of men and individuals in these groups and to make them stand out as discontinuous figures, against a continuity barely good enough to be used as a backdrop. A truly total history would cancel itself out . . . a history of the French Revolution cannot simultaneously and under the same heading be that of the Jacobin and that of the aristocrat." In a formal sense, Lévi-Strauss does not denigrate history; he simply argues that "historical knowledge has no claim to be opposed to other forms of knowledge as the supremely privileged one," but there is a strong suggestion that the only really satisfactory way to make sense of history would be to apply to it the method of myth analysis that Lévi-Strauss is exhibiting in his study of South American mythology! Whether such an argument could possibly have any appeal to professional historians or philosophers of history it is not for me to say. Certainly it lies far off the beaten track of conventional anthropology.

The anthropologist's main lament is rather different. The technique of analysis that Lévi-Strauss employs with such skill and seeming success in the analysis of myth grew out of his early exercises in the analysis of formal marriage systems, notably in *Les Structures élémentaires de la parenté*. In this work the conventions of matrimonial exchange were shown to constitute a system of communication between social groups; in the same way, conventions of cooking have now been shown to constitute a system of communication between Man and Nature. This analogy is not preposterous. Human brains devised styles of cooking, and human brains devised rules of marriage—the two codes of thought may well link up. But Lévi-Strauss has not tried to show that they in fact link up; he has simply moved off to study other things.

This is a pity. Compared with cooking and music and the peculiarities of naming systems, the study of kinship and marriage is dull and pedestrian stuff, but, for an anthropologist, kinship is the hard core, and for some of us Lévi-Strauss's retreat to the land of the Lotus Eaters is, to some extent, a matter for regret.

8
SCIENCE BY ASSOCIATION
DAVID MAYBURY-LEWIS

Lévi-Strauss has, almost overnight, become an institution. In France he is widely and appropriately regarded as the antithesis to Sartre's thesis. Intellectual journals throughout the world have broken out in a rash of symposia devoted to his ideas, occasionally interspersed with highbrow press conferences, bearing titles such as conversations with (or *entretiens avec*) Claude Lévi-Strauss. *Newsweek* celebrated the English translation of *La Pensée sauvage* with a full-page article, which was followed at a predictable and deceptively nonchalant interval by the apotheosis of an essay in *Time*. Clearly, structuralism is "in." But what is all the fuss about? The excitement has, after all, been caused by some highly technical books in social an-

From The Hudson Review, Vol. XX, No. 4 (Winter 1967–68), pp. 707–711. Copyright © 1968 by the Hudson Review, Inc. Reprinted by permission.

thropology, a discipline whose findings do not normally hit the headlines.

The idea behind structuralism is basically very simple. Its essence is an insistence on formal analysis that aims to produce explanatory models of social systems. Lévi-Strauss, taking his cue from Saussure and the structural linguists of the 1930s, set out years ago to uncover the grammar and syntax of human societies. In his classic work on the elementary structures of kinship, published in 1949, he argued that the marriage systems of certain kinds of society could be viewed as communication systems in which women (among other things) were messages. This was perhaps ony a variation on the old idea that any social system could be treated as a system of exchange, but Lévi-Strauss took the argument much further. These particular exchange systems, he suggested, were not only codes, but they were homologous with other codes in the same societies. Marriage arrangements might be shown to have the same structure as the distribution of meat from a slaughtered animal, the services performed by a barber, or a people's beliefs about life after death. They "said" the same thing in the idiom of the society in question. The job of the social anthropologist was therefore to find out what a society was trying, either consciously or unconsciously, to "say."

This, very baldly stated, has been the leitmotiv of Lévi-Strauss's work. From marriage systems he turned to the societies of Central Brazil, where he had himself done fieldwork, and suggested how the "language" of their institutional and intellectual arrangements could be interpreted. He followed this up with a book on totemism, in which he argued that the widespread custom of associating a human group with some nonhuman emblem or totem should be understood as a classificatory procedure. So, in a society where different clans recognize different animal species as their totems, this can be taken as a symbolic statement to the effect that one clan is to another as one species to another, that is, discrete. However, the actual nature of the relationships expressed in such symbolic statements can be grasped only when the complete system of classification and the nature of the analogy beween the natural series (in this case, the animal species) and the social series (in this case, the clans) has been understood. Hence, the study of totemism is only a particular branch of the study of human systems of classification, and it is this grand theme that is treated in *The Savage Mind*.

Lévi-Strauss starts off by demolishing the comfortable assumption that a wide gulf, or indeed a gulf of any sort, separates primitive thought from the thinking of civilized people (by which we normally mean ourselves, whoever we are). Anthropologists have demonstrated beyond question that peoples possessing only a rudimentary technology may nevertheless have a thorough, systematic, and detailed knowledge of their environment in all its aspects. Nineteenth-century scholars were inclined to believe that such primitive science was a fluke, acquired either accidentally or as a by-product of simple technical activities pursued in a "follow-your-nose" spirit. In fact, Sartre resuscitated just such arguments in his *Critique de la raison dialectique*. Lévi-Strauss will not accept them. Instead, he forces us to admit that such knowledge must have been acquired as a result of minute observation combined with genuine speculative interest. This speculation seeks order at all costs. More than that, it postulates a total system of connections in which everything in the universe has its place. In *The Savage Mind*, Lévi-Strauss unravels the logic behind such systems and, in so doing, presents us with an argument about the nature of all human thinking. Savages are clearly not the only ones given to savage thought. It is simply a mode of thinking that can be found anywhere and at any time. It proceeds as logically as our own "scientific" thought and obeys the same laws. It is the terms of this savage thought that differ. It tends to be expressed in concrete statements that refer to special characteristics of plants, animals, stars, topography, weather, human society, a whole host of things drawn at random from the inventory of a society's concepts. It is thus impossible to predict which features a society will choose as vehicles for its thought and often hard to understand why it has selected those it uses. One can only seek to decipher its code, to grasp the associations of those special features that give symbolic meaning to the statements in which they occur, and in this way to understand the system of categories that make up its way of thinking.

Lévi-Strauss does this with an argumentative subtlety and stylistic elegance that have dazzled his colleagues and brought critics to the verge of ecstasy. His own thought makes breathtaking associative leaps, so that reading him is an exciting experience even for the most skeptical. Here surely is the secret of the strange fascination that structuralism exercises over anthropologists and nonanthropologists alike. Lévi-Strauss can perceive connections where none were thought to exist. He can produce order where we had resigned ourselves to chaos, and we are suitably grateful.

Has the analysis of myth got bogged down? Lévi-Strauss gives it a new direction by insisting that myths do not try to explain natural phenomena but rather use natural phenomena as a medium of explanation, as they try to resolve the contradictions with which man is inevitably faced. Have anthropologists discussed totemism so exhaustively that they hardly know what it means anymore? Lévi-Strauss provides a formulation that enables them to see that someone who makes a statement like "I am a wallaby" is not necessarily feeble-minded or possessed of a prelogical mentality. Nor does he stop there. Totemic societies have traditionally been thought of as radically different from societies with caste systems. In the first, a man who is wallaby may not marry a woman who is wallaby, but must seek a wife from another totemic group. The essence of the second is that a man must marry within his caste. Lévi-Strauss argues that, formally speaking, these two codes represent similar but inverse solutions to a social problem; that they can be, and in the past actually have been, transformed into each other. In the one system, castes are heterogenous. They specialize in certain services that they perform for each other. In such a system, women are therefore decreed to be heterogenous too and cannot be interchanged between castes. On the other hand, in a totemic system the constituent groups do not really perform services for each other, although they may pretend to, for example by performing rites to ensure the abundance of their own species of game animal. Women are there-fore decreed to be interchangeable and are in fact exchanged between groups. Castes and totemic groups are thus two means of effecting social integration based on reciprocal services, al-though they appear to be entirely different social languages.

Later he takes the argument in a different direction. To-temism, he suggests, is not only a way of thinking, it is also an etiology. Totemic societies explain themselves in terms of a Weltanschauung that incorporates change into itself while remaining ostensibly immutable. They are in sharp contrast to those societies that admit the notion of flux as part of their self-image and therefore explain themselves by history. This accounts for what Lévi-Strauss calls the "totemic void," the fact that the great civilizations of Europe and Asia show little trace of totemic institutions, for explanations by classification and explanations through history are mutually exclusive. Of course, he concedes, all societies are processes. This does not mean, however, that they are all equally seen to be so by their own members.

This leads him into a final peroration, in which he takes issue with Sartre not only over the possibility of distinguishing between primitive and civilized thinking but also over the privileged position that Sartre and others tend to accord to historical explanations in social science. He argues devastat-ingly that historical statements about process are no less infer-ential, though they are often thought to be so, than sociological ones. However, one cannot help feeling that this critique of Sartre has been put in as a final chapter less because it winds up the argument of the book than because this was a con-venient and not too irrelevant place for Lévi-Strauss to go another round with his opponent for the benefit of the Parisian intelligentsia.

Here we come to the heart of the problem. How does one really evaluate a book like The Savage Mind, which is trying to do so many things at once? One does not do it justice by enumerating its major themes, for its arguments are too nu-merous and varied. Besides, the peculiar flavour of the book derives from the erudite range of its examples and its striking analogies. Savage thought is compared to the lace collar in a Clouet painting, while the paintings of Central Australian aborigines are like the mannered water-colours done by old maids (for they are both snobs). In fact, Lévi-Strauss's thought is as richly and unpredictably associative as that of the societies he discusses. After a while one gets used to it. When he tells us that the ideas of a given people remind us at once of . . . one braces oneself for an analogy so recondite that it may take considerable acrostic ability to perceive its relevance. And then there are the epigrammatic inversions so characteristic of his style. Of caste systems and totemic societies he says, for example: "castes naturalize a true culture falsely, totemic groups culturalize a false nature truly" (p. 127).

The total effect of his writing is so pregnant and elliptical that it is frequently difficult to discover what he means to say. No wonder the translation of La Pensée sauvage led to such divergences between author, editors, and translator that the translator's name has (at her request) been removed from the book. The fact of the matter is that Lévi-Strauss is often hard to follow, not because of the complexity of his thought, but because of the baroque ambiguities of his style. This places his critics in an invidious position. It may seem churlish to ask what he means when he has said it so memorably, and the people who do so are often thought of as spoil-sports. Yet the question must be asked.

The elegant prose glides easily over unargued assumptions, inconvenient evidence, and the occasional contradiction. Totemism, we are told, is a system of classification. Later it is assumed to be a system where totemic groups exchange women. But all totemic societies do not prohibit marriage between people of the same totem, or even confine totems to single social groupings, as Lévi-Strauss himself recognizes elsewhere in his book (p. 125). Totemism and historical explanations are held to be antithetical, yet they appear to coexist in Africa. Even if we accept that what we have hitherto called totemism is nothing but a special type of classificatory procedure, this does not tell us why some people feel their totems are sacred, others feel that they are inedible, and others feel that they are nothing in particular. This is, of course, a problem of a different order, and it would be foolish to reproach Lévi-Strauss for not doing what he never intended to. But his grand synthesis does seem on occasion to be not very illuminating.

Take, for example, the discussion of names that is central to The Savage Mind. He is provocatively witty about the naming of birds, dogs, cats, and racehorses, but when it comes to humans, his elaborate discussions and lengthy formalizations boil down to the suggestion that names classify people. This observation is immensely significant for some societies (the ones from which Lévi-Strauss draws his examples) where names form a well-defined system into which the named person is introduced. For the majority of human societies, however, the proposition is only true in the formal sense that to name something is to assign it to some sort of class. It may be suggestive to call this "treating individuation as classification," but the notion does not really lead anywhere when we come to consider the functions of names in an alien society, unless of course it happens to be one of the special type from which Lévi-Strauss generalizes.

I find all this a little disturbing. Lévi-Strauss appears to take unwarranted liberties with his evidence. He sacrifices precision of expression to verbal pyrotechnics, and when the display is over, it is not always clear what can be done with his grandiose theoretical constructs. Not only does he spin metatheories but he expresses them in metaphors, and one cannot help noticing that when he comes down from the clouds and deals with specific cases, he is often trivial or just plain wrong. But it is unreasonable to expect anybody to be always theoretically brilliant, or even regularly right. It is undeniable that some of Lévi-Strauss's insights have done precisely what we expect of structuralism, helped us to see things in a new way. In this respect, they have been revolutionary. Furthermore, there are few people who write as stimulatingly as he does about Man. If I continue, then, to wonder ungratefully whether or not he is right, that after all is my job as an anthropologist.

9

THE NATURE OF REALITY

COLIN M. TURNBULL

Any reader would be justified in expecting a book entitled *The Savage Mind* to deal, among other things, with totemism. Unfortunately, there are many, particularly in the ranks of professional anthropology, who would expect the subject matter to be almost exclusively totemic; to them this might even mean exclusively the totemic system of the Australian aborigines, which, by virtue of being the most complex system known, is too often mistakenly thought to contain all that need be known about totemism. There is little in this book that will appeal to such tiny minds, and its true value will escape others who are similarly myopic. On the other hand, those who would be the first to proclaim themselves as disciples of the author of this remarkable book are equally likely to reap but partial

From *Natural History*, Vol. LXXVI, No. 5 (May 1967), pp. 58, 60, 62–63.

benefit if they expect Claude Lévi-Strauss, genius of French anthropology, to be saying something unduly complicated simply because he is Claude Lévi-Strauss.

The author has the strange reputation of having reduced human society to mere mathematical equations, and of being abstract in his thought, as in his approach to anthropology, to the point where he can pursue his own thoughts only by means of computers. It is somehow never allowed to emerge that Lévi-Strauss is not an inhuman machine, but a warm, incredibly sensitive human being, with emotions just as powerful as those of anyone else. It might not be wrong to say that he is also a dedicated human being, and the object of his dedication is the true understanding of man. Perhaps he would, to be perverse, insist that the object of his devotion was society rather than man, but this work shows a profound concern for and understanding of man the individual, just as it tells us about man as a social particle.

This is not to say that The Savage Mind is an easy book, for Lévi-Strauss is not given to facile generalizations. As a true scientist he treats his subject, and his readers, with respect. He considers different points of view and conflicting evidence, and supports every statement with fact. Any one of us might find ourselves in possession of facts that would lead us to disagree here and there with some of the conclusions drawn or with some of the interpretations given, yet the bulk of the evidence is clear and unequivocal.

Lévi-Strauss is not likely to wish to see himself as a knight in shining armor, and his devotees would be still more dismayed at such iconoclasm. Yet, consciously or otherwise, he has devoted his life to the shattering of our ignorance concerning "savage man," a term that, with dry Gallic humor, he persists in using. The Savage Mind continues the battle, undermining still further the ground upon which stand those who would dismiss primitive man simply because of the superficial strangeness of his ways and the apparent difference between his mode of thought and ours. The book is, however, far more than an attempt to clear up old misconceptions. It is an eloquent appeal for a positive approach, in which we are urged to look to primitive culture for a better understanding of mankind and of human society. It succeeds in this in an unexpected way, for it will make the reader question the whole nature of social reality. To show the usage of abstract terms in primitive languages, Lévi-Strauss cites a Chinook example: to render the statement "the bad man killed the poor girl," the Chinook would say, rather, "the man's badness killed the girl's poverty." This is interesting linguistically, but it is of even greater importance in terms of social philosophy, and one wonders whether the Chinook, or other primitive peoples who show similar discernment, do not have a better grasp of the essence of reality than we do.

With regard to the thought of primitive man, Lévi-Strauss points out that Neolithic man was already heir to a long tradition of scientific thought. Agriculture, the domestication of animals, pottery, weaving—all these things and more cannot have been arrived at by mere perceptions of natural phenomena, only by a logical mental process. The book proceeds to illustrate that process as it can be seen at work in divers aspects of primitive culture. Of these aspects, illustrative of the process of primitive thought, totemism is merely included as one that in itself has no reality as a social institution, but rather as a system of thought. Here is an example of how the reader of this book not only will discover more about how primitive man thinks but will arrive at a better understanding of social organization in primitive society. Lévi-Strauss sees totemism as a classificatory system rather than as an "institutional reality." He does not see it merely as a somewhat facile (and "primitive" in its other sense) means of tying two worlds together, but rather as a sensitive appraisal of the similarity of certain differences that exist both in nature and in human culture. Differences and distinctions of the kind so clearly symbolized in totemic systems exist in the practical world in which human societies are formed. Totemism expresses a system for ordering these distinctions and differences that can be transferred to different levels. No society can survive in disorder. On the one hand, primitive man recognizes disorder all around him; on the other, he perceives a system of order in certain natural phenomena. By transferring this system of ordered relationships to the level of his own experiences, he introduces stability and resolves chaos.

Games, in primitive society, Lévi-Strauss points out, recognize the principle of differentiation, and indeed introduce inequality where previously none existed by forcing a stable situation to the point where one side is winner and the other loser. In the same way primitive religion is concerned with the same kind of distinctions and differences, but it takes inequality and reduces it to a great and all-pervading equality, finally equalizing the greatest and most obvious inequality of all, that between the living and the dead.

Lévi-Strauss sees myth as another example of the concern of the primitive mind for ordered relationships. Myth is not concerned, as has so often been thought, with the explanation of natural phenomena. Rather it is concerned with facts of a logical order, using natural phenomena to explain them.

For instance, the many myths told by the forest pygmies concerning the relationship between elephants and mice, or other small animals, are not told because the pygmies are particularly interested in elephants and mice, let alone in trying to explain how elephants and mice get along together. The focus of interest is on quite another plane. The facts are as follows: in the forest there are villagers as well as pygmies; the villagers are tall and consider themselves superior; they follow an economy that is directly in competition with that of the pygmies. The villagers cut the forest to plant their fields; the pygmies need the forest as it is in order to hunt. In his myths the pygmy explains these facts by showing that a similar situation exists in the animal world and is ordered to everyone's satisfaction. The large clumsy elephant who destroys the forest in his search for food is constantly being outwitted by the smaller and more clever animals; the smaller animals are constantly able to avoid the larger ones, and even to take advantage of them by trickery. The pygmy sees, in the actual situations around him, in the natural phenomena he understands so well, the patterns and systems of order that he needs to solve his own human situation.

Primitive thought is designed to meet not practical needs but intellectual ones. As a true scientific system of thought the one thing it will not tolerate is disorder. It is this passion for order, recognizing is as indispensable for survival, that characterizes the savage mind. This book shows the same zealous devotion, reaching out into all corners of social activity, lending color and direction wherever it touches. Customs that before seemed strange now appear as eminently logical and comprehensible; logic that before seemed remote and isolated is shown to be immanent and functional. The world of the primitive is no longer remote and unreal, nor indeed primitive, let alone savage. It is immediate, dynamic, and very real; if savagery is to be found, it is more easily found in our own unthinking attitudes toward a world we do not understand.

Lévi-Strauss not only helps us to comprehend primitive society but also helps us to respect it and, if we will, to learn from it. He writes with ease and elegance and with an ever-present humor that makes his exposition, even at its most difficult, pleasurable as well as worthwhile. It is anthropology at its finest, for it is written by an anthropologist who is also human.

10
LÉVI-STRAUSS'S UNFINISHED
SYMPHONY: THE ANALYSIS OF MYTH

BOB SCHOLTE

In current French intellectual circles, structural methods and investigations are definitely "à la mode." The name of this "school's" most illustrious representative—Claude Lévi-Strauss —has become virtually an academic household term. Innumerable Frenchmen and quite a few others feel called upon to offer homage to this "Pope of the Left Bank" or to chastise his disciples for their alleged "intellectual imperialism." But whether pro or con, one important fact is abundantly clear: the philosophic influence and cultural dominance of structural anthropology far exceed the restricted domain of ethnological inquiry or the stately corridors of the "laboratoire d'anthropologie sociale." Not only in Paris but elsewhere, cinematog-

From *Natural History*, Vol. LXXVIII, No. 2 (February 1969), pp. 24–26, 100–101.

raphers and musicians, aestheticians and literary critics, popular journalists and erudite commentators, professional philosophers and intellectual historians, sociologists and cultural anthropologists continue to add their critical assessments and varied opinions to a growing body of secondary literature on structuralism, its intellectual possibilities and theoretical limitations. This popular acclaim—whether French-continental or Anglo-American, laudatory or critical, judicious or irresponsible—does attest to the remarkable influence and intellectual importance of Lévi-Strauss's gigantic achievements. Though at times embarrassing to Lévi-Strauss himself, his many books are often best sellers and the constant subject of heated debates and learned interpretations. As one French critic was led to observe, whether we are Marxists or phenomenologists, Thomists or existentialists, we are all of necessity structuralists.

The *raison d'être* for Lévi-Strauss's phenomenal success is a complex one, though one reason clearly stands out. He is a French savant par excellence, a man of extraordinary sensitivity and human wisdom, an encompassing mind of considerable erudition and philosophical scope, a deliberate stylist with profound convictions and convincing arguments. These rare qualities are evident in all of Lévi-Strauss's writings, which explains why even his minute ethnographic analyses and specific ethnological arguments are avidly read and critically examined by interested laymen and knowledgeable scholars alike. *The Raw and the Cooked* (the first of four volumes devoted to the comparative study of myth) happily and ably carries on this scholarly and humanistic tradition. And the book adds yet another chapter to the tireless quest for a scientifically accurate, aestheically viable, and philosophically relevant cultural anthropology. The opening pages of the introductory "Overture" attest to the scientific continuity of purpose: to search for "an inventory of mental patterns, to reduce apparently arbitrary data to some kind of order, and to attain a level at which a kind of necessity becomes apparent, underlying the illusions of liberty." The study of mythology is an especially privileged domain for his deterministic understanding of "objectified thought and its mechanisms" since myths, unlike various marriage rules or lesser classificatory systems, "signify the mind that evolves them by making use of the world of which it is itself a part," that is, "an image of the world which is already inherent in the structure of the mind." Myth's quest for intelligibility is not, however, without its "objective correlate," its concrete realization in the domain of expressive imagery and sensed reality. In fact, myth is like music (the supreme mystery of the human sciences and the key to their progress): both are able to "act simultaneously on the mind and the senses, stimulating both ideas and emotions and blending them in a common flow, so that they cease to exist side by side, except insofar as they correspond to, and bear witness to, each other." Finally, this anthropological delineation of a "science of the concrete" constitutes a philosophical testament to the intellectual cogency and existential viability of human thought—primitive or civilized. As Lévi-Strauss concludes in the as yet untranslated second volume of *Mythologiques*, mythic thought contains within itself the objective seeds of aesthetic illumination and scientific intelligibility, not as an evolutionary stage in man's intellectual progress, but as a uniquely creative expression of one sociocultural variant of the diverse human condition.

The substance of mythology, like other modalities of man's intellectual activities, forms a response to what Lévi-Strauss—like Jean-Jacques Rousseau before him—considers a universal and fundamental anthropological problem: the transition from animality to humanity, instinct to intellect, literal to figurative, continuous to discrete, and from nature to culture. To render this monumental passage from the one to the other intelligibly, mythology carves out various domains of meaning and renders them explicable by mediating the given oppositions between them. For example, the mythic origins of the domestic fireside mediate between the "naturally" raw and the "culturally" cooked, the legendary waters mediate between the sky above and the earth below, religious funeral rites between the living and the dead, and so on. Lévi-Strauss traces the dramatic and complex contours of this integrative symphony of the mythic spheres by means of a detailed and exacting examination of the indigenous legends and primitive myths of American Indian culinary practices and cultural beliefs. The ethnographic data and ethnological analyses offered in these volumes simply defy a summary statement. In *The Raw and the Cooked* alone, 187 myths and their variants from over 80 tribes are discussed. In virtually every instance, a given myth is carefully described and intimately related to the totality of its sociocultural environment, its geographic, technoeconomic, sociological, and cosmological contexts. The elements of the myths are further shown to pertain to the human senses (auditory, tactile, olfactory, and gustatory) and to other modes of intellectual classification (botanical, zoological, organic, aesthetic, ideological, and religious). It is the domain of the human senses (so inexcusably neglected by anthropologists), however, that stand out as the mediators par excellence between the literally given and the symbolically meaningful. For example, the activity of cooking, the area of the cuisine, and the attendant gustatory code are significant because "not only does the cooking mark the transition from nature to culture, but through it and by means of it, the human state can be defined with all its attributes, even those like mortality which might seem the most unquestionably natural." This intellectualist conclusion about the meaning of food and food preparation does not, of course, make Lévi-Strauss's *Mythologiques* simply the anthropological version of the *Larousse Gastronomique*; but it is perhaps fitting that a French *philosophe* could rephrase the German Feuerbach's contention "Man is what he eats" to read "Man is what he thinks he eats." Nor does this conclusion even begin to exhaust the wealth of ethnographic data and the numerous ethnological analyses presented in *The Raw and the Cooked*. Thus, Americanists will find a series of suggestive historical reconstructions based on structuralist principles, while anthropological theorists may examine a number of methodological arguments on such perennial issues as the relation between form and content, myths and their transformations, "symbolist" and "functionalist" explanations, etc. We cannot go into these questions here, but those interested will find Lévi-Strauss's book indispensable reading.

One final question should be asked, one that inheres in the very organization of The Raw and the Cooked (whose Table of Contents includes such musical forms as Overture, Theme and Variations, Symphony in Three Movements) and reflects on the general scope and possible limitations of structural investigations: What is the anthropological meaning of Lévi-Strauss's celebration of comparative mythology, especially given its intimate kinship to the nature and understanding of music? Both myth and music mediate man's crucial passage from nature to culture by integrating the syntactically constituted and symbolically conscious domains of his intellectual reflections and esthetic creations with the neurologically determined and unconscious silence of his physiochemical nature and bioecological constraints. In structural explanation generally, the latter invariably underlie and account for the former. In the present context, this means that mythology and music—profoundly important as they are—can do no more than "bring man face to face with potential objects of which only the shadows are actualized, with conscious approximations—of inevitable unconscious truths." In other words, behind the joyful and creative enactment of mythic literature or the encompassing and self-reflective composition of musical forms looms the more determinist and quite mechanical reality of a cybernetic and esthetically indifferent unconscious. If structural investigation is to understand and explicate the implicit workings of this unconscious and universal brain, it must become the silent listener to the rhythms and pulsations of that unconscious; it can no longer hope to speak explicitly about the human condition or man's cultural products. That is, if Lévi-Strauss is to remain consistent with his own stated premises, structuralism is either reduced to inexplicable silence, like a concert audience, or to artistic metaphor, like the poet-musician. In the final analysis, the intellectually reflective and scientifically deliberate study of the infrastructural and hidden unconscious reality of myth "is itself a kind of myth."

11
SCIENCE OR BRICOLAGE?

DAVID MAYBURY-LEWIS

Du miel aux cendres is precisely the sort of sequel one would have expected to *Le Cru et le cuit* (1964). It is in its way a total Lévi-Straussian experience, which the *aficionados* are certain to enthuse over. From its dust jacket, taken from a 1554 copy of a book on hunting in the library of Fountainebleau castle, to the woodcuts that illustrate it, the book is an aesthetic treat. Sections of it are introduced by excerpts in Latin from Roman authors calculated to establish an atmosphere of erudite eclogue. But the maze of diagrams, couched in Lévi-Strauss's own parody of logical notation, warns the reader that there is hard work ahead. After a brief résumé of *Le Cru et le cuit*, we are plunged into the analysis of a further 166 myths,

Reproduced by permission of the American Anthropological Association from the *American Anthropologist*, Vol. 71, No. 1 (1969), pp. 114–121.

largely in order to elucidate the symbolic significance of honey and tobacco in the thought of the South American Indians.

Allusions to honey and tobacco abound in myth, literature, and popular sayings, and they are by no means confined to South America. Lévi-Strauss considers them in the special context of South American myth and draws from them a cosmic significance that only his most devoted followers are likely to find convincing. Nevertheless, the book will give great pleasure to anyone who enjoys intellectual acrostics and delights in fearless scholarship. It is essential reading for those who take a serious interest in South American Indians or in the study of myth. I found, however, that reading it for review was the most exasperatingly onerous task I can remember assuming. A reviewer must, after all, try to evaluate the argument of a work under review, and a major difficulty, though not the only one, with *Du miel aux cendres* is to find out precisely what the argument is. The style of the work does not help. It is a sort of Chinese puzzle, full of diversions, false trails, metaphoric asides, and inconclusive perorations. The serious reader, who either cannot or will not allow himself to be borne along unresisting on the waves of verbiage, will spend much of his time trying to remember what the point of a given section is supposed to be. By the end, he may still be trying to unravel the argument.

After the appearance of *Le Cru et le cuit*, it was claimed that anthropologists would no longer be able to consider "the content of myths to be unimportant or unworthy of attention *per se*" (N. Yalman, in *The Structural Study of Myth and Totemism*. E. Leach, ed. 1967:72). I doubt that they ever did. In the past they often ignored myths because their attention was focused elsewhere, which is not the same thing at all. Alternatively, they did not quite know what to do with myths once they had them. Well, Lévi-Strauss has now shown what he thinks ought to be done with them. He is convinced that myths are statements in some sort of metalanguage that his approach enables him to decode. Even those who do not accept his renderings of their meaning are unlikely, after these books, to doubt that such decoding is possible. There is no doubt that *Le Cru et le cuit* charted a new course in the study of myth. The trouble with *Du miel aux cendres* derives from that fact. It is no longer a pioneering work and cannot claim any critical forebearance on that score. Technically, it is a continuation of *Le Cru et le cuit* and cannot properly be appreciated without constant reference to the latter. Moreover, it ends abruptly, leaving the reader up in the air with the promise of yet another volume to come. The old virtues are still in striking evidence and have already earned respectful accolades in the intellectual weeklies. But what was pardonably experimental in *Le Cru et le cuit* becomes frankly irritating in its sequel. There is no reason why anthropological readers should any longer grant the author a willing suspension of their disbelief. The time has come, however provisionally, to take stock.

Lévi-Strauss points out that honey is ambiguous: now toxic, now delicious, now maleficent, now associated with all the good things of this world. There is, he suggests, a similar polarity in the role of tobacco, and honey and tobacco form a pair of mythic opposites. It should be noted that honey and tobacco are treated throughout like algebraic symbols, so that myths that make no mention of either are said to be dealing with honey/tobacco issues, to be related to such issues, or to be transformations of such issues. Since honey is seductive, myths dealing with seduction or any uncontrollable passion may be treated as honey myths. Similarly, tobacco requires burning, so that its role in myth is treated as part of the study of those myths where there is reference to burning, smoke, cooking, and the origin of fire. In *Le Cru et le cuit* an entire system of myths relating to the origin of fire was discussed. It was also argued that myths about the origin of wild pig systematically invoked the action of smoke/tobacco. But wild pigs are held to be prototypical of meat, and meat is the item par excellence requiring the action of fire. Tobacco thus enters meat myths, which are a prerequisite for fire myths. Surely, then, there must be a system of tobacco myths, explaining the origin of tobacco. Similarly, honey is symmetrical with tobacco. Honey enters myths that explain the origin of feather necklaces (and feathers are often burned to make smoke).

Surely there is, therefore, a system of myths explaining the origin of honey, and surely all these systems form a group of systems.

Du miel aux cendres is about the isolation and analysis of these systems. Lévi-Strauss points out the associations of the honey/tobacco notions with the wet/dry opposition, and this leads to a discussion of the mythic significance of climate and constellations, of periods of fasting and periods of abundance. The final section of the book, piquantly entitled "The instruments of darkness," seeks to establish the symbolic significance of sounds, and even of smells and physical states. By the interpretation, some would say the manipulation, of associations of ideas in myths, Lévi-Strauss argues that the relationships between certain types of sound are analogous to and thus represent the relationships between notions that the myth seeks to express. The rationale for this analogy is not, however, made clear in his lengthy treatment of the topic. In any case, the nub of the argument is that in South American myth the honey idea is seen as such a potently seductive force that it severs the link between man and the supernatural, whereas the function of the tobacco idea is to recreate, or at any rate to maintain, this link.

The conclusions drawn from all this are characteristically sweeping. We are told, and this is a direct outcome of the argument of *Le Cru et le cuit*, that cooking "seen in its pure state" (i.e., the cooking of meat) and alliance similarly looked at (i.e., exclusively as a wife-giving and wife-taking relationship between brothers-in-law) express in Indian thought "the essential articulation of nature and culture" (p. 259). The myths tell us furthermore that with the appearance of a neolithic economy and the consequent multiplication of peoples and diversification of languages, social life encountered its first difficulties, which resulted from population growth and a chancier composition of family groups than the models allowed for. Thus, motifs relating to famine, fasting, and the absence of fire are interpreted as the abolition of cooking, or as a sort of return to nature. Nature itself is ambiguous, offering either unbearable privations leading to famine or a natural (as opposed to cultural) abundance, and the polarity of honey ideas symbolizes these contradictory aspects (p. 356). South American myths, and by implication myth in general since evidence is also adduced on occasion from the Old World, are all variations on a grand theme of the relationship between nature and culture. At one stage, Lévi-Strauss suggests that the myths he is discussing describe the fall from a golden age, when nature was prodigal, through a bronze age when man had clear ideas and distinct oppositions at his disposal that enabled him to dominate his environment, to a state of misty indistinction where nothing can be properly possessed or preserved since everything is confused (p. 221).

What is one to make of all this? Above all, what is the evidence behind such hyperbole? Lévi-Strauss discusses his procedures at the beginning of Le Cru et le cuit. Lest I be accused of yet another of those obtuse failures of comprehension with which his critics are commonly charged these days, I shall quote the passage in French. In speaking of his undertaking (entreprise) and the objections to it, which he anticipates from mythographers and specialists in tropical America, he explains:

Quelle que soit la façon dont on l'envisage, elle se développe comme une nébuleuse, sans jamais rassembler de manière durable ou systématique la somme totale des éléments d'où elle tire aveuglément sa substance, confiante que le réel lui servira de guide et lui montrera une route plus sûre que celle qu'elle aurait pu inventer [1964:10].

The image of a nebulous method, blindly sucking its substance from the myths but nevertheless confident that the Real (or the True?) will keep it on the right track, is hardly one to inspire confidence or even to be taken seriously. Unfortunately, a great deal of what Lévi-Strauss writes cannot be taken seriously. His style is packed with similar conceits. The total effect is notoriously unclear—there are passages in both books that are unintelligible even to Frenchmen—and it systematically obscures important issues, dismissing them elegantly and epigrammatically just as a conjurer's patter distracts attention from what is really happening. In this instance he is smoothly skirting an issue left unresolved in both books, namely, the precise status of his interpretations of myth. What is this reality that he feels confidently will guide his enquiry? Is it to be found in his conclusions? If so, what sort of a reality do they represent? Again we are fobbed off with an epigram that has been much quoted. Lévi-Strauss proposes to show not so much how men think in myths but *"comment les mythes se pensent dans les hommes, et à leur insu"* (1964:20). But what does this mean, if anything? As for the crucial question of whether his interpretations of myths may be no more than something he chooses to read into his own manipulations of them, a sort of intellectual haruspication, Lévi-Strauss replies serenely that it does not matter:

For, if the final goal of anthropology is to contribute to a better knowledge of objective thought and its mechanisms, it comes to the same thing in the end if, in this book, the thought of South American Indians takes shape under the action of mine, or mine under the action of theirs [1964:21].

In this way, he sidesteps the real difficulty, which is how to get at the thought of South American Indians at all.

The way he sets about it is certainly unorthodox. He is dealing, he tells us, with mythology but sees no reason therefore to ignore the evidence of tales, legends, pseudohistorical traditions, ceremonies, and ritual (1964:12). His refusal to be bound by traditional distinctions or to be drawn into sterile definitional discussions is surely laudable. But some distinctions, nevertheless, have to be made and some working definitions provided. Lévi-Strauss never tells us how he knows whether a story is a myth or not or why he selects the "myths" that he does for consideration. He anticipates the objection that he may have selected his myths in order to prove his points, ignoring those that might serve as contrary evidence, and replies with two separate arguments. First, by *reductio ad absurdum*, he suggests that such an objection is utopian, for it requires an analysis of all myths before a comparative analysis of any myths can be undertaken. But this argument is in itself absurd.

Nobody expects a scholar to examine all the evidence in such a field. He is expected merely to state clearly how he selects the evidence he does examine and to show that he has made a serious attempt to ensure that there is not contrary evidence available and ignored. Alternatively, Lévi-Strauss argues that it is possible to write the grammar of a language without knowing all the words that have ever been uttered in it. He proposes therefore to provide at least the outline of a syntax of South American mythology (1964:16), without feeling bound to consider every myth ever recorded from that continent. This linguistic analogy, which has been the leitmotiv of all his work, will be discussed briefly below. For the moment it is enough to note that Lévi-Strauss ignores some of the conventional precautions of mythography. He presents some myths in paraphrase, some only in partial versions. He does not as a rule consider how the myth was collected, by whom, from whom, and what sort of a story it was supposed to be. This might not be of much significance for some purposes. But Lévi-Strauss on occasion goes into a microscopic *explication de texte*, where the style of a myth, its precise words and their associations are all considered as evidence for highly abstract theorizing. Under the circumstances it is reasonable to expect that he should take more care to establish his texts and their contexts.

For example, a crucial point in the complex pastiche developed in both books is Lévi-Strauss's contention that the jaguar of the Central Brazilian fire myths is married to a human wife. His evidence for this is a parenthesis in one of the Kayapó versions of the myth. None of the other Gê versions mentions that she is human. They do not mention that she is *not* human either, but if she were a female jaguar, this would hardly be necessary. Inquiries carried out among the present-day Kayapó, Apinaye, Sherente, and Shavante, all of whom know the story well, have provoked categorical assertions that the jaguar's wife was indeed a jaguar. One must therefore consider the Kayapó variant on which Lévi-Strauss bases his argument to be a curious anomaly rather than a typical text. Lévi-Strauss may of course argue that these Indians really think of the jaguar's wife as a human and of the jaguar as a brother-in-law, in spite of what they say.

I find the argument unconvincing, but in any case this is quite different from his statement that the Gê are explicit on the point (1964:91).

This brings us to the central difficulty. How does one attempt to validate the analysis of a myth? One might turn to the other aspects of the culture of the people who tell it. Yet in these books there is surprisingly little evidence adduced from ritual, a domain to which one might expect a scholar to turn for clues to mythical symbolism. There is much mention of sociological evidence, but this "evidence" turns out on inspection to have a curious status in the argument. When it is elaborately detailed, as for the Bororo (1964:45–52), it transpires that it has only the most tenuous connection with the subsequent analyses of myth. On the other hand, the "*armatures sociologiques*" to which Lévi-Strauss does link the myths are extremely general and abstract, consisting mostly of combinations built out of oppositions such as conjunction/disjunction, male/female, kinship/alliance (p. 37). Most myths could be expressed in these terms, especially if the oppositions are assigned as arbitrarily or even as metaphorically as Lévi-Strauss assigns them. Thus, the elaborate superstructure of interpretation rests on weak sociological foundations. But this does not appear to matter, for the relationship between social arrangements and mythical structure is postulated at such an abstract level as to be quite nondiscriminatory. Virtually any society could be shown to be appropriate for any myth, provided that the tellers lived in the proper environment. This is convenient, for it enables Lévi-Strauss to use and closely analyze myths from societies about which very little is known. At the same time it renders his analyses comparatively impervious to the progress of ethnography, for, if an earlier report is proved incorrect, it is unlikely to affect the myth analysis. In sum, these interpretations of myth do not require us to establish the ethnography.

The crucial evidence, it is soon clear, comes from ecology and from the myths themselves. Lévi-Strauss argues that myths are not told in order to explain natural phenomena. Rather they use the elements of the environment as symbols in a discourse that deals with the vital problems affecting man, or at least affecting the tellers of the myths. So he combs the literature for information about terrain, climate, flora, fauna, constellations, and anything else which might help him to elucidate the language of myth in given societies. The most helpful sources for his purpose are therefore ethnoscientific treatises, but there are few of these for South America, or indeed for anywhere else in the world. Nevertheless, he sets out with extraordinary industry and ingenuity to determine the salient characteristics of natural phenomena in order to speculate on how such features are likely to be perceived. From such speculations he derives a sort of dictionary of potential symbols. Such potentialities only acquire meaning, however, from their position in the constituent elements of myth and the relationship among such elements. Lévi-Strauss usually elucidates this in terms of a dialectic of bipolar oppositions. His insistence in a footnote (p. 74) that he does not always use binary models is accurate but misleading. The fact is that his interpretations of myth, the theoretical assumptions behind them, and the very style in which they are couched all rely heavily and monotonously on binary oppositions. So too did his programmatic paper, "The Structural Study of Myth," and the canonical formula it contained (Anthropologie structurale, 1958:252), which was expressly suggested as holding for all myths and which has, on Lévi-Strauss's own admission, guided his work ever since (pp. 211–212). But how does one arrive at these myth structures, or rather, how does one evaluate such postulated formulas once they are arrived at?

Mary Douglas wrote of one of Lévi-Strauss's earlier myth analyses (La Geste d'Asdiwal): "Although I have suggested that the symmetry has here and there been pushed too hard, the structure is indisputably there, in the material and not merely in the eye of the beholder" (in Leach 1967:56). But this is a faulty perception of the difficulty. If I read a myth, select certain elements from it, and arrange them in a pattern, that "structure" is bound to be in the material unless I have misread the text or demonstrably misrendered it. The fact of its being there does not, however, indicate that my arrangement is anything more than my personal whim. As a matter of fact, in the case of *La Geste d'Asdiwal*, it is quite possible to emphasize other arrangements that are equally inherent in the myth, especially if one uses the full text and not the abridged version presented by Lévi-Strauss. A myth is therefore bound to have a number of possible "structures" that are both in the material and in the eye of the beholder. The problem is to decide between them and to determine the significance of any of them.

Lévi-Strauss arrives at his structures by determining the referents of mythical symbols from a study of popular sayings, ethnography, and ecology, and then postulating the relationship of these symbols to one another. In order to do this, he frequently deals with groups of myths, selected by him as relating to a single theme. The structure or message (for Lévi-Strauss it amounts to the same thing) that emerges from them is the message of them all, although it may be a set of permutations on a mythic statement. Once such a group has been assembled, Lévi-Strauss feels justified in building the structure out of one feature from one myth and another from another myth, where neither feature appears in the myth containing the other. Having done so, he argues that the groups can be transformed into other groups by the systematic application of certain procedures. The validity of these groups, depending as they do on considerable interpretative abstraction, is open to question. Yet Lévi-Strauss treats them from start as firmly established. This confusion of his method with its results is exemplified by the way in which he deals with a group of "equations" that generate the six variations of a group he calls "The Frog's Feast." In a series of lengthy and ingenious analyses of myths taken from the Guianas, the Chaco, the Tupi, and the Gê, he argues that it is possible to trace a series of transformations. An Arawak myth describes how a woman marries a man and introduces him and his people to honey. When he inadvertently utters her name in public, she turns into a bee and flies away. Bee is here a woman. In a Warrau myth a man marries a girl, shows himself a miraculous and prodigious hunter, but finally turns into a bee and dissolves into honey. This gives the transformation of bee-woman into bee-man. Subsequent transformations deduced occasionally cryptically, from this corpus are bee-man into frog; frog into frog-woman; frog-woman into jaguar-woman; jaguar-woman into jaguar-man; jaguar-man into jaguar-woman. The two final transformations double back on themselves. In Lévi-Strauss's words:

Just as a seamstress finishing her work folds back the border of her material and sews it on the reverse side where it cannot be seen so that the whole thing does not unravel, [so] the group is completed by turning back the sixth transformation over the fifth one like a hem [p. 220].

On the next page we are told that, because the sixth transformation takes us back to the theme preceding the first one, this shows that there is no need to look further; the group, thus bounded at one of its extremities, is a closed one. But this is to mistake his procedure for his discovery. The sequence and the group are both postulates that depend on each other. One cannot be confirmed by reference to the other.

This type of "confirmation" abounds in the *Mythologiques*. There are references to similar "verifications." There is even talk of "proof." Lévi-Strauss speaks of his rules of method, of his predictions, of their confirmation. He shows his working in a series of diagrams, equations, and graphs, using a notation that imparts an air of science or, at the very least, of rigorous logic to the enterprise, so that it has duly been accepted in some circles as a "science of myth." The kindest thing to be said about such pretensions is that they should be taken as more Lévi-Straussian metaphor. They need not, indeed they cannot, be taken seriously. The rules that are so eloquently discussed are nevertheless imprecisely formulated and intuitively applied. The "verifications" depend on a tissue of assumptions that the reader is supposed to take on trust. Even the pseudological notation, which is undoubtedly convenient, does not mask the fact that Lévi-Strauss is quite casual about relationships that are crucial to his arguments, such as distinction, opposition, and contradiction. For those who find the interpretations implausible, there is little supporting evidence in the "verifications."

This problem of validation is the central difficulty, not only in Lévi-Strauss's analyses of myth, but in all of his structuralism. Unfortunately, he does not recognize it. Again and again he proposes his own theory as the only logically satisfactory solution, when this means it is the only solution that follows from his assumptions. At the beginning of this sustained investigation of myth he could write: "In spite of the formal perspective which it adopts, structural analysis thus validates ethnographic and historical interpretations which we proposed over twenty years ago and which [though] considered overbold at the time, have constantly gained ground [ever since] [1964: 17]." Yet this passage refers to certain papers on the social structures of Brazil that are notorious for their unverifiable speculations, unwarranted inferences, and untenable conclusions. (I am at present preparing a work that sets out the evidence for these categorical assertions.) This is not to say there is nothing in these papers that a specialist in the area would find acceptable or useful. But significantly the useful ideas they contain are not the interpretations Lévi-Strauss erroneously believes to have been validated, but certain general theoretical suggestions. The *Mythologiques* are similarly full of provocative suggestions. Some of them are tossed out as hypotheses about topics on which the author says he is no specialist and into which he does not wish to venture. Certainly it is this imaginative boldness that makes Lévi-Strauss exciting to read, but he can indulge in it at little risk. Since his ideas are infrequently stated as testable propositions, they are not normally refuted. If any of them, however unspecific, are taken up, however tenuously, by area specialists, then he may claim they have been "validated." At the very worst, they are simply left as exciting hypotheses. But when the excitement has died down, it still remains to be seen whether they lead anywhere and which, if any of his suggestions are "right."

Yet even if these theses are unprovable or unproven, this does not necessarily mean that they are inconsiderable or even implausible. This is why *Du miel aux cendres* is so tantalizing. There is so much of it that feels right. Nobody could doubt after reading it that Lévi-Strauss has correctly perceived the paradoxical aspects of the power of honey and tobacco symbolism in South America. He has demonstrated that there are recurrent themes in myth, not merely in the traditional folkloristic sense of textual motifs, but structural messages that may be expressed by varying symbols. His brilliant suggestions concerning the nature of mythic structure have certainly opened new perspectives in the anthropological study of symbolism. Meanwhile, the details of his investigations fascinate even where they fail to convince. Sights, sounds, smells, textures, tastes, their ramifications throughout the environment, their intellectual associations, all are investigated and codified, so that his is a cultural anthropology in its widest sense, peering into those recesses of human activity that anthropologists so often ignore or find inexplicable. But it is all pushed too far. In detail it often achieves self-parody, as when bull-roarers are said to have the function of chasing away women because they expel all the feminine terms from the periodic chain of marriage alliances, which offers a sociological equivalent of the cosmological chain formed by the alternation of night and day, thus:

$$\left(\overline{\triangle = \bigcirc} \; \overline{\triangle = \bigcirc} \; \overline{\triangle = \bigcirc} \; \overline{\triangle = \bigcirc}\right) \equiv \left(\text{day-night, day-night, day-night, day-night, etc.}\right) \left(\text{p. 363}\right)$$

In general, Lévi-Strauss throws out ideas that he does not investigate satisfactorily. Instead, he simply piles on more ideas, till his whole enterprise looks less like a science than a piece of his own *bricolage*.

Finally, one is led to wonder, as others have wondered before (e.g., Douglas 1967), whether peoples all over the world, or even the peoples of South America, really construct such elaborate myth systems in order to transmit coded messages about nature and culture, wife-givers and wife-takers. And should these myths then be treated as hymns or as five-finger exercises? Lévi-Strauss does not discriminate. But an analysis of his own work is illuminating for it reveals an obsession with the nature/

culture opposition and the notion of alliance. The patterns of Lévi-Strauss's thought emerge clearly, but what of the Indians, the tellers of the myths? It is not enough to say that structural analysis will reveal what they are trying to say in them simply because myth is a language and structuralism was successful in linguistics. Myth is not language, it is like language. The analogy is useful, but it has its limitations. In language the message is consciously communicated and consciously received by native or fluent speakers. It is not found at the level of syntax. Yet by compiling a syntax of myth, Lévi-Strauss claims to be decoding its unconscious message. Nor do linguists expect to find language universals at the level of syntax, yet Lévi-Strauss implies that there may be a universal language of myth, and he speaks of "la pensée mythique" as he sets about writing a grammar for it. There may be indeed, but if so it differs radically from ordinary languages and the same rules cannot be held automatically to apply to them both. So it will not do to suggest, as Leach does (1967:xviii), that those who are sceptical about Lévi-Strauss's revealed syntax of a pan-South American myth language are like the diehards who refused to believe in the deciphering of linear B. The analogy is a false one. After all of Lévi-Strauss's dialectical ingenuity we still do not know who is supposed to be saying what and in what language to whom.

12
CONNAISSEZ-VOUS LÉVI-STRAUSS?

ROBERT F. MURPHY

In the social sciences, *Les Structures élémentaires de la parenté* stands as a monument. It is at once the most important anthropological study of kinship since Lewis Henry Morgan's *Systems of Consanguinity and Affinity of the Human Family* (1871) and the most creative advance in social thought since the time, a half-century past, of Emile Durkheim, Georg Simmel, and Max Weber. This is admittedly an extravagant and incautious statement, and it is made in the face of grave personal doubts about some of the basic premises of the work. Nonetheless, *The Elementary Structures of Kinship* is a book that cannot be ignored by any serious student of society, for its underlying subject matter is the nature of man and the definition of the human situation.

From *Saturday Review*, May 17, 1969, pp. 52–53. Copyright 1969 Saturday Review, Inc.

The volume is the major opus of the celebrated Claude Lévi-Strauss, Professor of Social Anthropology at the Collège de France and ethnographer of Brazilian Indians. When first published in 1949, the book drew only part of the attention that its subject matter warranted. Written by an ethnologist for other ethnologists, it was read by most French anthropologists, many English anthropologists, and few American anthropologists—a gradient that reflected facility with French rather than doctrinal schisms. Lévi-Strauss complains in the preface to the second edition, the translation of which is here reviewed, that this linguistic provincialism has resulted in considerable misunderstanding of the work. His French, one might add, has a certain elegance that makes it obscure to the foreign reader and troubles French graduate students in anthropology as well. Even more discouraging than the language barrier for the potential reader was the virtual unavailability of the book. French publishers apparently assume that reading is a class-linked phenomenon, for Les Structures was issued in a printing so limited that it was soon exhausted. Those in libraries either fell apart (the work was miserably manufactured) or were stolen, and the few remaining copies were treasured by their owners the way bootleg copies of Henry Miller used to be.

While Les Structures lay untranslated and unavailable, the fame of the study spread through commentaries on it written by those who had read it, and by a few who had not. Lévi-Strauss also published other, less technical works, which were translated and widely distributed in paperback form. The most famous of these was Tristes Tropiques, a poignant and beautiful evocation of life among Brazilian Indians, which could well have been subtitled "Lévi-Strauss in the Underworld." The subsequent appearances of Structural Anthropology, Totemism, The Savage Mind, and the first of his volumes on mythology consolidated Lévi-Strauss's position as one of the most famous anthropologists of our age but also elevated him into the peculiarly French role of Great Academician. His vogue has spread throughout the United States, of course, making him as unavoidable at cocktail parties as the cheese dip. Novelists attempt to adopt his métier, students of comparative literature now read Bororo mythology for clues to Joyce, and philosophers have found a new respectability for ontology. No worse fate could befall any ethnographer, including being eaten by one's informants.

The contents of *The Elementary Structures of Kinship* will be a source of surprise, and even dismay, to the prospective reader who thinks he is to be treated to an anti-Sartre polemic. The bulk of the tome is concerned with the custom of cousin marriage and, more specifically, marriage with the cross-cousins. Cross-cousins are the children of the father's sister and of the mother's brother, making this a rather specialized topic, but the author goes beyond this fine detail to consider why in certain societies marriage with the mother's brother's daughter is preferred and the other form proscribed, and vice versa. Given the additional consideration that these forms of marriage occur only in remote and exotic societies, and only in a minority of them, one may wonder why Lévi-Strauss has become a culture hero of the established literati and the subject of a lead article last year in the *New York Times Magazine*.

It is perhaps the very arcane nature of the subject matter that makes this a great book, for Lévi-Strauss has the gift that allows some to see the universe in a speck of dust and him to see man's fate in the most obscure of social transactions. Cousin marriage is of importance to him because it is an elemental form of reciprocity, which, in turn, is man's means of meeting the contradictions of the natural order and thus transcending it to assert his humanity. Lévi-Strauss sets about his task by posing a fundamental opposition between the realm of nature and the level of culture. Within nature, sexuality is distinguished as the most social of instincts, but its expression manifests the contradictory tendencies of randomness and involution, or promiscuity and incest. The orderly exchange of women between groups through marriage at once resolves the antithesis, endows women with the dual status of natural object and cultural value, and sets in motion a cycle of reciprocity that is the primary means of distinguishing and then allying social groups through setting a definition of their otherness. In plainer language, the basic "we-they" distinction within human society is set by the rules of incest coupled with the laws of reciprocity. Among the latter rules or norms, those regarding the preference for marriage with one or another, or both, cross-cousins are the most elementary means of guaranteeing that he who gives a woman in marriage will have the expectation of getting one back as a wife.

The varieties of cross-cousin marriage, however, are each related to different kinds of cycles of exchange of women; that is, they are connected with different social systems. Though the demonstration of this point occupies the middle part of the volume, the arguments set forth are highly technical and need not be raised here. What is important is that Lévi-Strauss has written a book on social structure from the point of view of marriage instead of devoting the usual positivistic attention to the definition, nature, and composition of social aggregates, and he has thereby uncovered structures that are not evident from the traditional empirical perspective. This may seem like a shift of focus from apples to oranges, but it would miss the point. Rather, he has directed his attention from apples to anti-apples, for this is certainly the relation beween kinship-defined groups and marriage. In short, Lévi-Strauss is a dialectician by virtue of mode of thought, methodology, and results, which take the form of reconstructions of reality. His structures are not immediately given within his data but are transformations of these facts, sets of oppositions between the facts, and the resolutions of these contradictions.

That he is a dialectician, but not a materialist, has evoked some comment, and the Lévi-Strauss phenomenon is frequently interpreted as a result of the Marxian disillusionment or as a new kind of right-wing revisionism. It would be a mistake to cast his theories in a political frame of reference, however, for they have little immediate relevance to doctrinaire disputes, despite Lévi-Strauss's membership in French Left intelligentsia. His dialectic is more the pre-Marxian variety, for he sees the structures of society to be isomorphic with the structures of mind. To Lévi-Strauss, the basic organization of thought processes is of an oppositional kind; the mind acts much like a digital computer in posing conceptual opposites, but it goes beyond this to find resolutions of these contradictions. The structures of society are similarly conceived as a set of oppositions, and these are congruent with, if not emergent from, those of thought. He finds these elusive structures in marriage exchange, in myths, and in the contrasts of distinctive sound features in language.

It is a timeless dialectic, frozen and crystalline, an underlying level of reality that can occasionally be glimpsed within the chaos of events. This may well be its appeal today.

The only other anthropologist to have been so celebrated by such an unlikely following was Lewis Henry Morgan, to whose memory the book is appropriately dedicated. The apostle of Morgan, however, was Friedrich Engels, whereas Lévi-Strauss will probably have Susan Sontag. There is no doubt that the book will be widely read by this new disciplehood, but the bitterly funny part of it all is that none of them will really be able to follow his arguments. For all but the small band of social anthropologists who specialize in the cloudy realm of kinship algebra, the only parts of the book that need be read are Chapters 1–7 and 28–29, which give the author's general views on reciprocity, marriage, and the incest taboo. This warning will not stop the established literari from chatting about Murngin section systems, just as German workmen once discoursed on Punaluan marriage, but their listeners should beware. The caveat is not simply professional arrogance, for the preface to the volume contains a lengthy indictment by the author of Rodney Needham's interpretation of his work. Dr. Needham, incidentally, is Reader in Anthropology at the University of Oxford and happens to be the general editor of the translation of the book. Connaissez-vous Lévi-Strauss?

The publication of this translation is a major event, and it is a pleasure to say that it is faithful to the original while preserving its beauty of style; Needham and his associates have done a magnificent job. The book itself will quicken the controversy over Lévi-Strauss's theories, but its sweep and magnitude should also elevate the level and style of social science discourse. The systematic dialectical mode, the theory of mind and society, and the nonempirical nature of his structures make this one of the most pioneering, and controversial, ventures in the history of the study of man. Edmund Leach has called the book "a spendid failure." It may well be just that, but it will tower in a tradition of scholarship that has been characterized by small and squalid successes.

13
ORPHEUS WITH HIS MYTHS

GEORGE STEINER

There can be no doubt of Monsieur Lévi-Strauss's influence on the life of ideas in France. It is, perhaps, second only to that of Sartre. But the exact nature of that influence is not easy to define. Much of Lévi-Strauss's work is highly technical. In their manner of expression and in the range of reference they assume, his more recent writings are exceedingly intricate, almost hermetic. How many among those who invoke Lévi-Strauss's name and what they take to be the method of his thought have, in fact, read La Pensée sauvage, the whole of the Anthropologie structurale, let alone Le Cru et le cuit? The difficulty itself may be part of the spell. As did Bergson, Lévi-Strauss has been able to project a certain tone, a presence nearly

From Language and Silence, by George Steiner (New York, Atheneum, 1967), pp. 239–250. Copyright © 1965, 1967 by George Steiner. Reprinted by permission of the publisher.

dramatic, in a culture that has traditionally seen ideas as highly individualized and that, unlike England, gives to philosophic discussion a public, emotionally sharpened context.

A page of Lévi-Strauss is unmistakable (the two opening sentences of *Tristes Tropiques* have passed into the mythology of the French language). The prose of Lévi-Strauss is a very special instrument, and one that many are trying to imitate. It has an austere, dry detachment, at times reminiscent of La Bruyère and Gide. It uses a careful alternance of long sentences, usually organized in ascending rhythm, and of abrupt Latinate phrases. While seeming to observe the conventions of neutral, learned presentation, it allows for brusque personal interventions and asides. Momentarily, Lévi-Strauss appears to be taking the reader into his confidence, *derrière les coulisses*, making him accomplice to some deep, subtle merriment at the expense of the subject or of other men's pretensions in it. Then he withdraws behind a barrier of technical analysis and erudition so exacting that it excludes all but the initiate.

But through his aloof rhetoric, with its tricks of irony and occasional bursts of lyric *élan*, Lévi-Strauss has achieved a fascinating, sharp-etched individuality. Rejecting the Sartrian view of ordered, dialectical history as yet another myth, as merely another conventional or arbitrary grouping of reality, Lévi-Strauss adds: "*Cette perspective n'a rien d'alarmant pour une pensée que n'angoisse nulle transcendance, fût-ce sous forme larvée.*" The sentence is characteristic in several ways: by its mannered Pascalian concision and syntax; by the implicit identification that Lévi-Strauss makes between his own person and the "abstract concretion" of *une pensée*; but principally by its note of stoic condescension. It is that note, the cool inward and downward look, the arrogance of disenchanted insight, that fascinates Lévi-Strauss's disciples and opponents. As the young once sought to mime the nervous passion of Malraux, so they now seek to imitate the *hauteur* and gnomic voice of the Professor of Social Anthropology at the Collège de France.

In making of anthropology the foundation of a generalized critique of values, Lévi-Strauss follows in a distinctive French tradition. It leads from Montaigne's subversive meditation on cannibals to Montesquieu's *Lettres persanes* and to his use of a comparative study of cultures and mores as a critique of ethical, political absolutism. It includes the large use made by Diderot, Rousseau, and the *philosophes* of travel literature and ethnography and extends to the moral polemic so carefully plotted in Gide's narratives of his African journeys. The *moraliste* uses "primitive" cultures, personally experienced or gathered at second hand, as a tuning-fork against which to test the discord of his own milieu. Lévi-Strauss is a *moraliste*, conscious in style and outlook of his affinities with Montesquieu and Diderot's *Supplément au Voyage de Bougainville*. The concept does not translate readily into "moralist." It carries a literary, almost journalistic stress that has no immediate analogy with, say, the Cambridge Platonists. The *moraliste* can use fiction, journalism, drama, as did Camus. Or he may, like Lévi-Strauss, work outward from what is, in its origin and technical form, a highly specialized field of interest.

Only the comparative anthropologist and ethnographer are equipped to pass judgment on the solutions that Lévi-Strauss puts forward to complex problems of kinship and totemism, of cultural diffusion and "primitive" psychology. The technical literature that has grown up around the work of Lévi-Strauss is already large. But the bearing of that work on the notion of culture, on our understanding of language and mental process, on our interpretation of history is so direct and novel that an awareness of Lévi-Strauss's thought is a part of current literacy. "Like Freud," remarks Raphaël Pividal, "Claude Lévi-Strauss, while solving special questions, has opened a new road to the science of man."

That road begins with the classic achievement in sociology and social anthropology of Durkheim, Hertz, and Mauss. In the last's "Essay on Certain Primitive Forms of Classification" (1901–1902) we see outlined important aspects of the study of taxonomy and "concrete logic" in *La Pensée sauvage*. As Lévi-Strauss makes clear in his own "Introduction à l'oeuvre de Marcel Mauss," it is to Mauss's way of thinking about kinship and language, and above all to Mauss's *Essai sur le don* of 1924, that he owes certain assumptions and methodologies that inform his entire work. It is in this essay that Mauss puts forward the proposition that kinship relations, relations of economic and ceremonial exchange, and linguistic relations are fundamentally of the same order.

Beginning with his paper on structural analysis in linguistics and in anthropology (*Word*, 1945) and his first full-scale treatise, *Les Structures élémentaires de la parenté* (1949), Lévi-Strauss has made this conjecture of essential identity the core of his method and world-view. Examining a specific problem of kinship nomenclature and marital taboos, Lévi-Strauss argues that the evidence can be sorted out only if the women exchanged in marriage are regarded as a *message*, allowing two social groups to communicate with each other and to establish a vital economy of rational experience. Beginning with the particular instance, Lévi-Strauss has elaborated the view that all cultural phenomena are a language. Hence, the structure of human thought and the complex totality of social relations can be studied best by adopting the methodology and discoveries of modern linguistics. What political economy is to the Marxist concept of history (the circumstantial, technical basis underlying an essentially metaphysical and teleological argument), the work of Saussure, Jakobson, M. Halle, and the modern school of structural linguistics is to Lévi-Strauss.

As summarized in the chapters on "Language and Kinship" in the *Anthropologie structurale*, Lévi-Strauss's image of culture can be expressed, quite literally, as a syntax. Through our understanding of this syntax, particular rites, processes of biological and economic exchange, myths, and classifications as they are set forth in native speech may be analyzed into "phonemes" of human behavior. This analysis will disclose the true interrelations of otherwise disparate or even contradictory elements, for like structural linguistics Lévi-Strauss's anthropology regards as axiomatic the belief that each element of social and psychological life has meaning only in relation to the underlying system. If we lack knowledge of that system, the particular sins, however graphic, will remain mute.

Speaking to the Conference of Anthropologists and Linguists held at the University of Indiana in 1952, Lévi-Strauss evoked the ideal of a future "science of man and of the human spirit" in which both disciples would merge. Since then he has gone further, and it is hardly an exaggeration to say that he regards all culture as a code of significant communication and all social processes as a grammar. According to Lévi-Strauss, only this approach can deal adequately with the question asked in each of his major works: How do we distinguish between nature and culture, how does man conceive of his identity in respect of the natural world and of the social group?

The actual way in which Lévi-Strauss applies the tools of structural linguistics, or, more precisely, the analog of linguistics, to deal with problems of kinship, totemism, and ecology among the Indian peoples of North America and the Amazon basin, has been much debated. The attack of George C. Homans and David M. Schneider on *Les Structures élémentaires de la parenté* (*Marriage, Authority, and Final Causes,* 1955) has been met in Rodney Needham's *Structure and Sentiment* (1962). A more subtle critique is argued in E. R. Leach's fascinating paper on Lévi-Strauss in the *Annales* for November-December 1964. Dr. Leach shows how strongly Lévi-Strauss's "linguistics of culture" reflect the techniques and logical presuppositions of contemporary information theory and linear programing. Myths and behavior patterns in primitive society store and transmit vital information as does the electronic circuit and magnetic tape in the computer. Lévi-Strauss regards mental and social processes as fundamentally binary, as coded in sets of positive and negative impulses, finally balancing out in an equation of belief or folk custom that is at once harmonious and economic. Hence, the binary elements that seem to govern so much of his argument: animality/humanity, nature/culture, wet/dry, noise/silence, raw/cooked. But, as Dr. Leach points out, the binary is not the only or necessary system of relations and information coding. Analog computers perform tasks that digital computers are not suited for. In particular, says Dr. Leach, the matrices that Lévi-Strauss sets up to tabulate linguistic-ethnic relations, or totemic and mythical conventions, do not allow for gradations of value, for partial choices between alternatives that are not unambiguously positive or negative.

This is a controversy from which the layman would do well to abstain. What is striking are the rich suggestions that Lévi-Strauss's "metalinguistics" bring to a general theory of culture, to poetics and psychology. In the *Anthropologie structurale*, for example, we find the notion that our civilization treats language with immoderation, wasting words in a persistent recourse to speech. Primitive cultures tend to be parsimonious: "verbal manifestations are often limited to prescribed circumstances, outside which words are used only sparingly." And it is characteristic of Lévi-Strauss's ironic moralism that the discussion of the grammar of marriage in primitive cultures—words and women being set in analogy as media of communication—should end with the aphorism: "A *l'inverse des femmes, les mots ne parlent pas.*"

Increasingly, the thought of Lévi-Strauss can be understood as part of that revaluation of the nature of language and symbolism whose antecedents may be traced to Vico and Leibniz, but whose most radical effects have been modern. No less than Wittgenstein's *Tractacus*, *La Pensée sauvage* and *Le Cru et le cuit* infer that man's place in reality is a matter of syntax, of the ordering of propositions. No less than Jung, Lévi-Strauss's studies of magic and myth, of totemism and *logique concrète*, affirm that symbolic representations, legends, image-patterns, are means of storing and conceptualizing knowledge, that mental processes are collective because they reproduce fundamental structural identities.

Where "domestic" and scientific thought strives toward the economy of a single code, "savage" thought is a semantic system perpetually regrouping itself and rearranging the data of the empirical world without reducing the number of discrete elements. Scientific methodology is obviously different from the "concrete logic" of primitive peoples. But not necessarily better or more advanced. Lévi-Strauss insists that "the science of the concrete" is a second major way of apprehending nature and natural relations. He argues that the great achievements of neolithic man—pottery, the weaving of cloth, agriculture, the domestication of animals—cannot have been the result of hazard or randomly perceived example. These brilliant "conquests," which "remain the substratum of our civilization," are the product of a science different from ours, but continuing a parallel life of its own. If magic had not proved to be a supple and coherent mode of perception, why should science in the experimental-deterministic sense have begun so late in man's history?

Lévi-Strauss does not see history as a case of linear progression (this is the crux of his debate with Hegelianism and Sartre's dialectical historicism). By making of history a transcendental value, a concealed absolute, Sartre excludes a major part of past and contemporary humanity from the pale of significant experience. Our sense of history, with its dates and implicit forward motion, is a very special, arbitrary reading of reality. It is not natural but culturally acquired. Chronology is an ever-changing code. The grid of dates we use for prehistory is based on an entirely different scheme of values and admissible data than the grid we use to conceptualize the period from, say, 1815 to the present. It is of the essence of primitive thought to be *intemporelle* (timeless, untimely), to conceive of experience in simultaneous and partial *imagines mundi*. But as Lévi-Strauss observes, such a mental praxis may not be unrelated to the world-picture of quantum mechanics and relativity.

Since *Tristes Tropiques* (1955), if not before, Lévi-Strauss has done little to mask the general philosophic and sociological implications of his technical pursuits. He knows that he is arguing a general theory of history and society, that his specific analyses of tribal customs or linguistic habits carry an exponential factor. Of late, as if by some instinct of inevitable rivalry, he has challenged Sartre and the relevance of the existentialist dialectic. This may, in part, reflect the circumstances of contemporary French intellectual life. More pervasive has been Lévi-Strauss's concern to delimit his own thought from that of the two principal architects of rational mythology, Marx and Freud. His work is in frequent self-conscious dialogue with theirs.

One of the crucial statements occurs in the opening, autobiographical section of *Tristes Tropiques* (in their ironic, detached intimacy, these chapters recall *The Education of Henry*

Adams, and it is Adams's fastidious agnosticism that Lévi-Strauss's own posture most resembles). Unfortunately, the entire argument is of extreme concision and difficulty. Lévi-Strauss records his initiation to Marxism at about the age of seventeen:

A whole world was revealed to me. Since which time, my passionate interest has never lapsed; and I rarely concentrate on unravelling a problem of sociology or ethnology without having, beforehand, braced my thought by reading some pages of the *18th Brumaire of Louis Bonaparte* or of the *Critique of Political Economy*.

Marx has taught us "to build a model, to study its properties and the different ways in which it reacts in the laboratory, in order to apply these observations to the interpretation of empirical data which may be far removed from what one had foreseen." (This is, one should note, a rather curious gloss on Marx, making of his concrete historicism an almost abstract phenomenology.)

In the *Anthropologie structurale*, Lévi-Strauss cites Marx's well-known remark that the value of gold as repository and medium of wealth not only is a material phenomenon but also has symbolic sources as "solidified light brought up from the nether world," and that Indo-Germanic etymology reveals the links between precious metals and the symbolism of colors. "Thus," says Lévi-Strauss, "it is Marx himself who would have us perceive and define the symbolic systems which simultaneously underlie language and man's relations to the world." But he goes on to suggest, and this is the crux, that Marxism itself is only a partial case of a more general theory of economic and linguistic information and exchange-relations. This theory will be the framework of a truly rational and comprehensive sociology of man. Not surprisingly, the Marxists have challenged the "totalitarian" claims of Lévi-Strauss's "science of man" and have attacked its irrationalist, "antihistorical" aspects (the general issues are carefully set out in Lucien Sebag's *Marxisme et structuralisme*).

In *Tristes Tropiques*, Lévi-Strauss relates Marxism to the two other main impulses in his own intellectual development and conception of ethnography: geology and psychoanalysis. All three pose the same primary question: "that of the relation between the experienced and the rational (*le sensible et le rationnel*), and the aim pursued is identical: a kind of super-rationalism seeking to integrate the former with the latter without sacrificing any of its properties." Which may be a very abstract way of saying that Marxism, geology, and psychoanalysis are etiologies, attempts to trace the conditions of society, of physical environment, and of human consciousness to their hidden source. Social relations, terrain, and collective imaginings or linguistic forms are, in turn, the primary coordinates of Lévi-Strauss's *étude de l'homme*.

As Lévi-Strauss advances more deeply into his own theory of symbolism and mental life, the Freudian analogs grow more obtrusive and, probably, irritating. Hence, the sporadic but acute critique of psychoanalysis throughout the *Anthropologie structurale*, the argument that Freudian therapy, particularly in its American setting, does not lead to a treatment of neurotic disturbance but to "a reorganization of the universe of the patient in terms of psychoanalytic interpretations." Hence, also, one may suppose, Lévi-Strauss's determination to appropriate the Oedipus motif to a much larger context than that put forward by Freud. In Lévi-Strauss's ethnic-linguistic decoding of the legend and of its many analogs among the North American Indians, the primary meaning points to the immense intellectual and psychological problem faced by a society that professes to believe in the autochthonous creation of man when it has to deal with the recognition of the bisexual nature of human generation. The Oedipus motif embodies not individual neurosis but a collective attempt to regroup reality in response to fresh and perplexing insights. Again, as in the case of Marxism, the Freudian theory of consciousness emerges as a valuable but essentially specialized and preliminary chapter in a larger anthropology.

How does *Le Cru et le cuit* fit into this powerful construct? It is a detailed, highly technical analysis of certain motifs in the mythology of the Indians of the Amazon, more exactly, in the creation myths of the Bororo and Gê peoples. The first volume is the start of a projected series and deals with one subtopic of the larger binary unit: nature/culture. This subtopic is the discrimination between raw and cooked foods as reflected in Indian myths and practices. Starting with one Bororo "key-myth," Lévi-Strauss analyzes significant elements in 187 Amazonian legends and folk-tales; by means of complex geographical, linguistic, and topical matrices, he shows that these myths are ultimately interrelated or congruent. The argument leads to the proposition that the discovery of cooking has profoundly altered man's conception of the relationship between heaven and earth.

Before the mastering of fire, man placed meat on a stone to be warmed by the rays of the sun. This habit brought heaven and earth, man and the sun into intimate juxtaposition. The discovery of cooking literally set back the sphere of the gods and of the sun from the habitat of man. It also separated man from the great world of animals, who eat their food raw. It is thus an immensely important step in the metaphysical, ecological, psychic severance of the genus *Homo sapiens* from his cosmic and organic surroundings. That severance (there are definite echoes from Freud's *Beyond the Pleasure Principle* and *Civilization and Its Discontents*) leads to the differentiation and strenuous confrontation between the natural and the cultural stages of human development.

But the design of the book reaches beyond even this large theme. To what Lévi-Strauss defines as the "primary code" of human language and the "secondary code" of myths, *Le Cru et le cuit* aims to add "a tertiary code, designed to ensure that myths can be reciprocally translated. This is why it would not be erroneous to regard this book itself as a myth: in some manner, the myth of mythology."

The formula is lapidary and obscure, but the idea itself is not new. It crops up in Giordano Bruno, in Bacon's *De Sapientia Veterum*, in which myths or "fables" are regarded as a transparent veil occupying "the middle region that separates what has perished from what survives," and in Vico. Lévi-Strauss is seeking a science of mythology, a grammar of symbolic constructs and associations allowing the anthropologist to relate different myths as the structural linguist relates phonemes and language systems. Once the code of myths is deciphered and is seen to have its own logic and translatability, its own grid of values and interchangeable significants, the anthropologist will have a tool of great power with which to attack problems of human ecology, of ethnic and linguistic groupings, of cultural diffusion. Above all, he may gain insight into mental processes and strata of consciousness that preserve indices (the fossils or radioactive elements of the palaeontologist and geologist) of the supreme event in man's history—the transition from a primarily instinctual, perhaps prelinguistic condition to the life of consciousness and individualized self-awareness. This, and the flowering of human genius and "concrete logic" during the neolithic era are, for Lévi-Strauss, realities of history far more important than the brief adjunct of turmoil and political cannibalism of the past 3000 years.

Proceeding from the linguistic axiom that all elements in a complex system are related and that their sense can be derived only from an analysis of their interrelations, of the place which the unit can occupy in the set, Lévi-Strauss weaves a host of apparently disparate Amazonian and North American hunt-and creation-myths into a unified pattern. In the course of the argument, he seeks to demonstrate that successive variants of a myth cannot be discarded as irrelevant, that the sum of related tales is a living aggregate, a code of cultural reinterpretation in which single elements are regrouped but not lost (the analogy being that of mathematical topology, which studies those relations that remain constant when configurations change). The result is a kind of moiré pattern that we learn to read as the physicist reads superimposed photographs of cloud-chamber particles.

Philosophically and methodologically, Lévi-Strauss's approach is rigorously deterministic. If there is law in the world of the physical sciences, then there is one in that of mental processes and language. In the Anthropologie structurale, Lévi-Strauss presages a time when individual thought and conduct will be seen as momentary modes or enactments "of those universal laws which are the substance of the human unconscious" (*des lois universelles en quoi consiste l'activité inconsciente de l'esprit*). Similarly, *Le Cru et le cuit* concludes with the suggestion of a simultaneous, reciprocal interaction between the genesis of myths in the human mind and the creation by these myths of a world-image already predetermined (one might say "programed") by the specific structure of human mentality. If human life is, basically, a highly developed form of cybernetics, the nature of the information processed, of the feedback and of the code, will depend on the particular psychosomatic construct of the mental unit. Digital computers and analog computers may learn to have different dreams.

Once more, the substance and empirical solidity of Lévi-Strauss's case can be judged only by the qualified anthropologist (is he right about this or that aspect of Bororo life and language?). But the general implications are wide-ranging. This is particularly true of the first thirty pages of *Le Cru et le cuit*, entitled "Ouverture." They constitute the richest, most difficult piece of writing Lévi-Strauss has produced so far. It is not easy to think of any text as tightly meshed, as bristling with suggestion and fine intricacy of argument since the *Tractatus*. At various points, in fact, the themes of the two works come into contact.

Some of the difficulty seems gratuitous. There is hardly a proposition in these opening pages that is not qualified or illustrated by reference to mathematics, histology, optics, or molecular chemistry. Often a single simile conjoins several allusions to different scientific concepts. Looked at closely, however, a good many of the scientific notions invoked are elementary or vaguely pretentious. How much mathematics does Lévi-Strauss really know or need to know? But this constant use of mathematical and scientific notations points to a much larger and more urgent motif. In "Ouverture" Lévi-Strauss is articulating a radical distrust of language. A theme that has been latent in much of his work now comes to the fore: set against the pure syntax and tautological efficiencies of mathematics, of symbolic logic, and of scientific formulas, traditional discourse is no longer a predominant or wholly satisfactory medium. By universalizing structural linguistics, Lévi-Strauss is, in fact, diminishing the unique genius and central authority of common speech. As storehouses and conveyors (the vacuum tube and the electronic impulse) of felt life and human conjecture, myths embrace words but go beyond them toward a more supple, inventive, universal syntax.

Yet even they fall short of the "supreme mystery among the sciences of man" which is music. That arresting formula concludes a dazzling rhetorical flight in which Lévi-Strauss contends that "to think mythologically" is to think musically. Wagner has proved the quintessential kinship of myth and musical statement. Among all languages, only music "unites the contrary attributes of being both intelligible and untranslatable." It is, moreover, intelligible to all—a fact that makes "the creator of music a being similar to the gods."

In consequence, Le Cru et le cuit is given the formal structure of a piece of music: overture, theme and variations, sonata, fugue, three-part invention, rustic symphony in three movements. The conceit is not new: one finds it in Baudelaire's theory of correspondance (to which Lévi-Strauss implicitly refers), in Mallarmé, and in Broch's Death of Virgil, a novel ordered in analogy with the changes of mood and rhythm in a string quartet. Lévi-Strauss does little, moreover, to enforce the musical mimesis. It remains a rather labored jeu d'esprit. But the underlying concept has a deep fascination. The idea that music and myth are akin, that they build shapes of being more universal, more numinous than speech, haunts the Western imagination. It is incarnate, as Elizabeth Sewell has shown, in the figure of Orpheus. He is myth himself and master of life through his power to create harmony amid the inertness of primal silence or the ferocity of discord (the fierce beasts pause and listen). His presence—order and perception as the condition of the mind when that condition is nearest music— is discernible in Pythagorean doctrine and in Bacon's Magna Instauratio; it has the energy of living myth in Rilke and Valéry. In its celebration of music and mathematics, in its proud obscurity and claim to be itself a myth unfolding, a song of the mind, Le Cru et le cuit is, in the literal sense, an Orphic book. Would that its opening measures were quoted from a stronger source than Emmanuel Chabrier's *A la musique*.

Le Cru et le cuit is work in progress, and it would be fatuous to pass any general judgment on the complex ensemble of Lévi-Strauss's achievement to this date. That it is one of the most original and intellectually exciting of the present age seems undeniable. Not one seriously interested in language or literature, in sociology or psychology, can ignore it. At the same time, this newest book exhibits to a disturbing degree characteristics latent in Lévi-Strauss's work, certainly since the early 1950s. It is prolix, often arbitrary, and maddeningly precious (a technical discussion of the relations between Amazonian myths and the zodiac is entitled *"L'Astronomie bien tempérée"*). The argument is decked out with an apparatus of pseudomathematical notations that appears to carry more weight and relevance than it actually does. At times, the hard, astringent scruple of Lévi-Strauss's best style yields to an odd, postromantic lyricism (Chabrier after Satie). It is as if the prophet were pausing to draw his mantle close.

Perhaps this is both the genius and the danger of the enterprise. It is not, primarily, as anthropology or ethnography that this fascinating body of work may come to be judged and valued, but as extended poetic metaphor. Like so much in Marx and Freud, the achievement of Lévi-Strauss may endure, to use a term from *La Pensée sauvage*, as part of "the mythology of our time." It is too early to tell; *Le Cru et le cuit* ends with a catalogue of myths, not with a coda.

14
THE ANTHROPOLOGIST AS HERO

SUSAN SONTAG

The paradox is irresoluble: the less one culture communicates
with another, the less likely they are to be corrupted, one by
the other; but on the other hand, the less likely it is, in such
conditions, that the respective emissaries of these cultures will
be able to seize the richness and significance of their diversity.
The alternative is inescapable: either I am a traveller in ancient
times, and faced with a prodigious spectacle which would be
almost entirely unintelligible to me and might, indeed, provoke
me to mockery or disgust; or I am a traveller of my own day,
hastening in search of a vanished reality. In either case I am
the loser . . . for today, as I go groaning among the shadows,
I miss, inevitably, the spectacle that is now taking shape. [From
Tristes Tropiques.]

From *Against Interpretation* by Susan Sontag (New York, Farrar,
Straus & Giroux, 1966), pp. 69–81. Copyright © 1963 by Susan
Sontag. Reprinted by permission of the publisher.

Most serious thought in our time struggles with the feeling of homelessness. The felt unreliability of human experience brought about by the inhuman acceleration of historical change has led every sensitive modern mind to the recording of some kind of nausea, of intellectual vertigo. And the only way to cure this spiritual nausea seems to be, at least initially, to exacerbate it. Modern thought is pledged to a kind of applied Hegelianism: seeking its Self in its Other. Europe seeks itself in the exotic—in Asia, in the Middle East, among preliterate peoples, in a mythic America; a fatigued rationality seeks itself in the impersonal energies of sexual ecstasy or drugs; consciousness seeks its meaning in unconsciousness; humanistic problems seek their oblivion in scientific "value neutrality" and quantification. The "other" is experienced as a harsh purification of "self." But at the same time the "self" is busily colonizing all strange domains of experience. Modern sensibility moves between two seemingly contradictory but actually related impulses: surrender to the exotic, the strange, the other; and the domestication of the exotic, chiefly through science.

Although philosophers have contributed to the statement and understanding of this intellectual homelessness—and, in my opinion, only those modern philosophers who do so have an urgent claim on our interest—it is mainly poets, novelists, a few painters who have lived this tortured spiritual impulse, in willed derangement and in self-imposed exile and in compulsive travel. But there are other professions whose conditions of life have been made to bear witness to this vertiginous modern attraction to the alien. Conrad in his fiction, and T. E. Lawrence, Saint-Exupéry, Montherlant among others in their lives as well as their writing, created the métier of the adventurer as a spiritual vocation. Thirty-five years ago, Malraux chose the profession of the archaeologist, and went to Asia. And, more recently, Claude Lévi-Strauss has invented the profession of the anthropologist as a total occupation, one involving a spiritual commitment like that of the creative artist or the adventurer or the psychoanalyst.

Unlike the writers mentioned above, Lévi-Strauss is not a man of letters. Most of his writings are scholarly, and he has always been associated with the academic world. At present, since 1960, he holds a very grand academic post, the newly created chair of social anthropology at the Collège de France, and heads a large and richly endowed research institute. But his academic eminence and ability to dispense patronage are scarcely adequate measures of the formidable position he occupies in French intellectual life today. In France, where there is more awareness of the adventure, the risk involved in intelligence, a man can be both a specialist and the subject of general and intelligent interest and controversy. Hardly a month passes in France without a major article in some serious literary journal, or an important public lecture, extolling or attacking the ideas and influence of Lévi-Strauss. Apart from the tireless Sartre and the virtually silent Malraux, he is the most interesting intellectual "figure" in France today.

Lévi-Strauss has assembled, from the vantage point of anthropology, one of the few interesting and possible intellectual positions—in the most general sense of that phrase. And one of his books is a masterpiece. I mean the incomparable Tristes Tropiques, a book that became a best-seller when published in France in 1955, but when translated into English and brought out here in 1961 was shamefully ignored. Tristes Tropiques is one of the great books of our century. It is rigorous, subtle, and bold in thought. It is beautifully written. And, like all great books, it bears an absolutely personal stamp; it speaks with a human voice.

Ostensibly, Tristes Tropiques is the record, or memoir rather, written over fifteen years after the event, of the author's experience in the "field." Anthropologists are fond of likening field research to the puberty ordeal that confers status upon members of certain primitive societies. Lévi-Strauss's ordeal was in Brazil, before the Second World War. Born in 1908 and of the intellectual generation and circle which included Sartre, Beauvoir, Merleau-Ponty, and Paul Nizan, he studied philosophy in the late twenties and, like them, taught for a while in a provincial lycée. Dissatisfied with philosophy, he soon gave up his teaching post, returned to Paris to study law, then began the study of anthropology, and in 1935 went to São Paulo as

Professor of Anthropology. From 1935 to 1939, during the long university vacations from November to March and for one period of more than a year, Lévi-Strauss lived among Indian tribes in the interior of Brazil. *Tristes Tropiques* offers a record of his encounters with these tribes—the nomadic, missionary-murdering Nambikwara, the Tupi-Kawahib, whom no white man had ever seen before, the materially splendid Bororo, the ceremonious Caduveo, who produce huge amounts of abstract painting and sculpture. But the greatness of *Tristes Tropiques* lies not simply in this sensitive reportage, but in the way Lévi-Strauss uses his experience—to reflect on the nature of landscape, on the meaning of physical hardship, on the city in the Old World and the New, on the idea of travel, on sunsets, on modernity, on the connection between literacy and power. The key to the book is Chapter Six, "How I Became an Anthropologist," where Lévi-Strauss finds in the history of his own choice a case study of the unique spiritual hazards to which the anthropologist subjects himself. *Tristes Tropiques* is an intensely personal book. Like Montaigne's *Essays* and Freud's *Interpretation of Dreams*, it is an intellectual autobiography, an exemplary personal history in which a whole view of the human situation, an entire sensibility, is elaborated.

The profoundly intelligent sympathy which informs *Tristes Tropiques* makes other memoirs about life among preliterate peoples seem ill at ease, defensive, provincial. Yet sympathy is modulated throughout by a hard-won impassivity. In her autobiography Simone de Beauvoir recalls Lévi-Strauss as a young philosophy student-teacher expounding "in his detached voice, and with a deadpan expression . . . the folly of the passions." Not for nothing is *Tristes Tropiques* prefaced by a motto from Lucretius' *De Rerum Natura*. Lévi-Strauss's aim is very much like that of Lucretius, the Graecophile Roman who urged the study of the natural sciences as a mode of ethical psychotherapy. The aim of Lucretius was not independent scientific knowledge but the reduction of emotional anxiety. Lucretius saw man as torn between the pleasure of sex and the pain of emotional loss, tormented by superstitions inspired by religion, haunted by the fear of bodily decay and death. He recommended scientific knowledge, which teaches intelligent detachment, equanimity. Scientific knowledge is, for Lucretius, a mode of psychological gracefulness. It is a way of learning to let go.

Lévi-Strauss sees man with a Lucretian pessimism and a Lucretian feeling for knowledge as both consolation and necessary disenchantment. But for him the demon is history—not the body or the appetites. The past, with its mysteriously harmonious structures, is broken and crumbling before our eyes. Hence, the tropics are *tristes*. There were nearly twenty thousand of the naked, indigent, nomadic, handsome Nambikwaras in 1915, when they were first visited by white missionaries; when Lévi-Strauss arrived in 1938, there were no more than two thousand of them; today they are miserable, ugly, syphilitic, and almost extinct. Hopefully, anthropology brings a reduction of historical anxiety. It is interesting that Lévi-Strauss describes himself as an ardent student of Marx since the age of seventeen ("Rarely do I tackle a problem in sociology or ethnology without having first set my mind in motion by reperusal of a page or two from the 18th *Brumaire of Louis Bonaparte* or the *Critique of Political Economy*") and that many of Lévi-Strauss's students are reported to be former Marxists, come as it were to lay their piety at the altar of the past since it cannot be offered to the future. Anthropology is necrology. "Let's go and study the primitives," says Lévi-Strauss and his pupils, "before they disappear."

It is strange to think of these ex-Marxists—philosophical optimists if ever such have existed—submitting to the melancholy spectacle of the crumbling prehistoric past. They have moved not only from optimism to pessimism, but from certainty to systematic doubt. For, according to Lévi-Strauss, research in the field, "where every ethnological career begins, is the mother and nursemaid of doubt, the philosophical attitude par excellence." In Lévi-Strauss's program for the practicing anthropologist in *Structural Anthropology*, the Cartesian method of doubt is installed as a permanent agnosticism. "This 'anthropological doubt' consists not merely in knowing that one knows nothing but in resolutely exposing what one knows, even one's own ignorance, to the insults and denials inflicted on one's dearest ideas and habits by those ideas and habits which may contradict them to the highest degree."

To be an anthropologist is thus to adopt a very ingenious stance vis-à-vis one's own doubts, one's own intellectual uncertainties. Lévi-Strauss makes it clear that for him this is an eminently *philosophical* stance. At the same time, anthropology reconciles a number of divergent personal claims. It is one of the rare intellectual vocations that do not demand a sacrifice of one's manhood. Courage, love of adventure, and physical hardiness—as well as brains—are called upon. It also offers a solution to that distressing by-product of intelligence, alienation. Anthropology conquers the estranging function of the intellect by institutionalizing it. For the anthropologist, the world is professionally divided into "home" and "out there," the domestic and the exotic, the urban academic world and the tropics. The anthropologist is not simply a neutral observer. He is a man in control of, and even consciously exploiting, his own intellectual alienation. A *technique de dépaysement*, Lévi-Strauss calls his profession in *Structural Anthropology*. He takes for granted the philistine formulas of modern scientific "value neutrality." What he does is to offer an exquisite, aristocratic version of this neutrality. The anthropologist in the field becomes the very model of the twentieth-century consciousness: a "critic at home" but a "conformist elsewhere." Lévi-Strauss acknowledges that this paradoxical spiritual state makes it impossible for the anthropologist to be a citizen. The anthropologist, so far as his own country is concerned, is sterilized politically. He cannot seek power, he can only be a critical dissenting voice. Lévi-Strauss himself, although in the most generic and very French way a man of the Left (he signed the famous Manifesto of the 121, which recommended civil disobedience in France in protest against the Algerian War), is by French standards an apolitical man. Anthropology, in Lévi-Strauss's conception, is a technique of political disengagement; and the anthropologist's vocation requires the assumption of a profound detachment. "Never can he feel himself 'at home' anywhere; he will always be, psychologically speaking, an amputee."

Certainly the earliest visitors to preliterate peoples were far from detached. The original fieldworkers in what was then called ethnology were missionaries, bent on redeeming the savage from his follies and making him over into a civilized Christian. To cover the bosoms of the women, put pants on the men, and send them all to Sunday school to mumble the gospel was the aim of an army of stony-eyed spinsters from Yorkshire and rawboned farmers' sons from the American Midwest. Then there were the secular humanists—impartial, respectful, hands-off observers who did not come to sell Christ to the savages but to preach "reason," "tolerance," and "cultural pluralism" to the bourgeois literary public back home. And back home there were the great consumers of anthropological data, building rationalist world views, like Frazer and Spencer and Robertson Smith and Freud. But always anthropology has struggled with an intense, fascinated *repulsion* toward its subject. The horror of the primitive (naïvely expressed by Frazer and Lévy-Bruhl) is never far from the anthropologist's consciousness. Lévi-Strauss marks the furthest reach of the conquering of the aversion. The anthropologist in the manner of Lévi-Strauss is a new breed altogether. He is not, like recent generations of American anthropologists, simply a modest data-collecting "observer." Nor does he have any axe—Christian, rationalist, Freudian, or otherwise—to grind. Essentially he is engaged in saving his own soul, by a curious and ambitious act of intellectual catharsis.

The anthropologist—and herein lies his essential difference, according to Lévi-Strauss, from the sociologist—is an *eye-witness*. "It is sheer illusion that anthropology can be taught purely theoretically." (One wonders why a Max Weber writing about ancient Judaism or Confucian China is permissible, if a Frazer describing scapegoat rituals among the Tagbanua tribe in the Philippines is not.) Why? Because anthropology, for Lévi-Strauss, is an intensely personal kind of intellectual discipline, like psychoanalysis. A spell in the field is the exact equivalent of the training analysis undergone by candidate psychoanalysts. The purpose of fieldwork, Lévi-Strauss writes, is to "create that psychological revolution which marks the decisive turning point in the training of the anthropologist." And no written tests, but only the judgment of "experienced members of the profession" who have undergone the same psychological ordeal, can determine "if and when" a candidate anthropologist "has, as a result of fieldwork, accomplished that inner revolution that will really make him into a new man."

However, it must be emphasized that this literary-sounding conception of the anthropologist's calling—the twice-born spiritual adventure, pledged to a systematic déracinement—is complemented in most of Lévi-Strauss's writings by an insistence on the most unliterary techniques of analysis and research. His important essay on myth in Structural Anthropology outlines a technique for analyzing and recording the elements of myths so that these can be processed by a computer. European contributions to what in America are called the "social sciences" are in exceedingly low repute in this country, for their insufficient empirical documentation, for their "humanist" weakness for covert culture criticism, for their refusal to embrace the techniques of quantification as an essential tool of research. Lévi-Strauss's essays in Structural Anthropology certainly escape these strictures. Indeed, far from disdaining the American fondness for precise quantitative measurement of traditional problems, Lévi-Strauss finds it not sophisticated or methodologically rigorous enough. Somewhat at the expense of the French school (Durkheim, Mauss, and their followers) to whom he is closely allied, Lévi-Strauss pays lavish tribute, throughout the essays in Structural Anthropology to the work of American anthropologists—particularly Lowie, Boas, and Kroeber.[1] But his nearest affinity is to the more avant-garde

---

1 Lévi-Strauss relates in Tristes Tropiques that although he had long been familiar with the writings of the French anthropologists and sociologists, it was a reading of Lowie's Primitive Society in 1934 or 1935 that effected his conversion from philosophy to anthropology. "Thus began my long intimacy with Anglo-American anthropology. . . . I started as an avowed anti-Durkheimian and the enemy of any attempt to put sociology to metaphysical uses."

Nevertheless, Lévi-Strauss has made it clear that he considers himself the true legatee of the Durkheim-Mauss tradition and recently has not hesitated to situate his work in relation to the methodologies of economics, neurology, linguistics, and game theory. For Lévi-Strauss, there is no doubt that anthropology must be a science, rather than a humanistic study. The question is only how. "For centuries," he writes, "the humanities and the social sciences have resigned themselves to contemplate the world of the natural and exact sciences as a kind of paradise which they will never enter." But recently, a doorway to paradise has been opened by the linguists, like Roman Jakobson and his school. Linguists now know how to reformulate their problems so that they can "have a machine built by an engineer and make a kind of experiment, completely similar to a natural-science experiment," which will tell them "if the hypothesis is worthwhile or not." Linguists—as well as economists and game theorists—have shown the anthropologist "a way to get out of the confusion resulting from too much acquaintance and familiarity with concrete data."

Thus the man who submits himself to the exotic to confirm his own inner alienation as an urban intellectual ends by aiming to vanquish his subject by translating it into a purely formal code. The ambivalence toward the exotic, the primitive, is not overcome after all, but only given a complex restatement. The anthropologist, as a man, is engaged in saving his own soul. But he is also committed to recording and understanding his subject by a very high-powered mode of formal analysis—what Lévi-Strauss calls "structural" anthropology—that obliterates

---

philosophical problems posed by Marx, Freud, and Sartre. And, on the level of technical analysis, he is fully aware of his debt to the French writers, particularly by way of the *Essai sur quelques formes primitives de classification* (1901–1902) by Durkheim and Mauss, and Mauss's *Essai sur le don* (1924). From the first essay, Lévi-Strauss derives the starting point of the studies of taxonomy and the "concrete science" of primitives in *La Pensée sauvage*. From the second essay, in which Mauss puts forth the proposition that kinship relations, relations of economic and ceremonial exchange, and linguistic relations are fundamentally of the same order, Lévi-Strauss derives the approach most fully exemplified in *Les Structures élémentaires de la parenté*. To Durkheim and Mauss, he repeatedly says, he owes the decisive insight that *"la pensée dite primitive était une pensée quantifiée."*

all traces of his personal experience and truly effaces the human features of his subject, a given primitive society.

In *La Pensée sauvage*, Lévi-Strauss calls this thought "anecdotique et géometrique." The essays in *Structural Anthropology* show mostly the geometrical side of his thought; they are applications of a rigorous formalism to traditional themes—kinship systems, totemism, puberty rites, the relation between myth and ritual, and so forth. A great cleansing operation is in process, and the broom that sweeps everything clean is the notion of "structure." Lévi-Strauss strongly dissociates himself from what he calls the "naturalistic" trend of British anthropology, represented by such leading figures as Malinowski and Radcliffe-Brown. British anthropologists have been the most consistent proponents of "functional analysis," which interprets the variety of custom as different strategies for producing universal social ends. Thus, Malinowski thought that empirical observation of a single primitive society would make it possible to understand the "universal motivations" present in all societies. According to Lévi-Strauss, this is nonsense. Anthropology cannot aim to understand anything more than its own proper subject. Nothing can be inferred from anthropological material for psychology or sociology, for anthropology cannot possibly get complete knowledge of the societies it studies. Anthropology (the comparative study of "structures" rather than "functions") can be neither a descriptive nor an inductive science; it occupies itself with only the formal features that differentiate one society from another. It has properly no interest in the biological basis, psychological content, or social function of institutions and customs. Thus, while Malinowski and Radcliffe-Brown argue, for example, that biological ties are the origin of and the model for every kinship tie, "structuralists" like Lévi-Strauss, following Kroeber and Lowie, emphasize the artificiality of kinship rules. They would discuss kinship in terms of notions that admit of mathematical treatment. Lévi-Strauss and the structuralists, in short, would view society like a game, which there is no one right way to play; different societies assign different moves to the players. The anthropologist can regard a ritual or a taboo simply as a set of rules, paying little attention to "the nature of the partners (either individuals or groups) whose play is being patterned after these rules." Lévi-Strauss's favorite metaphor or model for analyzing primitive institutions and beliefs is a language. And the analogy between anthropology and linguistics is the leading theme of the essays in *Structural Anthropology*. All behavior, according to Lévi-Strauss, is a language, a vocabulary and grammar of order; anthropology proves nothing about human nature except the need for order itself. There is no universal truth about the relations between, say, religion and social structure. There are only models showing the variability of one in relation to the other.

To the general reader, perhaps the most striking examples of Lévi-Strauss's theoretical agnosticism is his view of myth. He treats myth as a purely formal mental operation, without any psychological content or any necessary connection with rite. Specific narratives are exposed as logical designs for the description and possibly the softening of the rules of the social game when they give rise to a tension or contradiction. For Lévi-Strauss, the logic of mythic thought is fully as rigorous as that of modern science. The only difference is that this logic is applied to different problems. Contrary to Mircea Eliade, his most distinguished opponent in the theory of primitive religion, Lévi-Strauss argues that the activity of the mind in imposing form on content is fundamentally the same for all minds, archaic and modern. Lévi-Strauss sees no difference in quality between the scientific thinking of modern "historical" societies and the mythic thinking of prehistoric communities.

The demonic character that history and the notion of historical consciousness has for Lévi-Strauss is best exposed in his brilliant and savage attack on Sartre, the last chapter of *La Pensée sauvage*. I am not persuaded by Lévi-Strauss's arguments against Sartre. But I should say that he is, since the death of Merleau-Ponty, the most interesting and challenging critic of Sartrean existentialism and phenomenology.

Sartre, not only in his ideas but in his entire sensibility, is the antithesis of Lévi-Strauss. With his philosophical and political dogmatisms, his inexhaustible ingenuity and complexity, Sartre always has the manner (which are often bad manners) of the enthusiast. It is entirely apt that the writer who has aroused Sartre's greatest enthusiasm is Jean Genêt, a baroque and didactic and insolent writer whose ego effaces all objective narrative; whose characters are stages in a masturbatory revel; who is the master of games and artifices, of a rich, overrich style stuffed with metaphors and conceits. But there is another tradition in French thought and sensibility—the cult of aloofness, l'esprit géometrique. This tradition is represented, among the new novelists, by Nathalie Sarraute, Alain Robbe-Grillet, and Michel Butor, so different from Genêt in their search for an infinite precision, their narrow dehydrated subject matter and cool microscopic styles, and, among film-makers, by Alain Resnais. The formula for this tradition—in which I would locate Lévi-Strauss, as I would put Sartre with Genêt—is the mixture of pathos and coldness.

Like the formalists of the "new novel" and film, Lévi-Strauss's emphasis on "structure," his extreme formalism and intellectual agnosticism, are played off against an immense but thoroughly subdued pathos. Sometimes the result is a masterpiece like Tristes Tropiques. The very title is an understatement. The tropics are not merely sad. They are in agony. The horror of the rape, the final and irrevocable destruction of preliterate peoples taking place throughout the world today—which is the true subject of Lévi-Strauss's book—is told at a certain distance, the distance of a personal experience of fifteen years ago, and with a sureness of feeling and fact that allows the readers' emotions more rather than less freedom. But in the rest of his books, the lucid and anguished observer has been taken in hand, purged, by the severity of theory.

Exactly in the same spirit as Robbe-Grillet disavows the traditional empirical content of the novel (psychology, social observation), Lévi-Strauss applies the methods of "structural analysis" to traditional materials of empirical anthropology. Customs, rites, myths, and taboo are a language. As in language, where the sounds that make up words are, taken in themselves, meaningless, so the parts of a custom or a rite or a myth (according to Lévi-Strauss) are meaningless in themselves. When analyzing the Oedipus myth, he insists that the parts of the myth (the lost child, the old man at the crossroad, the marriage with the mother, the blinding, etc.) mean nothing.

Only when put together in the total context do the parts have a meaning—the meaning that a logical model has. This degree of intellectual agnosticism is surely extraordinary. And one does not have to espouse a Freudian or a sociological interpretation of the elements of myth to contest it.

Any serious critique of Lévi-Strauss, however, must deal with the fact that, ultimately, his extreme formalism is a moral choice, and (more surprisingly) a vision of social perfection. Radically antihistoricist, he refuses to differentiate between "primitive" and "historical" societies. Primitives have a history; but it is unknown to us. And historical consciousness (which they do not have), he argues in the attack on Sartre, is not a privileged mode of consciousness. There are only what he re-vealingly calls "hot" and "cold" societies. The hot societies are the modern ones, driven by the demons of historical progress. The cold species are the primitive ones, static, crystalline, harmonious. Utopia, for Lévi-Strauss, would be a great lowering of the historical temperature. In his inaugural lecture at the Collège de France, Lévi-Strauss outlined a post-Marxist vision of freedom in which man would finally be freed from the obligation to progress, and from "the age-old curse which forced it to enslave men in order to make progress possible." Then

history would henceforth be quite alone, and society, placed outside and above history, would once again be able to assume that regular and quasi-crystalline structure which, the best-preserved primitive societies teach us, is not contradictory to humanity. It is in this admittedly Utopian view that social anthropology would find its highest justification, since the forms of life and thought which it studies would no longer be of mere historic and comparative interest. They would correspond to a permanent possibility of man, over which social anthropology would have a mission to stand watch, especially in man's darkest hours.

The anthropologist is thus not only the mourner of the cold world of the primitives, but its custodian as well. Lamenting among the shadows, struggling to distinguish the archaic from the pseudoarchaic, he acts out a heroic, diligent, and complex modern pessimism.

15

WHAT IS STRUCTURALISM?

PETER CAWS

Primitive people, Claude Lévi-Strauss tells us, have a passion for naming, classifying, and establishing relations between things, without much regard to the accuracy of the classifications or the objective validity of the relations. In this they resemble the French. It is no accident that Paris should be the world capital of fashion, one of the most complex and most arbitrary significative systems ever devised by man (and it is no surprise that the structuralist Roland Barthes should have devoted his latest book, *Système de la mode*, to a solemn analysis of this system). Nowhere is the preoccupation with system—or for that matter with fashion—more evident than in French intellectual life. Since World War II there have been two major fashions in French thought: the first was existentialism, which lasted until the early fifties, and the second,

From *Partisan Review*, Vol. XXXV, No. 1 (Winter 1968), pp. 75–91. Copyright © 1968 by Partisan Review.

which took hold in the late fifties and early sixties and is now at its peak—or perhaps somewhat past it—is structuralism.

Neither existentialism nor structuralism has had the character of a movement in the strict sense of the term, in contrast to such prewar fashions as surrealism and Marxism. Marxism was naturally allied with the Party; surrealism was identified with André Breton and his followers. In both cases, of course, there extended from the center an intellectual region within which people wished to claim the title "surrealist" or "Marxist," although they might be disowned by the hard-core disciples. The center, for existentialism, was much less well defined; unlike Breton, Sartre never assumed the role of pope. In the case of structuralism, there is not really a center at all. The founding father is generally agreed to be Lévi-Strauss, but there are at least four other people who occupy essentially independent leading positions, namely, Jacques Lacan, Louis Althusser, Barthes, and Michel Foucault. To make matters worse, structuralist habits and beliefs are quite consistent with those of many other intellectual movements. Movements succeed but do not replace one another; surrealism and Marxism are still very much alive, and Althusser is a prominent Marxist. Lacan, for his part, is a dedicated and fundamentalist Freudian who was strongly influenced by surrealism. The others have less striking doctrinal commitments, but they come from diverse professional fields—Lévi-Strauss from anthropology, Barthes from belles lettres and literary criticism, Foucault from philosophy. Little wonder that the standards of clarity and distinctness learned from Descartes by every student in the *lycées* have, confronted by the structuralist phenomenon, broken down completely. A kind of despair can now be detected on the part of French commentators on the intellectual scene; a recent article in the *Quinzaine Littéraire* entitled "Où en est le structuralisme?" begins as follows: " '. . . In the momentary world of commercialized concepts, eclecticism is the rule.' This statement of Alain Badiou characterizes precisely the intellectual debauch to which the pseudoschool which has been named *structuralism* has given rise." The article makes the point that while there is a more or less identifiable set of contemporary activities properly called structuralist, the indiscriminate use of the term has made it almost useless.

A careful examination of what lies behind the fashion, however, reveals a quite definite, and I think very important, common element in structuralist thought that fully warrants the view that men as different as those named above form a single school, not at all deserving of the *Quinzaine's* epithet "pseudo-"; the only trouble is that to call this school "structuralism," while not actually misleading, fails to indicate what is most significant about it and what binds its members together. The name says something interesting about the origins of the movement in structural anthropology and structural linguistics, but the line of thought that has emerged from the confrontation of those disciplines has more to do with linguistic and cultural products (myths, works of literature) and their relation to the problem of human subjectivity than with any concept of structure in the more obvious sense. Obviously, there are structures in language and in culture, such as Navajo grammar or Tibetan marriage customs, and one might, to consider the anthropological case only, have expected that "structuralism" would have taken as its task the analysis of such objects in terms of the interrelation of their elements, by contrast to the "functionalism" of Malinowski, for example, which conducted its analyses in terms of social and psychological purpose. There is, in fact, an anthropological structuralism of precisely this sort, associated mainly with the name of Radcliffe-Brown. But the obvious structures, while not unimportant, are not what Lévi-Strauss is chiefly interested in. For him the really significant structures are beneath the surface, as it were—although all such spatial metaphors are dangerous—and may have a series of quite different embodiments at the level of apparent structure. A remark in his address to a Conference of Anthropologists and Linguists at Indiana in 1953 gives one of the clearest early indications of the line structuralist thought was to take. After commenting on the similarity of problems encountered in the two fields he said, ". . . we have not been sufficiently aware of the fact that *both* language and culture are the product of activities which are basically similar. I am now referring to this uninvited guest which has been seated during this Conference beside us, and which is *the human mind.*"

The event that has brought structuralism most vividly to the attention of the English-speaking world has been the publication of a translation of Lévi-Strauss's *La Pensée sauvage.* It has been pointed out by a number of critics that the translation of the title (*The Savage Mind*) is unfortunate, and in fact it manages, with a single literalism, to throw the emphasis off to a quite extraordinary degree. The book is about systems of thought in so-called primitive societies, and the "savage" mind suggests a contrast with the "civilized" mind to be found in more "advanced" societies. All the terms in quotes, at least to the extent that they suggest a hierarchy of value (as they inevitably do) would be rejected by Lévi-Strauss. The trouble with "savage" in English is that it now has only one level of meaning; while it was once possible to use the term in a more or less descriptive way ("the friendly savages") it has come to mean hopelessly uncivilized or downright ferocious. "*Sauvage,*" on the other hand, has the connotations of "wild" in English as it applies to plants and animals that are not at all ferocious but on the contrary represent a special kind of natural value (*un canard sauvage* is a wild duck, not a savage duck). "*La pensée sauvage*" is therefore, as Lévi-Strauss himself remarks, "mind in its untamed state," and it represents not just the mind of savages but the human mind, and therefore our mind. It is this relevance of his work to contemporary man's understanding of himself that has placed Lévi-Strauss at the center of the current intellectual scene.

It is worth noting that the universality that Lévi-Strauss attributes to mind does not involve him in the absurdity, as some have suggested, of maintaining that there is no essential difference between primitive societies and modern ones. The difference, however, he sees as one of social organization and not as involving essentially a disparity of mental powers or even of patterns of thought. In an interview (one in a series with Georges Charbonnier, published as an issue of *Les Lettres nouvelles* in 1961) he compares the two types of society to two types of machine, clocks, and steam engines: primitive societies, like clocks, use a constant input of energy and "have a tendency to maintain themselves indefinitely in their initial state, which explains why they appear to us as societies without history and without progress"; modern societies, on the other hand, like thermodynamic rather than mechanical machines, "operate in virtue of a difference of temperature between their parts . . . (which is realized by different forms of social hierarchy, whether slavery, serfdom, or class distinction); they produce much more work than the others, but consume and progressively destroy their sources of energy." This is not doctrinaire Marxism of the kind that is to be found in Althusser, for example, but it does represent a willingness, common to all the structuralists, to take Marx seriously and to admit the validity of many of his criticisms of Western civilization, an attitude that is in refreshing contrast to the polarity of disapproval and defiance that still clings, now somewhat vestigially, to discussions of such questions in the United States. In fact, I think it is possible to account for the difference in other than social terms without abandoning the structuralist approach (and without, of course, mitigating the social consequences), but that is getting ahead of the exposition.

It has by now become a commonplace of linguistics that the oldest languages are not necessarily the simplest, from the point of view either of grammar or of vocabulary. The complexity of ancient (and of primitive) grammar has always been a puzzle, although in the structuralist context it is easy enough to see it as a manifestation of a constant mental complexity; the standard account of the complex vocabulary, however, has been that it answered to certain strictly practical needs of the users of the language—as reflected in the fact, for example, that there are seven Eskimo words for "snow." But Lévi-Strauss amasses a great quantity of evidence to show that the naming of details of variation in the natural environment, among primitive people, goes far beyond any possible considerations of utility and amounts to what he calls a "science of the concrete"—not always accurate by the standards of modern classification (although far more so than early ethnologists were prepared to believe), but having in the primitive intellectual world just the function that science, in its nonutilitarian aspect, has in ours, namely, that of organizing the totality of experience into a coherent whole. Using the resources of this rich descriptive language the primitive mind shows a tendency to build intelligible structures on more abstract levels: magic, which corresponds to science in its practical aspect (and which sometimes works, although that is not of the first importance); myth, which corresponds to literature; totemism, which corresponds to morality in providing rules of conduct of a satisfyingly rigorous nature, offenses against which are suitably dangerous. Modern man thinks of these things as childish curiosities that he has long since outgrown, failing to see that science is his magic, literature and other forms of entertainment his myths, morality his totemism.

Part of what conceals from us our interior link with the primitive is a habit, inculcated by the development of modern science, of looking for the *proper* way of building these various structures, on the assumption that the main function of language is to communicate truth and that consistency is a greater virtue than creativity (except, of course, within the carefully marked-off region known as "art"). We have all become engineers with concepts, working from plans and anxious to get the structure right. The primitive, however, is not an *ingénieur* but a *bricoleur* (a word for which there is no really satisfactory English equivalent). He puts together his structures from whatever comes in handy, without special concern for the congruity of their elements. *Bricolage* is the kind of thing that is made out of tar paper and baling wire; the *bricoleur* is the handyman, the tinkerer, who gets surprisingly practical (and often aesthetic) results from the most unlikely material. One of the fundamental theses of *La Pensée sauvage* is that the structure is all-important, the material largely irrelevant; it is as though the mind had to busy itself about something of sufficient complexity but cared very little about the nature (or the logical level) of its components. Lévi-Strauss gives many examples of homologous mythical structures in which elements and relations change places from one tribe to another, sometimes arriving at what in Western eyes would be a complete contradiction;

the native informer, however, recognizes the same structure beneath the contradiction and cannot understand why an apparent inconsistency matters.

Although the "same" structure can sustain different embodiments, that does not mean that the primitive mind apprehends it as disembodied. This is one of the most elusive but most important points in structuralist theory. As Jean Pouillon puts it in his "Essai de définition," at the beginning of a recent issue of *Les Temps modernes* devoted to structuralism:

Structuralism is not formalism. On the contrary, it challenges the distinction between form and matter, and no matter is a priori inaccessible to it. As Lévi-Strauss writes, "form defines itself by opposition to a content which is exterior to it; but structure has no content: it is itself the content, apprehended in a logical organization conceived as a property of the real."

The world becomes intelligible as it becomes structured, primarily through the agency of language, secondarily through the agency of magic, totem, and myth. There are many languages and many myths; structuralism finds that they are homologous, and capable of being generated out of one another by means of suitable transformations. Language, myth, and so on represent the way in which man has been able to grasp the real, and for him they constitute the real; they are not structures of some ineffable reality that lies behind them and from which they are separable. To say that the world is intelligible means that it presents itself to the mind of the primitive as a message, to which his language and behavior are an appropriate response— but not as a message *from elsewhere*, simply as a message, as it were, in its own right. I am aware that this way of talking seems obscure, and uncomfortably reminiscent of McLuhan, but it is the way Lévi-Strauss has chosen to express the natural assumption of intelligibility with which mind confronts the world. The message, furthermore, is unitary, a fact that modern man easily forgets: ". . . we prefer to operate with detached pieces, if not indeed with 'small change,' while the native is a logical hoarder: he is forever tying the threads, unceasingly turning over all the aspects of reality, whether physical, social or mental. We traffic in our ideas; he hoards them up." And in this way he avoids the fragmentation we frequently lament in our own lives. But it would be a mistake to suppose that he has access to a kind of conceptual stability denied to us, by virtue of some now-lost insight into things as they are. He looks for no such insight and therefore does not miss it; it is enough to be engaged in the structuring activity, whatever form it may take, to be relieved of any uneasiness about lack of foundations or of meaning or of the other things for which modern man, anguished and alienated as he is, often yearns so eloquently.

If mind in its natural state finds this psychic equilibrium so easily, how does it come about that modern man has such difficulty in adjusting himself to the conditions of his existence? We may have moments of equilibrium, significantly enough when we are wholly engaged in some activity (as might by now be expected, it doesn't matter much *what* activity, whether athletic, intellectual, or artistic), but left to our own reflective devices we tend to be a bewildered and discontented lot. This bewilderment and discontent manifest themselves in all sorts of projects for self-improvement, self-realization, even self-discovery, all of which the primitive would find completely mystifying. He is in the fortunate condition of not knowing that he has a self, and therefore of not being worried about it. And the structuralists have come to the conclusion that he is nearer the truth than we are, and that a good deal of our trouble arises out of the invention of the self *as an object of study*, from the belief that man has a special kind of being, in short from the emergence of humanism. Structuralism is not a humanism, because it refuses to grant man any special status in the world. Obviously, it cannot deny that there are individual men who observe, think, write, and so on (although it does not encourage them in the narcissistic effort of "finding themselves," to use the popular jargon). Nor does it deny that there are more or less cohesive social groups wth their own histories and cultures. Nothing concrete recognized or valued by the humanist is excluded, only the theoretical basis of humanism. In order to clarify this point it is necessary to consider the central question of structuralism, which comes to dominate all discussions of it, namely, the status of the *subject*.

The subject, first of all, is a linguistic category, the "vantage" (to use an expression due to Benveniste) of verbs in the first person. As such it is important only for purposes of clarity in reference; it avoids confusion beween persons. (Strictly speaking, the first person refers to the subject *"I"*; the other "personal" subject *you* and the "nonpersonal" subject *he*, however, do not lend themselves as readily to overinterpretation.) The subject is a vantage-point in nonlinguistic senses too: *I* look at the world from a particular point of view, *I* act upon it from a particular strategic location. So far there is no difficulty about the matter. But—whether under the influence of Greek philosophy, or Christianity, or Renaissance humanism—Western man began to look for a more substantial embodiment of the subject than that provided by his own contingent and transient body as percipient and agent, or by his linguistic habits as a mere point of reference. Just as the assertion that the world is a message now elicits the immediate response "from whom?" so the intelligibility of the world seems to be addressed to something more basic and more permanent than the momentary and evanescent subject of particular utterances or particular actions. If God had to be invented to originate and sustain the world, man had to be invented to perceive and understand it. Men therefore began to ask "What am I?" in a nonlinguistic sense, much as they also asked "What is matter?" or "What is gravity?" They began, in other words, the long and frustrating attempt to get the subject out into the world so that it could be examined objectively. But this involves a logical mistake and can easily lead to a psychoanalytic disaster.

The psychoanalyst among the structuralists is of course Lacan, and he has devoted a large part of his work to the problem of subjectivity. Lacan's career began at least as early as Lévi-Strauss's, and it is evident from his collected writings (*Ecrits*, 1966) that he represents a genuinely independent source for structuralism. His reputation in France rests mainly on his Seminar at the *Ecole Pratique des Hautes Etudes,* whose members hold him in a regard reminiscent of that in which Wittgenstein was reputedly held by his students at Cambridge. Lacan has been in no special hurry to get his ideas into general circulation, and there is no systematic development to be traced. Starting always from Freud, he wanders by circuitous paths and in a highly personal, extremely difficult and often irritating style, compounded with verbal preciosity, hermetic allusions and a kind of half-concealed amusement at the whole enterprise, into various problematic corners of contemporary thought. The impressive thing is that (once the barrier of style has been surmounted) he consistently throws light on them from a completely original angle.

What makes Lacan a structuralist is his insistence on the central place of language. "Whether it wishes to regard itself as an agent of cure, of development, or of inquiry," he writes, "psychoanalysis has but one medium: the word of the patient. . . . We shall show that there is no word without response, even if it is greeted only with silence, as long as there is a hearer, and that that fact is the clue to its function in analysis." This shows at once the parallel with Lévi-Strauss, although with a difference of scale: the message is particular rather than universal. The structure of language is, as before, the key to the structure of mind. On the opening page of *Ecrits,* in a short introduction to the collection as a whole, Lacan provides a characteristic example of his own style and a characteristically involuted formulation of a problem:

"Style is the man himself," we repeat, without seeing in it any malice, nor being troubled by the fact that man is an uncertain reference. . . .

Style is the man, let us adopt the formula, only to extend it: the man to whom one addresses oneself?

This would simply be to satisfy the principle we have put forward: that in language our message comes to us from the Other, and to enunciate it to the limit: in an inverted form. (And let us remember that this principle is applied to its own enunciation. . . .)

But if man were reduced to being nothing but the point of return to our discourse, would not the question come back to us what is the point of addressing it to him?

Once the urge to dismiss this as pretentious rubbish has been overcome, it begins to reveal a preoccupation that, as much as anything else, is the hallmark of structuralist activity. The reference to self-reference, the idea of language doubling back on itself, are examples of that *dédoublement* of which recent French writers have become so fond. (It would not be improper, according to Lévi-Strauss, to think of his own work as "the myth of mythology." They are important because the subject, for Lacan, turns out to be a kind of *dédoublement*, a matching of consciousness with the world, of speaker with hearer, of the signifier with the signified. The latter terms are from the linguistics of Saussure and are of crucial significance to the structuralists. Whereas the civilized mind thinks itself capable of taking an objective stance and judging the adequacy of language or symbol (the signifier) to their meanings (the signified), the view of mind that emerges from ethnology and psychoanalysis suggests that the two realms are autonomous and that mind *is* precisely this adequacy, so that such objectivity is impossible.

This point is made again and again, in different forms and different occasions, in the writings of Lacan. The subject is an activity, not a thing; the Cartesian *cogito* comes closer to representing it correctly than any view of the self as substance, but even the *cogito* gives too strong a sense of continuity and permanence, so that it would perhaps be better to say "*cogito ergo sum*" *ubi cogito, ibi sum.* The subject produces itself by reflecting on itself, but when it is engaged on some other object, it has no being apart from the activity of being so engaged. The idea that it had objective being and could be studied scientifically, according to Lacan, was a direct consequence of the sucess of science in throwing light on the rest of the world. The troubled Viennese came to Freud because he was a scientist and had the prestige that went with that identification; but when Freud looked for the subject in the light of science he found instead the unconscious, the Other, as Lacan puts it. Freud's own subjectivity, of course, was engaged on this quest, and its discovery by itself would have been, again, a case of impossible self-division. Although Lacan never quite puts it this way, one could sum up the conclusion of his argument against the possibility of a science of the subject by saying: *the subject cannot be the object of science because it is its subject*. When the analyst tries to get at "the subject which he calls, significantly, the patient," what he finds is not the true subject at all, but only something called into being by his questioning: "that is to say, the fish is drowned by the operation of fishing. . . ." The final image of the subject, in the most recent writings, is the Moebius strip, or as Lacan calls it "the interior eight," which from two surfaces produces one, or from one two, depending on the starting point. What Lacan seems to be saying is that the subject cannot give an analytic account of itself, only paradoxes, hints, and images; and this being the case, "there is no science of man." "There is no science of man, because the man of science does not exist, only its subject." "It is known that I have always felt a repugnance for the term *sciences humaines*, which seems to me a call to slavery itself."

One of the most powerful structuralist blows against traditional humanism was administered by the publication in 1966 of Michel Foucault's *Les Mots et les choses*. The starting point for the reflections that resulted in the book, he says in the preface, was a text of Borges, which is worth quoting for itself as well as for the light it throws on the structuralist enterprise.

This text cites "a certain Chinese encyclopedia" where it is written that "animals are divided into: a) belonging to the Emperor, b) embalmed, c) tame, d) suckling pigs, e) mermaids, f) fabulous, g) dogs running free, h) included in the present classification, i) which behave like madmen, j) innumerable, k) drawn on camel-skin with a very fine brush, l) et cetera, m) which have just broken their leg, n) which from a distance look like flies."

And Foucault continues:

In our astonishment at this taxonomy what strikes us with sudden force, what, because of its setting, is presented to us as the exotic charm of another system of thought, is the limitation of our own: the stark impossibility of thinking *that*.

Why, Foucault asks, do we find Borges's imaginary Chinese classification so preposterous? Into what intellectual straitjacket has our own history forced us? And he concludes that our resistance to this kind of spontaneous absurdity, our demand for logical coherence even where it is unnecessary, is again a product of the invention of *man* as an embodiment of analytic reason. Until early modern times, individual subjectivity and collective subjectivity were absorbed in Discourse, a human activity (a linguistic one, which in context amounts to the same thing) constituting the world as intelligible and summing up all that could be said about it. The rise of science led to the fragmentation and dissolution of this conceptual and linguistic unity, by drawing attention to separable properties of the world —biological, economic, philological—and pursuing them independently. But it then became apparent that in some sense all these inquiries were about the same thing; only instead of recombining into a single activity, they were thought of as pointing to a single entity—Man. Man thus appeared to have achieved his own objectification. The present perplexity of the so-called humanities indicates, however, that that conclusion was premature; the picture of man that they present to us turns out to bear little resemblance to the real thing. Humanism has been a detour from which we may be beginning to return to the main track: Foucault concludes with a more or less confident prediction that man will disappear "like a face drawn in sand at the edge of the sea."

This must not be misunderstood as a prophecy of doom. Men will still be here, facing the same problems in the same way, with the exception that the particular aberration called *man* will have been done away with. All attempts to classify and predict individual human behavior quickly encounter limits that show them, in all but a few cases (and all these to some extent pathological), to be futile. Rational, humanist aesthetics, for example, yielded when put into practice a wooden imitation of art; art began to revive in this century when the surrealists and others preached liberation from ortho- dox canons and advocated the free play of the unconscious. The havoc that the social sciences are capable of wreaking sur- rounds us on every side. There is nothing wrong with the social sciences, of course, if they are inquiries into group behavior or even individual behavior carried on by somebody for whom that behavior constitutes an object; they become dangerous only when ignorant people believe what they are told about them- selves and become what the social scientist says they are. Struc- turalism, in effect, advocates an engagement with the world, an abandonment of too much self-examination in favor of partic- ipation in some significative activity, which in structuring the world will bring the subject into equilibrium with it. What activity is a matter of wide choice. There is nothing partic- ularly worthy, as the existentialists thought, in political or even in artistic activity; any number of others are capable of em- bodying the structure of mind.

Art and politics, nevertheless, as two of the most compre- hensive structures available, have come in for special attention, and above all literature, since it employs directly the very archetype of structure, namely, language itself. But there is more than one kind of structuralist criticism, and the overlap with other preoccupations is greater here than anywhere else. The great triumph of the structural method, which imitated the sciences in producing new knowledge, remains in fact the work of the Marxist critic Lucien Goldmann on Pascal and Racine, in the course of which he was able to reconstruct some parts of the Jansenist movement that had been forgotten and furthermore to find evidence that they had in fact existed (the relevant works are, of course, Le Dieu caché and Correspon- dance de Martin de Barcos, abbé de Saint-Cyran). I have not included Goldmann in the list of structuralists because much of what I have taken to define the movement does not apply to him, and his own method, which he calls "genetic struc- turalism," rests very heavily on the notion of literature as an embodiment (often in spite of the intentions of the writer) of some collective social attitude appropriate to a class or a period. Structural criticism in the wider sense does not limit itself to collective or social or historical considerations, although it does not ignore them either. The work *is* a structure; the critic uses it as a point of departure. One of the striking things about this criticism, in fact, is its habit of getting a great deal more out of a work than the author or for that matter his historical period could possibly have put into it. Foucault, in *Les Mots et les choses*, spends the whole first chapter on a painting of Velásquez, "The Maids of Honor," from which he extracts by hindsight and free elaboration a whole theory of the "absence of the subject" (another pivotal concept of structuralism). And Althusser, who has applied structuralist techniques to a "rethinking" of Marx, is said in a recent essay in *Aletheia* to have developed a complete apparatus "for putting oneself in condition to read Marx so as to think profitably not only what Marx wrote but also what he thought without writing."

This last claim, it should be noted, is not made by Althusser himself and was not necessarily meant kindly. The same article calls Althusser's works (*Pour Marx; Lire Le Capital*) "limiting cases of interpretation" and suggests that what is presented there is not just Marx but something much more, which Marx indeed could not have created, since he did not enjoy the advantages of the intervening hundred years. And this is quite in keeping with the principles of structuralist criticism. The clearest statement of these principles is to be found in Barthes's *Critique et vérité*, a response to Picard's *Nouvelle critique ou nouvelle imposture*, in turn an attack on Barthes's *Sur Racine*. Picard, a typical humanist, had become indignant at the way in which Barthes had, in his view, tampered with literary and historical objectivity, with the "facts" about Racine. (Another common element in structuralist thought is its distrust, in the so-called *sciences humaines*, of the flat empiricism of the natural sciences, principally because in the human context a great deal of interpretation goes into deciding what the facts are.) Barthes points out that there could be a "science" of literature only if we would be content to regard the work simply as a "written object," disregarding its sense in favor of all its pos-

sible senses, disregarding its author in favor of its more generalized linguistic origins—treating it, in fact, as the ethnologist
treats a myth. What criticism does, by contrast, is to produce
one of the possible senses of the work, to construct alongside
it, as it were, another work (the interpretation) as a hypothesis in the light of which the details of the original become
intelligible. "The book is a world," says Barthes. "The critic
confronted by the book is subject to the same conditions of
utterance as the writer confronted by the world." But the critic
can never replace the reader; the individual also confronts the
book at a particular time, in a particular context; it becomes
part of his experience, presents itself to him with a certain
intelligibility, as a message (from whom?); it engages him in
another episode of the structuring activity that makes him what
he is. An old book is not (unless the reader takes pains to
make it so) a bit of antiquity; it is a bit of the present; consequently Racine can still be read, and new critical views about
Racine, possible only in the light of contemporary events, can
find in him without distortion meanings that he and *his* contemporaries could not even have understood. Similarly, Althusser
is justified in his rethinking of Marx; indeed, all works have
constantly to be rethought if they are to be more than archae-
ological curiosities.

The consideration of structuralist criticism brings us back to
Lévi-Strauss. The critic never says all there is to be said about
a book; his reading is always an approximation that we know
to be inadequate, even if we do not know what would constitute
an adequate reading—even if it makes no sense to imagine such
a reading. Similarly, language never formulates the world adequately, nor does myth, nor does science—inspite of its (now
abandoned) aspiration to completability in principle—nor does
history. These structures change in time (they can, to use structuralist jargon, be considered in diachronic as well as in synchronic aspects); also, which is not the same thing, they are
dynamic, having complex interrelations among themselves.
The respect in which I think Lévi-Strauss does not exploit the
full resources of his own method in distinguishing between
primitive and modern societies has to do with this complexity

of interrelation of structures. If mind emerged, as it surely did, under evolutionary pressure that required an order of complexity in behavior greater than that of any other form of life, if when the evolutionary pressure was off, it devised language as a means of keeping that complexity in dynamic equilibrium with its world, then it seems to me the way was opened for a kind of amplification of complexity by shifting language from the side of the object to the side of the subject, where mind (now ramified with language) became capable of handling an even greater objective complexity and indeed required it in order to maintain equilibrium. We are perhaps today in one of the later stages of such an exponential development.

If that should be the case, we might well cultivate the totalizing quality of the primitive mind, of which Lévi-Strauss speaks at the end of La Pensée sauvage. It is there (in the course of a polemic against Sartre) that he refers also to "this intransigent refusal on the part of the savage mind to allow anything human (or even living) to remain alien to it." This allusion to one of the oldest mottoes of humanism may seem an odd conclusion to a discussion of an antihumanist point of view; but I think the truth is that here again Lévi-Strauss does not go far enough. To restrict the sphere of concern to the human, or even to the living, does not do justice to mind as its own history has revealed it. The structuring activity that keeps the subject in balance with the world is and must be all-encompassing. To quote Pouillon once more, "structuralism forbids us to enclose ourselves in any particular reality." The fact that we abandon a restrictive humanism, however, does not mean that we cease to be men. If structuralism had a motto it might well be: Homo sum, nihil a me alienum puto.

The danger with attitudes as generous as this is, of course, that they may in the end become completely uncritical. A theory that applies to everything does not distinguish between different things and might as well apply to nothing; if every human activity allows a structuralist interpretation, the fact that any particular activity does so ceases to be instructive. The structuralist thesis seems to me to bear the stamp of truth, but there is a penalty for arriving at the truth, namely, that in at least one important respect nothing remains to be done. Here again there is an illuminating parallel with existentialism, and one that I think throws a good deal of light on the difference in habits of thought between French intellectuals and Anglo-American ones (especially philosophers). Once one sees that the conscious subject is isolated and alone or that the variety of human activity is to be accounted for by an inveterate urge to build intelligible structures, everything appears in a new light, nothing is ever the same again—but for the most part the old problems remain problematic, at any rate from the analytic point of view. The fact that existentialism and structuralism do not lend themselves to theoretical elaboration may account for their unpopularity with Anglo-American thinkers whose tastes run to the technical and the abstract.

The French, on the other hand, never seem to tire of elaboration in the direction of the discursive and the concrete: literary philosophy permits the repetition of the same truth in a variety of ways, philosophical literature and belles lettres permit its demonstration in a variety of contexts. The best structuralist writers have developed these forms to a point of great finesse. Jacques Derrida, the most recent star of the movement, exemplifies the philosophical mode brilliantly in his collection *L'Ecriture et la différence*, published in Paris last summer; Barthes remains the master of the literary mode, and his lecture on "La Mythologie de la Tour Eiffel," given during a stay in the United States, was a perfect example of it. In the vein of his earlier *Mythologies*, it showed that while structuralism may leave unchanged the structure of the world at large, it *structures* for us the various parts of the world with which we come in contact—a process, in Barthes's own words, of "conquest by the intelligible." Its great contribution has been to provide a strategy for this conquest, to claim once again for intellect a territory we had all but abandoned to the absurd.

16
LÉVI-STRAUSS AND THE PRIMITIVE
ROBERT L. ZIMMERMAN

Why are we so fascinated by the primitive? Why do we continue to investigate primitive man? Is it because we envy his simplicity and spontaneity? Does his animality excite and "eroticize" us? Or is it because our desire for self-knowledge —indeed, for more than that, for a self, an identity—drives us beyond our own beginning to the beginning of our race? Do we somehow know, as Hegel put it, that to become a person one must "ingest" the history of the race, become a We in order to become an I?

Although all the above explanations no doubt have something to do with our continued investigation of the primitive, the last seems to me the most compelling. It is therefore somewhat paradoxical that one of the results of this investigation has been the fairly widespread acceptance of the view that,

From Commentary, Vol. XLVI, No. 5 (May 1968), pp. 54–61.

after all, the primitive is *not* like us; rather, he is a preman, a savage, a creature one cut above the beast. Most of us, in other words, have come to believe that the history of the race is analogous to the history of an individual, in that it has a beginning stage that is outgrown in time and that stands to what comes after it as the potential stands to the actual, the complete and the developed to the incomplete and undeveloped.

This view has had some formidable champions, among them Auguste Comte, Sir James George Frazer, Lévy-Bruhl, and Hegel. In our time, it has had a formidable critic: Claude Lévi-Strauss, the distinguished French social anthropologist. In his many works, Lévi-Strauss has argued that this interpretation of the primitive is factually and theoretically indefensible. *The Savage Mind* contains perhaps the most thorough presentation of Lévi-Strauss's position, and is for this reason worth summarizing at some length, although it should be stated at the outset that no summary of the argument can do justice to its complexity or to the vast amount of evidence introduced to defend it.

In *The Savage Mind*, Lévi-Strauss undertakes an analysis of primitive thought in general—which, he argues, far from lacking a conceptual structure, rests upon a remarkably rich and complex one—and of primitive scientific thought in particular —which he argues is full-blown scientific thought and not, as we have been used to hearing, some prelogical, nonrational counterfeit of it. Although primitive science is tied to the world of perception and imagination—the phenomenological world of the felt, immediate qualities of things—and organized in aesthetic and mythological terms, it does not follow, according to Lévi-Strauss, that it is therefore an inferior or theoretically defective science. It represents rather a method of approaching nature that is only *other than*, not less than, the one employed by modern science. As he puts it, there are

. . . two distinct modes of scientific thought . . . two . . . levels at which nature is accessible to scientific enquiry: one . . . that of perception and imagination: the other at a remove from it. It is as if the objects of science . . . could be arrived at by two different routes, one very close to, and the other more remote from, sensible intuition.

The order of nature, that is to say, appears *on* its sensible surface as well as *beneath* it; the perceptible order of things reflects the imperceptible order of things, and is thus reachable by two routes: one travels by way of the sensible features and felt qualities of things; the other penetrates to what lies beneath and beyond them. Thus:

Wild cherries, cinnamon, vanilla, and cherry are grouped together by the intellect as well as by the senses because they all contain aldehyde, while the closely related smells of wintergreen, lavender, and banana are to be explained by the presence of ester. On intuitive grounds alone we might group onions, garlic, cabbage, turnips, and mustard together even though botany separates liliceae and crucifers. In confirmation of the evidence of the senses chemistry shows that these different families are united on another plane: they contain sulphur.

To be sure, not every link on the surface of nature signifies or reflects a link in its depths. But to say this is only to demonstrate the imperfect nature of a science based on the secondary properties of things, not to show that such a science is illegitimate.

The primitive, in other words, seeks the order of his world in sensible terms and thus creates a science based on the sensible aspects of things. But this is not all. His search, according to Lévi-Strauss, is motivated not merely by a utilitarian but also by a theoretical interest. If it were otherwise, we could not explain, among other things, the existence in the primitive's language of terms that refer to objects or features of objects having little or no practical value. For example, although Indians of the northeastern United States and Canada derive no economic benefit from reptiles, they nevertheless possess a herpetology with distinct terms for each genus of reptile and other terms applying to particular species and varieties. And even when a known object *does* afford an economic benefit to the tribe, the process of "over-knowing" that takes place and the elaborate terminology that is created to express it suggest an interest or a drive that is more than practical. Thus, for instance, "The Hanunóo have more than a hundred and fifty terms for the parts and properties of plants. . . . Over six hundred named plants have been recorded among the Pinatubo . . . and one hundred terms [for] parts and characteristics of plants."

Furthermore, if the utility of an animal be taken as the reason for its being known, then the knowledge the primitive has of certain animals that, in his mind, have curative properties (like spiders for fertility, worms for rheumatism, or frozen bear excreta for constipation) must be said to be truly astounding. For surely it is absurd to claim that the primitive came to know about spiders, worms, and frozen bear excreta because they cured respectively, sterility, rheumatism, and constipation. It seems more likely, as Lévi-Strauss observes, that ". . . animals are not known as a result of their usefulness; they are deemed useful . . . because they are first of all known."

Consider also the divination of omens. Among the Iban or Sea Dayaks of South Borneo, the songs and cries of certain birds are taken to be guides to the future: "The rapid cry of the Crested Jay . . . is said to resemble the crackle of burning wood and so presages the successful firing of a family's swiddens. The alarm cry of the Trogon . . . is likened to the death rattle of an animal being slain and augurs good hunting." Clearly, the resemblances and associations between the cries and what they suggest are independent of any practical considerations. They are, rather, the spontaneous products of "free association": the apprehension of the phenomenological qualities of the cries. It is because this "logic" is at work that the cries become omens and take on signification. In other words, it is only *after* the cry has been associated with some event and been given a "meaning" that it begins to function in a practical way, namely, as evidence of what is to occur.

In his science, then, the primitive exhibits a theoretical interest. He strives to detect the order and connections among the objects in his world to satisfy his "instinct" for order and connectedness. Contrary to the widely held belief, the primitive is not a "savage" who is governed only by his bodily impulses and who thinks, if at all, in merely utilitarian terms. His desires are not limited to those things that are "good to eat"; he is as much desirous of those things that are "good to think." Thus, if we accept the dual premise that disinterested inquiry and classification—whatever the principle of that classification might be—is the core of a genuine science and that primitive science is an instance of such distinterested inquiry and classification, we come with Lévi-Strauss to the conclusion that primitive science is genuine science.

Lévi-Strauss continues his assault on the myth of the primitive savage by turning to the phenomena of totemism and totemic classification. Through an analysis of these phenomena —first undertaken in *Totemism* and present in its basic conclusions throughout the body of his writings—Lévi-Strauss tries to show that, contrary to this myth, primitive thought rests upon a rich and complex conceptual structure. More specifically, he argues, negatively, that totemism is an illusion and that the classic understanding of it is wrong (among other things, this understanding holds that members of a clan identify it with the totemic object and literally believe it to be their ancestor); positively, he argues that totemism represents a highly sophisticated mechanism for ordering or classifying that has as its (unconscious) goal the differentiation and integration of units within society. Classification in terms of totemic objects stands in relation to *social* entities or phenomena as classification as such stands in relation to *natural* entities and phenomena: both, that is, signify and ratify the diversity-within-unity of what is. What this means can perhaps best be illustrated by some examples. In *Totemism*, Lévi-Strauss describes an Australian tribe ". . . which names its moieties after the parts of a tree. In the Ngeumba tribe Gwaidmudthen is divided into *nhurai* (butt) and *wangue* (middle) while Gwaigulir is equivalent to *winngo* (top). These names refer to the different portions of the shadow of a tree and refer to the positions taken up in camping." And in *The Savage Mind*, speaking about the class of the Chicksaw tribe, he observes:

The Racoon people . . . live on fish and wild fruit, those of the Puma lived in the mountains . . . and lived principally on game. The Wild Cat clan slept in the daytime and hunted at night . . . Members of the Bird clan were up before daybreak. . . . the people of the Red Fox clan were professional thieves . . . the Redskunk lived in dugouts underground.

What these examples illustrate is the classificatory function of totemism. The totemic naming system is a device, a structure, a mechanism for distinguishing among and correlating the various groups within a tribe. As Rousseau observed (Lévi-Strauss is indebted to him in this), totemism, by superimposing a set of natural entities upon a set of social entities, translates the latter into the former. The facts of social life—such as the functions of different clans, their hunting duties and positions, spatial location within the village, position in the hierarchy, exogamous relations—are thus "coded" in terms of a symbolism or notation derived from the totemic objects themselves, that is, from nature. The set of totemic objects, with its perceived internal distinctions and its overall "organicity," stands in a symbolic or metaphorical relation to the set of units that comprise the social organism. Totemism is thus based upon symbolic or metaphoric reasoning. It can be thought of as a logic generated by a phenomenal awareness of an analogy between nature and society or among sets of things that contain similar differences. It provides a calculus for social ordering and makes the structure of society lucid and thinkable. Or—what comes to the same thing—it is a code that metaphorically represents the units within society, their various roles, and the relations they bear to one another.

There is much to say about this enormously fertile and provocative interpretation of totemism. Not only does it salvage the phenomenon of totemism that, as classically conceived, had virtually become meaningless because of the wealth of counter-instances raised against it (for example, the many clans that did not identify with the totemic object or in which totems were chosen willy-nilly with no pretense of literal ancestry); not only does it remove totemism from the narrow framework of magic or religion and place it within the broader framework of taxonomical activity as such; but, with one stroke, it re-establishes the continuity between primitive and modern man. It accomplishes this because the function of totemism is now seen as a function that any and every society in search of co-hesion and interplay must somehow symbolize and underwrite through some mechanism or other. In other words, as Lévi-Strauss observes, when we deal with totemism:

We are . . . dealing not with an autonomous institution which can be defined by its distinctive properties and is typical of certain regions of the world and certain forms of civilization, but with a modus operandi which can be discerned even behind social structures traditionally defined in a way diametrically opposed to totemism.

Deciphering the totemic code, the significations of the to-temic objects both in themselves and as they relate to each other, is a complicated process. The meaning of an object or an event is a function of that with which it is paired or asso-ciated, and since such pairing is rather variable (although not arbitrary), to re-establish the semantic value of a totemic name, or the relations among a group of totemic names, becomes a difficult task. This, of course, is an instance of the larger diffi-culty of deciphering the meanings of objects and events as such. For as we saw with respect to the meanings of bird cries, the linked entities (that is, the cry and the event it brought to mind) are connected by an "informal" logic, a logic that uti-lizes the modalities and "feels" of things. Such a logic, although not in itself irrational (we can understand the relations it fixes once we know what those relations are) is not based on reason and is thus difficult to reconstruct rationally.

Furthermore, primitive logic, the logic behind totemic and all primitive classification, utilizes many poles of reference in its ordering procedures. Thus, according to Lévi-Strauss, al-though the basic structure or movement of primitive logic is the unification of opposites, the correlation of differences through pairing or binary thinking, this movement takes place in many ways and on many levels. In primitive logic, objects can be paired in terms of contiguity and/or resemblance. These, in turn, are "many-valued" terms. That is, resemblances can be based on considerations that are sensory (similar smells), metaphoric (bird cries), or almost anything else (among the Luapula of South India, the function of construction links bees and carpenters); contiguity, on the other hand, can be based on a juxtaposition that is diachronic or synchronic, static or dynamic. In addition, primitive logic will pair things that are compatible and things that are incompatible, objects whose presence excludes one another as well as objects whose activities include one another. And so on. Thus, although the "logic of the concrete," as Lévi-Strauss calls it, is a procedure of thought that orders and introduces system into what appears disordered and systemless, it does so in many different and subtle ways.

Nonetheless, once one grasps the way this logic "goes," all the classificatory schemata that operate within primitive societies become theoretically susceptible of analysis, since all of them make use of the same logical principles, or variants of these principles. Not only, for example, are colors, smells, foods, animals, plants, and inanimate objects associated in terms of resemblance and contiguity but natural events (such as sunrise or sunset), a region of space (such as the sky), an animal activity (such as the cry of a bird), and human events (for example, a man dies, a pregnant woman's body swells) are also given "meaning" in terms of the same principles in that they are associated with events that resemble them or are contiguous with them (in any one of the number of ways two entities or events can be similar or contiguous). These various classifications or quasi-classifications are thus *structurally* isomorphic or at least are constructed in terms of the same set of logical principles.

Furthermore, just as the theoretical impulse behind these classifications is the unification of multiplicity, the establishment of connections among separate entities, so the impulse of society, so to speak (an unconscious impulse analogous to the "unconscious" grammar of a language) is the creation of liaison structures among its various component parts; thus, Lévi-Strauss argues, borrowing an insight from Marcel Mauss, relations among subgroups within society, like exogamous ties or the ritualistic interchange of gifts, all serve the same end and are governed by the same logic. In each of these cases, atomic units are taken up into a structure that makes them parts of an organic whole. As such they are homologous and intertranslatable.

Once social reality is conceived in this way as a logical system, any number of logical relations among social phenomena becomes apparent. Thus, a structure that has been used on one level with respect to a certain content can be transposed onto another level with respect to a different content. For example, food prohibitions—based upon a belief in the reincarnation of an ancestor in the form of a plant or an animal—reappear on the level of language as a prohibition against uttering any of the homophones of the name of the deceased. Or a structure that has appeared in one tribe can appear as an inverted or transformed structure in a different tribe. In certain tribes, before a man dies, he sometimes indicates the animal in whose form he will be reincarnated; this becomes the animal that his descendants are henceforth forbidden to eat. In other tribes, a child will observe a food prohibition connected with an animal that the village "wise men" had associated with his mother's pregnancy. The content of these "systems"—food prohibitions, notions of reincarnation, etc.—can vary enormously, but the structures, the forms they assume, recur throughout, though sometimes in shapes that are transmuted versions of one another; and since these transmuted structures, according to Lévi-Strauss, are logically related, they admit, once we have learned the logical principles behind them, of structural interpretation. Hence, if we could gather all the data relating to a tribe's technoeconomic, social, and religious structures, we could, with the help of a computer, determine all the logical principles at work in the ordering techniques of that tribe and show these structures and that society to be like a vast set of logically generated transformations. Using logic, cybernetics, game theory, and the like, the anthropologist can "unlock" the primitive society.

Primitive logic, then, however subtle, variable, and kaleidoscopically shifting it may be, is certainly a logic. Moreover, according to Lévi-Strauss, it is an ". . . elementary logic . . . the least common denominator of all thought . . . an original logic. . . ." As such, it lies not only behind primitive thought (that is to say, all the ordering systems that primitive thought elaborates, as well as the structures of primitive life), but behind all thought and all life. And because it is omnipresent, it follows that there is really no such thing as "The Primitive Mind," or "The Modern Mind"; there is only "Mind-As-Such." To be sure, "Mind-As-Such" exhibits different contents at different times (primitive science, for instance, deals with the secondary properties of things, while modern science deals with the primary properties of things), but its structures do not vary (in the cases of both primitive and modern science, different contents are ordered and systematized in terms of opposition, contiguity, resemblance, etc.). We might add that it is the belief in such a Mind, or the efficacy of believing in such a Mind, with its invariant structures, that has convinced Lévi-Strauss that he can construct a model of Man and Society that will encompass all men and all societies. Indeed, it is just such a model that his work as a whole is an attempt to construct. By legitimizing the search for this model, or for closer and closer approximations to it (an activity that, although not antagonistic to empirical research, is not empirical research), Lévi-Strauss has significantly affected modern anthropological inquiry.

Lévi-Strauss's account of the savage mind is, of course, not immune from criticism; indeed, the very range and daring of his claims render debate probable. One can, for example, wonder whether he has not confused a phase of a developed science, that of classifying, with the essence of a developed science, that of constructing theoretical entities or models. Few would doubt —certainly in the light of the evidence Lévi-Strauss presents— that primitives classify or that primitives classify (at least some of the time) for the sake of classifying—that they are driven by a theoretical and not merely by a utilitarian interest. And, I suppose—although here there would be some controversy— many would at least be responsive to Lévi-Strauss's speculations, carefully hedged as they are, about the isomorphism that exists between the primary and the secondary qualities of things, between what appears and what is inferred. In the area of epistemology, philosophers since Berkeley have been skeptical about the legitimacy of the distinction altogether; and psychologically, men have always balked somewhat at the notion that their perceptions and feelings yield up only a "subjective" reality, a realm of "phenomenal" events that exist only "in" and "for" their minds. The bias in favor of the given, of what is directly perceived and felt, is not something we have outgrown. Many of us still can't really believe that the colors and tastes and smells of things are not really real, or that what looks like human behavior in animals is really a mechanical response to a mechanical stimulus, or that what we introspect as our reasons for acting are not really the springs of our action. This, in the broadest sense of the word, "explains" why philosophers like Bergson, Whitehead, Dewey, Peirce, James, and Husserl have refused to succumb to the rationalized Parmenidean universe of science.

Yet even if we grant all this—that the primitive classifies, that the method he uses in classifying is formally congruent with the methods of modern science, and that he classifies for the sake of classifying—it does not necessarily follow that primitive science is full-blown science. One feels somewhat hesitant here, since the meaning of science is not unequivocal and since the term is, to a degree, normative as well as descriptive. Nevertheless, it is commonly agreed that what is fundamental to developed, full-blown science—modern science—is not *classification* but *explanation*, and that the core of modern science is the construction of explanatory models and the testing of them through the verification of their implied, observable consequences. Notwithstanding the difficulties philosophers of science have run into in trying to pin down the concept of explanation, one thing is clear: *classification is not explanation*, and an inquiry into nature that merely classifies is not a scientific inquiry in the full sense of that term.

Thus, contrary to Lévi-Strauss, it is tempting to say that primitive science provided "Mind-As-Such" with a long period of time during which it looked at nature and, after a fashion, classified it. That this was a necessary precondition for science goes without saying; but because it did only this primitive science must be thought of as a precursor to a more profound inquiry into nature, that is, as a precursor to, and not an equal of, modern science.

The issue is sharpened when we recognize that, in its most general sense, Lévi-Strauss's entire enterprise is at odds with his thoughts about primitive science. For if the essence of science is classification then the field that he himself engages in, anthropology, is something other than, or more than, science. For surely what Lévi-Strauss does is not classification; rather, in constructing models of "Mind-As-Such," he is seeking to delineate the set of invariant structures behind all human thought and life. This activity transcends mere classification and reintroduces the very distinction he is seeking to eliminate. Conversely, if what Lévi-Strauss does is science, then what the primitive does is not science but rather a phase in the development of science. This is a crucial distinction.

In addition, we might also question the value of Lévi-Strauss's rationalism. As we saw, the forms of human thought and life are for him, in the end, determined by rational and logical principles. When primitive man thinks, his thought is logical. To be sure, the logic at work is not a conventional logic; it is a "concrete," "felt," "aesthetic" logic; it is "many-valued" and turns on many "axes." Nevertheless, it reveals itself to such conventional logical techniques as those of game theory, cybernetics, structural linguistics, and the logic of classes. It is thus systematic, it is not antagonistic to the laws of Aristotelian logic, and, more generally, it constitutes an ordering system that is both amenable to and reconstructable in terms of linear, sequential, "ordinary" thought. In addition, notwithstanding the complexities involved, it can be seen according to Lévi-Strauss that social phenomena like totemism, gift-giving, or the exogamous relations among clans are determined by rational ends, that is, the ends of societal order, stability, and coherence. Thus, the image that emerges of man and society is of an organism that has set itself rational goals and has chosen rational, or what it takes to be rational, means to achieve these goals.

Before entering upon a criticism of Lévi-Strauss's rationalism, one must, first of all, bear in mind what he is *not* implying by this term. He does not, for instance, mean that men always reach conclusions that are rational or that social phenomena are always produced by means of careful rational deliberation. To interpret him in his fashion would be to misperceive the level of generality in his rationalism. Lévi-Strauss is not talking about the *content* of human thought and life but about its form: it is not the material, the "filling," but the structure of these phenomena that he would call rational and logical. Thus, from the point of view of their structures, as classificatory and ordering systems of nature, modern and primitive science are both logical and rational just as primitive and modern kinship systems, as classificatory and ordering systems within society, are both logical and rational. Once we recognize the nature of Lévi-Strauss's rationalism, its generality and formality, we should be less intuitively opposed to it; at the same time, however, we should also be less concerned or intellectually engaged with it. For given its generality and its abstractness, it seems to be a claim about man that at times borders on the trivial and insignificant and at times arbitrarily stretches and mishandles the meanings of terms. Is it not trivial to say that primitive and modern science are alike because they both are mechanisms that order nature? Considered as ordering mechanisms, any two human inquiries into nature are alike: men always order in some way or other when they inquire, even if they do so in a disorderly fashion. And do we not arbitrarily stretch and mishandle the meaning of the term "logic" if we apply it both to what Russell and Whitehead did in *Principia Mathematica* and to what the primitive does in divining bird cries or attributing medicinal value to spiders? Is it not trivial to say that primitive and modern kinship systems or marriage prescriptions are alike because they both are mechanisms that order relations among the elements within a society? What social institution *isn't* such a mechanism? Do we not, finally, arbitrarily stretch the meaning of the term "rational," if we use it to denote both a system that marks and codes distinctions and relations within a society metaphorically, and a system that marks and codes such distinctions and relations nonmetaphorically? Surely the term "rational" denotes the latter and has as a boundary condition that it cannot be used of the former. To say that the former system is rational but relies on the imagination, while the latter system is rational but relies on the intellect is like saying that all humans are males but some are he-males and some are she-males.

One might set this latter point against a different background. Intuitively, we believe that man is both rational and irrational. Man is rational when he practices science and irrational when he relies on magic; man is rational when he uses his intelligence to decide the future course of events and irrational when he continues to rely on the mechanisms or institutions of magic. Now it is precisely this that Lévi-Strauss seems to deny. It would seem that these antitheses or oppositions have no place in his model. For according to that model man is rational both in practicing science and in relying on magic; man is rational both in using intelligence and in not using it; man is rational both in discarding ineffective mechanisms or institutions and in not discarding them. Surely the term "rational" is being misused when it is employed to identify such diverse, even contradictory human actions.

Finally, we might wonder at the discontinuity between nature and man that Lévi-Strauss's theories seem to imply. For in his rejection of the coming-into-being of man, in his insistence that man qua "Mind-As-Such" always was, he is in effect rejecting the existence of prehumans who mediated the transition from nature to man. That is, in rejecting the notion that the primitive was a "Savage," a preman, he is also rejecting the notion that man as we know him evolved through a series of human-like forms.

Now, to be sure, the claim that there is discontinuity within nature is no longer objectionable (at an earlier time this would have been thought to be virtually a logical impossibility). Indeed, in areas like subatomic physics and quantum mechanics, discontinuity has virtually become a confirmed fact. However, two considerations must be dealt with. First, the discontinuity for which Lévi-Strauss argues occured allegedly on the macroscopic level. Yet on this level all our experience points to the omnipresence of continuity, and in deference to this omnipresence, physicists have generally confined discontinuity to the microscopic subatomic level. The discontinuity that Lévi-Strauss alleges is thus exceedingly counterintuitive. Second, Lévi-Strauss does not deal with the possibility that the discontinuity within nature that he proposes may be not a discontinuity at all but rather a result of our inability to find those prehuman forms that would fill in the gap and eliminate the discontinuity, or even a result of our way of looking at and investigating primitives. That is, it may be that the alleged discontinuity is in fact a result of our inquiry's being incomplete or distorting, and not at all an objective fact about nature. (This was precisely the response of many to the finding of discontinuity in physics.) The importance of this possibility is obvious: one cannot ascribe to nature what is properly a consequence of one's method of inquiry. But Lévi-Strauss, even though he seems clearly aware of the issue—indeed, he speaks of it often in Tristes Tropiques—nonetheless, seems essentially to disregard it. Moreover, his commitment to the construction of the model of "Mind-As-Such" seems not to allow him to consider it seriously, for the logic of models and of model-making tends to subvert the the subjective-objective distinction. This is why all model-making—Lévi-Strauss's, it seems to me, not excepted—runs the risk of becoming arbitrary and subjective, of becoming, in some cases, sheer speculation and indulgence in metaphysics.

Lévi-Strauss's belief in the existence of a Super-Mind, that is, a quasi-Kantian set of invariant structures that all minds, and products of minds like societies, exhibit, leads him to some interesting reflections about human history. In a general sense, his theory of history is anti-Marxian. This is all the more interesting since he often has suggested that his thought is greatly indebted to Marx. Thus, In Tristes Tropiques, he says: "rarely do I tackle a problem in sociology or ethnology without having first set my mind in motion by a re-perusal of a page or two from the 18th Brumaire of Louis Bonaparte or the Critique of Political Economy." And in The Savage Mind, speaking of

Sartre, he says that "in both our cases Marx is the point of departure of our thought." Nonetheless, at bottom, his thought moves in quite a different direction from that of Marx. What separates them is their respective attitudes toward historical change.

For Marx it seems clear that history is developmental. Man unfolds in history and, like a seed, slowly comes to fruition. Moreover, the forms of life and of social organization at any given time are a function of the distance yet to be traveled and of the obstacles that impede, but paradoxically also further, the process; although dialectical, history for Marx is progressive. Time measures the progress of history; if it contains the seeds of contradiction, it also contains the seeds of consummation.

For Lévi-Strauss, on the other hand, it would seem that history and time are not developmental and progressive; they do not lead to successively better states of society and relations among men or even to a basic alteration of man's modes of consciousness and styles of living. (It is, by the way, on this point, although not solely on this point, that Lévi-Strauss criticizes Sartre in the last chapter of *The Savage Mind*. For Sartre, at bottom, retains a Marxian view of time and history. Thus, for example, Sartre distinguishes superior and inferior modes of consciousness in terms of historical position and context, and he is unwilling to grant that the primitive possesses "complex understanding," since such understanding could not have existed at that level of historical development.) For Lévi-Strauss, history is a series of combinations or clusters of modes of consciousness and life, individual and social, spread out in time. These different clusters represent the different contents or events that "fill in" the structures of "Mind-As-Such" in different historical epochs. Thus, the existence of totemic clans, exogamy, gift-giving, etc., in the particular "piece" of history occupied by a primitive group represents the content or set of events in terms of which "Mind-As-Such" has "organicized" these particular group of men living in that particular time. Those combinations that actually become manifest represent only some of the combinations that *could* have come about. The set of possible modes of consciousness and life is probably large but finite.[1] The diversity they exhibit, however, should not hide the fact that behind them, like Plato's Forms and Hegel's Categories, stand the invariant and recurring structures that they subserve and from which they derive their reality.

Lévi-Strauss rarely deals with the factors that lie beneath the structures of "Mind-As-Such." He does, however, speak of phenomena like demographic expansion, wars, and drought, as the generative factors underlying empirical change. Yet all these seem in the end reducible to the physical forces of nature. Thus, in speaking of the laws of primitive logic, the "original" and "elementary" logic that is the source of all thought, Lévi-Strauss remarks that these laws are "a direct expression of the structure of the mind (and behind the mind, probably of the brain)." And lest the parenthetical "probably" be misconstrued, he goes on to say in *The Savage Mind*:

. . . the ultimate goal of the human sciences [is] not to constitute, but to dissolve man. The preeminent nature of anthropology is that it represents the first step in a procedure which involves others. Ethnographic analysis tries to arrive at invariants beyond the empirical diversity of human societies. . . . However, it would not be enough to reabsorb particular humanities into a general one. This first enterprise opens the way for others . . . which are incumbent upon the exact natural sciences: the reintegration of culture in nature and finally of life within the whole of its physico-chemical conditions.

And, he adds, "the opposition between nature and culture . . . seems to be of primarily methodological importance."

---

1 Thus, speaking of customs in *Tristes Tropiques*: "The ensemble of a people's customs has always its particular style; they form into systems. I am convinced that the number of these systems is not unlimited, and that human societies, like individual human beings . . . never create *absolutely*; all they can do is to choose certain combinations from a repertory of ideas which it should be possible to reconstitute . . . one could eventually establish a periodic chart of . . . elements analagous to that devised by Mendeleev. In this, all customs, whether real or possible, would be grouped by families, and all that would remain for us to do would be to recognize those which societies had . . . adopted."

The activities of the physical energies that govern all things have no point, no goal, no consummation; equally as surely one cannot speak of them as "progressing." And since these activities underlie the empirical and structural events that constitute human history, that history in turn cannot be said to progress. History and time are merely the space within which, on one level, the structures of Mind and the contents of those structures, exhibit their respective permutations and combinations. We have thus not progressed beyond the primitive; we have merely turned up on a different roll of the dice.

Now this vision of man and history, Lucretian in its broad outlines, can have a purgative and cathartic effect; it can loosen the grip of existence. Seen from the Olympian, timeless perspective of structuralism, our concrete concerns—our hopes, our struggles, our despairs—lose their flesh and blood, their urgency. The reality of our strivings and our failures, of our struggles with ourselves and others over principles and ideals, of our moral visions and political revolutions—in short, our humanity—fades, and like a God (or a crab) we are released from the demands and anxieties of being human. Seeing it all from this remote, transcendent vantage-point produces a detachment, a disinterest, a purely theoretical frame of mind: our passions are subdued, calmed, muted. It would be folly if, knowing this truth about things human, one remained within the frustrating, painful world of the passions. In understanding and resigning before the reality of what is—the reality of human insignificance and cosmic indifference—man fulfills his destiny: self-realization lies in the adjustment of our humanity to our intellect.

Thus, if Lévi-Strauss's structuralism is Marxian, it is because it accepts Marx's demand that man be studied scientifically; its heresy, on the other hand, from a Marxian point of view, is its abstract, idealist conception of man as nonhistorical, nonsocial, nonexistential Mind, and its undialectical mechanistic materialism that minimizes the reality of human purposes and principles, reads history as indifferent to such purposes and principles, and places no obligation upon us to work for them. In these rejections lies the offensiveness of structuralism—its trivialization of our deepest instincts.

But to find structuralism offensive is neither to disprove it factually nor even to judge it wrong on the basis of some (necessarily relative) set of moral values. For structuralism makes no factual claim but rather offers a way of interpreting facts; and any formative appraisal of it must be relative and arbitrary. Nevertheless, one cannot but be struck by its many internal irregularities and inconsistencies. While rejecting the reality of the passions, structuralism passionately seeks release from them; while denying the reality of man's earthliness and finitude, it not only commits itself to a disciplined study of these phenomena but plays them off as a means of enlisting support for itself; while it implies an apolitical posture, it, in effect, pragmatically, seems to support the status quo and to express an ideology as conservative as historical Catholicism; while it implicitly prescribes that man seeks fulfillment in intellect, it denounces prescription; while it concerns itself with the forms and structures of human thought and life and, indirectly, minimizes the reality of the content of human thought and life, it presents us nevertheless with its own clear message, namely, the dignity of the intellect and the folly of the passions; and while denying the existence of cross-cultural Truth, it solemnly, even scientifically, announces its existence. All these inconsistencies within structuralism testify to the unavoidable reality of the very things that structuralism seeks to minimize and discredit.[2]

Is primitive man then a savage different *in kind* from us, or is he essentially identical with us? The work of Lévi-Strauss does not provide us with the answer—but then, neither does the work of any anthropologist. This, however, should produce a cynicism about anthropology within us only if we misconceive the nature of the question, that is, if we believe it to be

---

2 This conception of man and history seems to involve two apparently incompatible philosophical views. On the one hand, in saying that man and human history are reducible to chemistry and physics, Lévi-Strauss is speaking like a materialist. On the other hand, in maintaining that man and human history are governed by the forms and categories, the invariant and recurring structures of Mind-As-Such, he is speaking like an idealist. And these two views, unless they are substantially qualified, contradict each other.

a rather straightforward empirical question amenable to the methods of scientific inquiry. It should be clear by now that the matter is not at all as simple as that. Rather, the nature of the question is perhaps best defined by its resemblance to such perennial philosophical questions as, "What is man?" "What is nature?" and "What is the relation between man and nature?" And with respect to these questions it is as important that we confront them and *attempt* to answer them as it is that we answer them conclusively. For only in that continuing confrontation do we define and redefine ourselves; and only by grappling with these questions of identity do we create an identity worth bothering about.

17
SARTRE VS. LÉVI-STRAUSS

LIONEL ABEL

I have been told that Sartre regards *Critique de la raison dialectique*, his second effort at a philosophical anthropology, as his major work of theory. However, since its publication in 1961 (only a small section of it has so far appeared in English translation), it has had little effect on thought or action in Europe or America. Certainly it has stirred up nothing like the excitement that followed the publication of *Being and Nothingness*. And though we are living in a period of radical reflection—of radical action, too, I'd say—the *Critique*, while it may find some interested readers, is hardly going to make excited disciples, anyway not in the West, and according to Raymond Aron (see his article in *Encounter*, June 1965), it is unlikely to have any kind of influence in the Communist world.

From *Commonweal*, Vol. LXXXIV, No. 13 (June 17, 1966), pp. 364–368.

If by the Communist world Aron means Russia, her satellites in Eastern Europe, and China, one cannot but agree with him. But there is the Third World, where Communism is a force, and in the Third World, I think, Sartre's latest philosophical work may well have a real impact.

What is the Third World? We use this term to refer to the underdeveloped countries, many of which are under the influence of Maoism, that is to say, China. But I have noticed that when Sartre speaks of the Third World, with which he identifies himself, he never refers to China explicitly, but only to Castro's Cuba, to Ho Chi Minh's North Vietnam, and to the new struggling nations of Africa. So he is ambiguous about China and, I suspect, wants to be. I take it that while he is disinclined to attack China politically, his interest is stirred not by China, but by that part of the world where there are what he calls in his *Critique* "groups in fusion," organizations that are not yet bureaucratized and that give individuals access to historical action. Sartre has committed himself unreservedly to such organizations in his *Critique*, and such organizations can still be found in those underdeveloped countries that have not yet made it on the international scene.

If Sartre's *Critique* has not yet influenced the Third World, I predict that it will, as soon, that is, as its theses are understood there. What is more, these theses are already understood, though in less sophisticated terms, by those intellectuals of the Third World who have taken up the struggle against colonialism. A case in point: Frantz Fanon, the Algerian revolutionary (a Negro born in Martinique, he was a psychoanalyst) who wrote *The Wretched of the Earth*, issued in 1965 in English with, not surprisingly, an introduction by Sartre. Now I do not know whether M. Fanon ever read Sartre's *Critique* in manuscript (Fanon died the year it was published) or had conversations with the author. But one does not have to assume that M. Fanon either read Sartre's *Critique* or talked with Sartre to account for the similarity and often identity of outlook between him and the French philosopher.

Here is Frantz Fanon on the native populations subject to colonial rule: "The native . . . is ready for violence at all times.

From birth it is clear to him that this narrow world, strewn with prohibitions, can only be called in question by absolute violence." And here is Sartre in his *Critique*, on the colonist: ". . . the colonial wars of the nineteenth century have achieved for the colonist an original situation of violence as his fundamental relation with the native . . ." Fanon: "The colonial world is a Manichean world . . ." Sartre: "In every way, action here becomes Manichean, and divides one from the enemy's forces by an absolute negation . . . they become *other than men*." Fanon:

. . . the native town . . . is a place of ill-fame, peopled by men of evil repute . . . It is a town of niggers and dirty Arabs. The look that the native turns on the settler's town is a look of lust, a look of envy; it expresses his dreams of possession—or manner of possession: to sit at the settler's table, to sleep in the settler's bed, with his wife if possible.

Sartre expresses a like judgment in rather different terms, since he is thinking of how the colonials regard the natives: ". . . it's a question of 'devils' or of 'savage imbeciles.' " Fanon boldly accepts the charge of the colonists. He writes:

The native is declared insensible to ethics; he represents not only the absence of values, but also the negation of values. He is, let us admit it, the enemy of values and in this sense he is the absolute evil. He is the corrosive element, destroying all that comes near him; he is the deforming element, disfiguring all that has to do with beauty or morality."

There are also theoretical points of agreement between the Algerian militant and the French philosopher. Sartre in his *Critique* shows a particular liking for spontaneously organized groups brought together for a single action. Fanon has a like feeling. Sartre also recognizes the instability and insufficiency of such groups for a struggle of any long duration. So does Fanon. And Sartre accepts the necessity of authoritarian terror in holding together militant groups, especially when their aims are historically justified. Once again, Fanon makes a like judgment. Finally—and this is perhaps the most interesting point of agreement—Sartre holds in his *Critique* that economic and sociological theories only become genuinely intelligible from the point of view of those who have undertaken a historical action; Fanon places the practical judgments of parties leading a struggle for independence above any kind of doctrine, even the doctrines of socialism.

There is a difference in tone, though, between the two writers, which Sartre notes perceptively in his introduction to Fanon's book. Sartre writes:

When Fanon says of Europe that she is rushing to her doom, far from sounding the alarm, he is merely concluding a diagnosis. . . . As to curing . . . no: he has other things to think about . . . for Fanon is not interested in us at all; his work— red hot for some—in what concerns us is as cold as ice; he often speaks of us, never to us.

Behind this difference of tone there is a difference not of theory but of situation. Fanon's *The Wretched of the Earth* expresses the thrilling prospect of historical action for peoples hitherto denied access to it. Sartre's introduction to Fanon's book expresses the disappointment and chagrin of Europeans (also Americans) who desire above all else an active role in the historical process and can see no way of attaining to it. In fact, Sartre's *Critique*, in its most interesting parts, concerns itself with those obstacles to historical action that the peoples of the so-called free world have recently confronted and been unable to surmount.

Are only the peoples of the underdeveloped countries able to act historically? And is historical action the only kind of action in which men can find significance? I suspect that Sartre has already answered these questions, and in a way negative to our hopes. And that is why, I think, his *Critique* has had little resonance in Europe or America. Sartre has nothing to say in it—politically, that is—to Europeans or Americans, except that they ought to support the action of the colonial peoples.

In his introduction to Fanon's book Sartre writes:

Today the native populations reveal their true nature, and at the same time our exclusive "club" reveals its weakness—that it's neither more nor less than a minority. Worse than that: since the others become men in name against us, it seems that we are the enemies of mankind; the elite shows itself in its true colors—it is nothing more than a gang.

Does this not amount to urging the Africans, the Asians, and the South Americans to come and get us—the Europeans and North Americans? And is there nothing for us in the advanced countries to do except side with the claims—not always reasonable—made against us by the peoples of the Third World? Is there nothing for white Americans to do except support the claims made against them by the Negroes? And is there nothing for European humanity—of which North Americans are a part—to do now but cheer the efforts made by the underdeveloped peoples to destroy it—and imitate it?

I am willing to grant Sartre—and Fanon too—that if every African does not finally get a white bathtub and some type of parliament, the world may be destroyed. So there is little point in asking whether for Africans to have bathtubs and parliaments is more important than for the world to endure. Doubtless to get these blessings, if they are indeed that, much blood will be shed. There will be many injustices, also inexpiable crimes. But we cannot stop the process we ourselves inaugurated. The European and American devotion to historical and technological development for more than a century cannot but be the dominating ideal for decades to come among the underdeveloped peoples.

But what can we make our ideal, we who have progressed enough to be sick of progressivism? Can it be just to cheer the progress of those to whom such progress is heartening, and sustain their hatred of us for being ahead of them? Can we do nothing more than aid them to catch up with us? Cannot Europeans and Americans help themselves?

For Europe is in trouble too, also North America, and not merely because the colonized peoples have taken up arms against colonialism and mean to pay us off for our sins. The fact is that for a long period of history these same sins were perfectly consistent with the continuity of European and American civilization and did not indicate that the humanity that created this civilization was in a state of crisis. Now it is. But why?

Once again, what can the ideal of Europeans and of North Americans be today? Also of the Soviet peoples, to whom progress is hardly more of a problem now than it is for us? Some years ago an Italian socialist, Andrea Caffi, said this to me:

Socialism has to have a new meaning. It must mean from now on that no one should be forced to do any kind of work which seems foolish to him or is harmful to others. Also it must mean that many more moments of human experience can now have a clear and intelligible meaning. With the present advance of technology such demands are not necessarily utopian, and anything less is unworthy of one who calls himself a socialist.

Think what such an ideal would mean if expressed to the Soviet peoples. In fact, it is being expressed to them right now, indirectly to be sure, by those artists and writers who have caught their interest and, unfortunately, the interest of the Soviet authorities.

At the outset I referred to Sartre's *Critique* as his second effort at a philosophical anthropology. *Being and Nothingness*, of course, was his first effort, and in that work he did speak to the people of the West. I must add here that, in my opinion, *Being and Nothingness* was more genuinely philosophical than is his *Critique*. It was not, like the latter, a generalization of anthropological and historical facts, assembled from all kinds of sources, but an attempt to think about man as the central object of our philosophical problems. As such, it implied an ethic, and Sartre announced he would follow it with an ethic, though many doubted that he could. Instead of making good his promise, he states categorically in his new work that philosophy cannot advance today beyond the philosophical position already taken by Marx (nobody, not even Sartre, knows exactly what that position is), and limits himself to generalizing anthropological and historical data in ways he thinks consonant with Marxist doctrine. So the Critique is not a genuinely philosophical work, nor does it even imply an ethic. It assumes the absolute validity of historical action, and of anything that might be done to gain access to such action. And it does not go beyond the view of ethics Sartre expressed in his book on Genêt, published in 1952, in which he wrote: "Thus a morality which does not explicitly assert that it cannot possibly be adhered to today contributes to the mystification and the alienation of men." In other words, no morality can be conceived of today whose precepts we will not be forced to violate.

The strongest attack on Sartre's Critique to date has come from another Frenchman—he happens to be Sartre's admirer and friend—Claude Lévi-Strauss, who was led to anthropology, he tells us, by his interest in philosophy. May I note here that according to the German thinker Martin Heidegger, the transformation of metaphysics into anthropology was achieved in France by none other than René Descartes. In any case, the two most powerful intellectual positions now being expressed in the land of Descartes are based on different conceptions of the past—and future—of man.

But Lévi-Strauss does not like at all the manner in which Sartre has derived his new anthropology out of Cartesianism. In La Pensée sauvage, Lévi-Strauss writes:

In fact, Sartre becomes the prisoner of his Cogito: the Cogito of Descartes gave one access to the universal but on the condition of remaining a psychological and individual being; Sartre, in sociologizing the Cogito, merely changes his prison . . . ; thus the approach of Sartre to the world and to man shows that narrowness traditionally seen in closed societies . . . . Descartes, who wanted to lay the foundations of physics, cut Man from Society. Sartre, who was trying to found an anthropology, cuts his society from other societies.

Right. But I must add that the society that Sartre now thinks his is that of the Third World's radicals. Turning Descartes's "I think" into the "We think" of a particular social group, the group he favors because it is capable of historical action, Sartre has cut himself off from all other groups, is forced to regard them as objects.

May I ask the reader not to hurry at this point over a problem only statable in abstract terms? Even in his *Being and Nothingness*, Sartre committed himself to do subject-object relationship in all the affairs of persons. Even in the relation between two individuals, according to Sartre, only one could be the subject and the other would have to be his (or her) object; one would have to be constituted by the other, and accept being thus constituted. Against this view, Merleau-Ponty pointed out that we can constitute others as constituting us, though the logic of this experience is still elusive; thus two can confront each other as subjects. But for Sartre, only one individual could be the subject, and now, in his *Critique*, only one social group.

In *La Pensée sauvage*, Lévi-Strauss goes on to attack Sartre's exaltation of historical action, and also to vindicate the possibility of moral behavior now; as against Sartre's conviction, similar to that of Communists like Brecht, that deeds can only be truly moral at some point in time. In making these judgments Lévi-Strauss has, it seems to me, taken a stand very much like that now being held by the radical spirits among American youth today. Does this mean that Lévi-Strauss is himself the prisoner of some particular group, as I suggest that Sartre is a prisoner of the group he favors, the radicals of the Third World?

By no means. The denial of history-making as an ultimate value, and the contention that action can and ought to be moral, do not exclude the communication of an individual with groups, or of one group with other groups. About this Lévi-Strauss is perfectly clear: I must say many of the young American radicals are not. Often they talk like Sartreans, and refuse communication even with those who might agree with them, but happen to be older. Such attitudes in the American youth are, I think, superficial and bound to pass, being inconsistent with their real interests, and have been given far too much attention by intellectuals like Lewis Feuer who are interested in attacking them.

History is a myth, Lévi-Strauss contends, and plays the same role in the mind of Sartre that the eternal past plays in the minds of primitives. Why is history a myth? Because the more detailed the information a historian gives us about the past, the less able he is to explain or interpret it. Also, an event has only to be sufficiently distant from us in time, or distanced from us by our thoughts, for it to lose whatever intelligibility it had. And whatever we ourselves may do in order to achieve what Sartre calls historical action, our deeds, when a certain time has passed, must become myths to those who come after us.

After he dismisses the value of historical action, Lévi-Strauss stresses the view that decent behavior, justice, and solidarity have been present in the most primitive communities. He writes in *Tristes Tropiques*: "The zealots of progress run the risk of underestimating and thus have known too little about the immense riches which our race has accumulated . . . the golden age which blind superstition situated behind or ahead of us is in us." And in *La Pensée sauvage*:

. . . each and every one of the tens or hundreds of thousands of societies which have coexisted, or succeeded each other, ever since man made his appearance on this earth, has availed itself of a moral certitude—the very one we ourselves can invoke—proclaiming that even in a society reduced to a tiny band of nomads, or a hamlet lost in the heart of the forest, the meaning and dignity of which human life is capable are to be found.

From the point of view expressed, or implied, here, the societies of Western Europe, as the societies being created in the new nations, are not at all representative of the kind of harmony that can and ought to prevail among men. Lévi-Strauss even thinks, with Rousseau, that our whole effort for progress and modernization was "ill-boding." To be sure, Europeans, North Americans included, are responsible for the present craze for progress and modernization. But I think we are also responsible at this point in our history to cure our own illnesses and not merely to endure the consequence of having spread them in other parts of the world.

And here I cannot but think of the efforts of the American youth to solidarize themselves with the American Negroes in their struggles for civil rights; also to create more genial and human conditions for learning on American campuses. What the American youth who took part in the Berkeley riots expressed most strongly was a lack of interest in progress as such. The aims of the American youth were immediate and moral, rather than prospective or political. They claimed that whatever they could accomplish they wanted to accomplish of themselves. They said they wanted to redress wrongs rather than to create the future. They were able to act, and they did not raise the question as to whether their action had historical meaning. They were interested in the immediate correction of what they considered to be present injustices, present ills. Mario Savio said: "I have a deep-seated suspicion of anyone who requires a theory to show that some practice is morally wrong." While the youth are not always this clear-headed, there can be no mistaking the point, the incidence, of their criticism. For surely in a developed world there must be something to be said about how things are done, also undone, by bureaucrats and officials, if you please, by the Establishment. I wonder if any of the young people in the Berkeley riots or in the Civil Rights movement has been influenced by Lévi-Strauss. Perhaps some have. But in any case, on the basis of what has been said and done by American youth in these movements, I should say that, for all the sympathy expressed by them for the American Negro, still oppressed in both the South and the North, and for those colonial peoples still struggling for advancement, the main interest of American youth is being directed toward the correction of those present injustices that efforts toward progress are often ready to ignore. It is as if the American youth felt—and how could anyone contravert this feeling?—that in the United States a high enough scale of abundance has been achieved for us to ask what this abundance is for, and how it is to be distributed. The American youth, I suggest, want to be their own heroes and will not delegate, as Sartre does, the burden of heroism to the underdeveloped nations of Africa and elsewhere.

This is a difficult age to be sure. And even Lévi-Strauss is not without his contradictions. When George Steiner accused him of having a "theory of history and of cultural hierarchy that is profoundly un-Marxian," Lévi-Strauss replied:

. . . Of course I am not a Marxist in the ordinary sense . . . something which can be true when we look at it from inside a culture is no longer true when we try to consider it from the outside. Therefore I am in full agreement with Marx, and even with Sartre, when they say that for a member of modern contemporary civilization things appear this way. History has a meaning and should have, because this is the only way to give a wider meaning to civilization itself. I can perfectly well claim, at the same time, that while this is true inside the society of the observer, it ceases to be true when we try to reflect a broader point of view and look at it from the outside.

Why should Lévi-Strauss have made such concessions to historicism, Marxist or Sartrean? And why was he willing to concede here the moral stand that distinguishes his own anthropology from the moral relativism of other schools? And is it right to say that something can be true when seen from inside society and yet ceases to be true when looked at from the outside? Would Lévi-Strauss then admit that the idea of keeping Negroes segregated is true from within the American South and false only when considered by people from the North? But this is exactly what the Southerners say and have said ever since the Civil War.

The trouble with this statement of Lévi-Strauss is that it tends to make his position less clear. What that position amounts to, as set forth in its purity in his anthropological writings, is that the civilized peoples of the developed countries may now rejoin their primitive brothers of the remote past. They can have access, if not to the making of further history, then to moral and ritual actions in which the whole meaning and dignity of life may be expressed. Surely the sense of Lévi-Strauss's main pronouncements as an anthropologist is a condemnation of Marxian historicism and an encouragement to regard it as devoid of truth. Our prospect now, I take it Lévi-

Strauss is really saying, is to become again like the primitives. There is certainly every indication that the American youth have this feeling, and no doubt came to it of themselves.

In the Third World, the idea of historical and technological progress will certainly be dominant for many decades. I do not see how Europeans or Americans can be unsympathetic to that ideal when it is held by others. We were the ones who originally advanced it. But I think too that it can no longer be our own ideal. What can the ideal for our world be? About this, Sartre, still concerned with progress and history, has said little to interest us; while Lévi-Strauss, taking the very remote past for a model, an inspiration, has told us something.

BIBLIOGRAPHY OF CLAUDE LÉVI-STRAUSS

BOOKS

La Vie familiale et sociale des Indiens Nambikwara, Paris, Société des Américanistes, Gonthier, 1948.

Les Structures élémentaires de la parenté, Paris, Presses Universitaires de France, 1949. Edition revue et corrigée, Paris, Mouton & Cie, 1967.

Race et histoire, Paris, UNESCO, 1952. Réédité chez Gonthier, Paris, 1967.

Tristes Tropiques, Paris, Plon, 1955.

Anthropologie structurale, Paris, Plon, 1958.

La Pensée sauvage, Paris, Plon, 1962.

Le Totémisme aujourd'hui, Paris, Presses Universitaires de France, 1962. Deuxième édition, Paris, P.U.F., 1965.

Mythologiques: Le Cru et le cuit, Paris, Plon, 1964.

Mythologiques: Du miel aux cendres, Paris, Plon, 1966.

Mythologiques: L'Origine des manières de table, Paris, Plon, 1968.

Entretiens avec Claude Lévi-Strauss, by Georges Charbonnier, Paris, Plon-Juilliard, 1961.

248   BIBLIOGRAPHY OF CLAUDE LÉVI-STRAUSS

ENGLISH TRANSLATIONS

Tristes Tropiques, translated by John Russell, New York, Criterion Books, 1961. (Published in London by Hutchinson and Company under the title *A World on the Wane*.) Chapters XIV, XV, XVI, and XXXIX of the French original are omitted.

Totemism, translated by Rodney Needham, Boston, Beacon Press, 1963.

Structural Anthropology, translated by Claire Jacobson and Brooke Grundfest Schoepf, New York, Basic Books, 1963.

The Savage Mind, Chicago, University of Chicago Press, 1966.

The Scope of Anthropology, translated by Sherry Ortner Paul and Robert A. Paul, London, Jonathan Cape, 1967. This is a translation of the "Leçon inaugurale faite le mardi 5 janvier 1960" at the Collège de France, and was first published in *Current Anthropology*, Vol. VII, No. 2, 1966.

"The Story of Asdiwal," translated by Nicholas Mann, in *The Structural Study of Myth and Totemism*, edited by Edmund Leach (A.S.A. Monographs, 5), London, Tavistock Publications, 1967.

The Elementary Structures of Kinship, translated from the revised edition by James Harle Bell and John Richard von Sturmer, and edited by Rodney Needham, Boston, Beacon Press, 1969.

The Raw and the Cooked, translated by John and Doreen Weightman, New York, Harper and Row, 1969.

Conversations with Claude Lévi-Strauss, by Georges Charbonnier, translated by John and Doreen Weightman, London, Jonathan Cape, 1969.

ARTICLES

1936

"Contribution à l'étude de l'organisation sociale des Indiens Bororo," *Journal de la Société des américanistes*, n.s., Vol. XXVIII.

"Entre os selvagems civilizados," *O Estado de São Paulo* (Coleção do Departamento municipal de cultura, 1), São Paulo, Brazil.

"Os mais vastos horizontes do mundo," *Filosofia, Ciências e Letras*, Vol. I, São Paulo, Brazil.

1937

"A civilisação chaco-santiaguena," *Revistas do Arquivo Municipal*, Vol. IV, São Paulo, Brazil.

Indiens du Brésil, Guide-catalogue de l'exposition, etc. (mission Lévi-Strauss), Paris, Muséum National d'Histoire Naturelle, Musée de l'Homme, Paris.

"Poupées Karaja," *Boletim de la Sociedade de Etnografia e de Folklore*, Vol. I, São Paulo, Brazil.

"La sociologie culturelle et son enseignement," *Filosofia, Ciências e Letras*, Vol. II, São Paulo, Brazil.

1942

"Fards indiens," *VVV*, Vol. I, No. 1.

Souvenir of Malinovski, *ibid.*

1943

"The Art of the Northwest Coast," *Gazette des Beaux-Arts*, Ser. VI, Vol. XXIV, No. 9.

"Guerre et commerce chez les indiens de l'Amérique du Sud," *Renaissance, revue trimestrielle publiée par l'Ecole Libre des Hautes Etudes*, Vol. I.

"The Social Use of Kinship Terms among Brazilian Indians," *American Anthropologist*, Vol. XLV, No. 3.

1944

"On Dual Organisation in South America," *América Indígena*, Vol. IV, No. 1, Mexico City.

"Reciprocity and Hierarchy," *American Anthropologist*, Vol. XLVI, No. 2.

"The Social and Psychological Aspects of Chieftainship in a Primitive Tribe: The Nambikwara of Northwestern Mato Grosso," *Transactions of the New York Academy of Sciences*, Series II, Vol. VII, No. 1.

1945

"L'analyse structurale en linguistique et en anthropologie," *Word, Journal of the Linguistic Circle of New York*, Vol. I, No. 2.

"Le dédoublement de la représentation dans les arts de l'Asie et de l'Amérique," *Renaissance, revue trimestrielle publiée par l'Ecole Libre des Hautes Etudes*, Vols. II and III, 1944–45.

"French Sociology," in *Twentieth Century Sociology*, edited by George Gurvitch and Wilbert E. Moore, New York. (French translation: *La Sociologie au XXe siècle*, Paris, Presses Universitaires de France, 1947.)

"L'oeuvre d'Edward Westermarck," *Revue de l'histoire des religions*, Vol. CXXIX, Nos. 1 and 2–3.

1946

"The Name of the Nambikwara," *American Anthropologist*, Vol. XLVIII, No. 1.

"La technique du bonheur," *Esprit (L'Homme américain)*, No. 127.

1947

"Le serpent au corps rempli de poissons," *Actes du XXVIIIe Congrès international des Américanistes*, Paris.

"Sur certaines similarités morphologiques entre les langues chibcha et nambikwara," *ibid.*

"La théorie du pouvoir dans une société primitive," in *Les Doctrines politiques modernes*, New York.

1948

"The Nambicuara," in *Handbook of South American Indians*, edited by Julian Steward, Bureau of American Ethnology, Smithsonian Institution, Washington, D.C., Vol. III.

"The Tribes of the Right Bank of the Guaporé River," *ibid.*

"The Tribes of the Upper Xingu River," *ibid.*

"The Tupi-Kawahib," *ibid.*

1949

"L'efficacité symbolique," *Revue de l'histoire des religions*, Vol. CXXXV, No. 1.

"Histoire et ethnologie," *Revue de métaphysique et de morale*, 54e année, No. 3–4.

"La politique étrangère d'une société primitive," *Politique étrangère*, No. 2.

"Le sorcier et sa magie," *Les Temps modernes*, 4e année, No. 41.

1950

"Documents rama-rama," *Journal de la Société des Américanistes*, n.s., Vol. XXXIX.

"Introduction à l'oeuvre de Marcel Mauss," in *Sociologie et anthropologie*, par Marcel Mauss, Paris, Presses Universitaires de France. Réédité en troisième édition, 1966.

"Préface à C. Berndt," *Women's Changing Ceremonies in Northern Australia*, Cahiers de l'Homme, Vol. I, No. 1, Paris, Hermann.

"Le Préface à K. Dunham," *Danses d'Haïti*, Paris, Fasquelle.

"Sur certaines objets en poterie d'usage douteux provenant de la Syrie et de l'Inde," *Syria*, Vol. XXVII.

"The Use of Wild Plants in Tropical South America," *Handbook of South American Indians*, edited by Julian Steward, Bureau of American Ethnology, Smithsonian Institution, Washington, D.C., Vol. VI.

1951

"Avant-propos," *Bulletin international des sciences sociales (numéro spécial consacré à l'Asie du Sud-Est)*, Vol. III, No. 4, Paris, UNESCO.

"Language and the Analysis of Social Laws," *American Anthropologist*, Vol. LIII, No. 2.

"Les sciences sociales au Pakistan," *Bulletin international des sciences sociales (numéro spécial consacré à l'Asie du Sud-Est)*, Vol. III, No. 4, Paris, UNESCO.

1952

"Kinship Systems of Three Chittagong Hill Tribes," *Southwestern Journal of Anthropology*, Vol. VIII, No. 1.

"Miscellaneous Notes on the Kuki," *Man*, Vol. LI, No. 284.

"La notion d'archaïsme en ethnologie," *Cahiers internationaux de sociologie*, Vol. XII.

"Le Père Noël supplicié," *Les Temps modernes*, 7e année, No. 77.

"Les structures sociales dans le Brésil central et oriental," in *Indian Tribes of Aboriginal America, Selected Papers of the 29th International Congress of Americanists*, Vol. III, edited by Sol Tax, University of Chicago Press.

"Le syncrétisme religieux d'un village mogh du territoire de Chittagong," *Revue de l'histoire des religions*, Vol. CXLI, No. 2.

Toward a General Theory of Communication, paper submitted to the International Conference of Linguists and Anthropologists, University of Indiana, Bloomington (mimeographed).

"La visite des âmes," *Annuaire de l'Ecole Pratique des Hautes Etudes* (Sciences religieuses), 1951–1952.

1953

Chapter One, in Results of the Conference, etc., *Supplement to International Journal of American Linguistics*, Vol. XIX, No. 2.

"Panorama de l'ethnologie," *Diogène*, No. II.

"Recherches de mythologie américaine (I)," in *Annuaire de l'E.P. H.E.* (Sciences religieuses), 1952–1953.

"Social Structure," in *Anthropology To-Day*, prepared under the chairmanship of A. L. Kroeber, University of Chicago Press.

"Structure sociale," *Bulletin de psychologie*, Vol. VI, No. 7.

1954

"L'art de déchiffrer les symboles," *Diogène*, No. 5.

"Place de l'anthropologie dans les sciences sociales et problèmes posés par son enseignement," in *Les Sciences sociales dans l'enseignement supérieur* (Rapports préparés par C.W. Guillebaud et al.), Paris, UNESCO.

"Qu'est-ce qu'un primitif?" *Le Courrier*, No. 8–9.

"Recherches de mythologie américaine (II)," in *Annuaire de l'E. P. H.E.* (Sciences religieuses), 1953–1954.

1955

"Diogène couché," *Les Temps modernes*, 10e année, No. 110.

"Les mathématiques de l'homme," *Bulletin international des sciences sociales* (numéro spécial sur les mathématiques), Vol. VI, No. 4. Reprinted in *Esprit*, 24e année, No. 10, 1956.

"Rapports de la mythologie et du rituel," in *Annuaire de l'E.P.H.E.* (Sciences religieuses), 1954–1955.

"The Structural Study of Myth," *Journal of American Folklore*, Vol. LXVIII, No. 270.

"Les structures élémentaires de la parenté," in *La Progenèse*, Centre International de l'Enfance (Travaux et Documents VIII), Paris, Masson.

1956

Compte rendu de G. Balandier, Sociologie des Brazzavilles noires, *Revue française des sciences politiques*, Vol. VI, No. 1.

"Le droit au voyage," *L'Express*, 21 septembre.

"The Family," in *Man, Culture and Society*, edited by Harry L. Shapiro, Oxford University Press.

"La fin des voyages," *L'Actualité littéraire*, No. 26.

"Jeux de société," *United States Lines*, Paris Review (numéro spécial sur les jeux).

"Les organisations dualistes existent-elles?" *Bijdragen tot de Taal-, Land- en Volkenkunde*, Vol. CXII, No. 2.

"Les prohibitions du mariage," in *Annuaire de l'E.P.H.E.* (Sciences religieuses), 1955–1956.

"Sorciers et psychanalyse," *Le Courrier*, No. 7–8.

"Structure et dialectique," in *For Roman Jakobson, Essays on the Occasion of his Sixtieth Birthday*, edited by Morris Halle, Le Haye, Mouton.

"Les trois humanismes," *Demain*, No. 35.

1957

Compte rendu de R. Briffault—B. Malinovski, Marriage: Past and Present, *American Anthropologist*, Vol. LIX, No. 5.

"Recherches récentes sur la notion d'âme," in *Annuaire de l'E.P. H.E.* (Sciences religieuses), 1956–1957.

"Le symbolisme cosmique dans la structure sociale et l'organisation cérémonielle de plusieurs populations nord- et sud-américaines," *Série Orientale Roma*, XIV, Institut pour l'Etude de l'Orient et de l'Extrême-Orient, Rome.

1958

Compte rendu de R. Firth, ed., Man and Culture: An Evaluation of B. Malinovski, *Africa, Journal of the International African Institute*, Vol. XXVIII, No. 4.

"Dis-moi quels champignons," *L'Express*, 10 avril.

"Documents tupi-kawahib," in *Miscellanea Paul Rivet, Octogenario Dicata*, Mexico.

"Le dualisme dans l'organisation sociale et les représentations religieuses," in *Annuaire de l'E.P.H.E.* (Sciences religieuses), 1957–1958 and 1958–1959.

"One World, Many Societies," *Way Forum*, No. 27.

Préface à M. Bouteiller, *Sorciers et jeteurs de sorts*, Paris, Plon.

1959

"Amérique du Nord et Amérique du Sud," *Le Masque*, Paris, Musée Guimet.

Art. "Mauss, Marcel," *Encyclopedia Britannica*.

Art. "Passage Rites," *Encyclopaedia Britannica*.

"Le Masque," *L'Express*, No. 443.

Préface à D. C. Talaysesva, *Soleil Hopi*, Paris.

1960

"Ce que l'ethnologie doit à Durkheim," *Annales de l'Université de Paris*, I.

"Compte rendu d'enseignement (1959–1960)," in *Annuaire du Collège de France*.

"Le dualisme dans l'organisation sociale et les représentations religieuses," in *Annuaire de l'E.P.H.E.* (Sciences religieuses), 1958–1959.

"Four Winnebago Myths, A Structural Sketch," in *Culture and History: Essays in Honor of Paul Radin*, edited by S. Diamond, Columbia University Press.

"La geste d'Asdiwal," in *Annuaire de l'E.P.H.E.* (Sciences religieuses), 1958–1959. Reprinted in *Les Temps modernes*, No. 179, March, 1961.

Leçon inaugurale faite le mardi 5 janvier 1960, Collège de France, Paris.

"Méthodes et conditions de la recherche ethnologique française en Asie," in *Colloque sur les recherches*, etc., Fondation Singer-Polignac, Paris.

"On Manipulated Sociological Methods," *Bijdragen tot de Taal-, Land- en Volkenkunde*, Vol. CXVI, No. 1.

"La structure et la forme. Réflexions sur un ouvrage de Vladimir Propp," *Cahiers de l'Institut de Science Economique appliquée* (Recherches et dialogues philos. et écon. 7), No. 99. Reprinted in *International Journal of Slavic Linguistics and Poetics*, 3, 1960, under the title "Analyse morphologique des contes russes."

"Les trois sources de la réflexion ethnologique," *Revue de l'enseignement supérieur*, 1.

1961

"La chasse rituelle aux aigles," in *Annuaire de l'E.P.H.E.* (Sciences religieuses), 1959–1960.

Compte rendu d'enseignement (1960–1961), in *Annuaire du Collège de France*.

Comptes rendus divers, *L'Homme*, Vol. I.

"La crise de l'anthropologie moderne," *Le Courrier*, No. 11.

"Le métier d'ethnologue," *Revue de l'Université des Annales*, n.s., No. 129.

1962

"La Antropologia, Hoy: Entrevista a Claude Lévi-Strauss" (par Eliseo Veron), *Cuestiones de Filosofia*, Vol. I, No. 2–3, Buenos Aires.

Compte rendu d'enseignement (1961–1962), in *Annuaire du Collège de France*.

Comptes rendus divers, *L'Homme*, Vol. II.

"Ethnologue avant l'heure," *Les Nouvelles littéraires*, 29 novembre (numéro spécial Rousseau).

"Jean-Jacques Rousseau, fondateur des Sciences de l'Homme," in *Jean-Jacques Rousseau* (Conférences organisées par l'Université ouvrière et la Faculté des Lettres de l'Université de Genève; conférences prononcées lors de la séance solennelle du 28 juin 1962, à la Salle de la Réformation à Genève), Neuchâtel, La Bacconnière.

"Les limites de la notion de structure en ethnologie," in *Sens et usages du terme structure*, edited by R. Bastide, Janua Linguarum, No. XVI, Le Haye.

"Sur le caractère distinctif des faits ethnologiques," *Revue des travaux de l'Académie des Sciences Morales et Politiques*, 115e année, 4e série, Paris.

"Les Chats de Charles Baudelaire," en collaboration avec R. Jakobson, *L'Homme*, Vol. II, No. 1.

1963

"Alfred Métraux, 1902–1963," *Journal de la Société des américanistes*, Vol. LII.

"The Bear and the Barber," *Journal of the Royal Anthropological Institute*, Vol. XCIII, part I.

Compte rendu d'enseignement (1962–1963), in *Annuaire du Collège de France*.

"Les discontinuités culturelles et la développement économique et sociale," *Table ronde sur les prémices sociales de l'industrialisation* (1961), Paris, UNESCO.

"Réponses à quelques questions," *Esprit*, No. 322.

"Rousseau, père de l'ethnologie," *Le Courrier*, No. 3.

"Marques de propriété dans deux tribus sud-américaines," en collaboration avec N. Belmont, *L'Homme*, Vol. III, No. 3.

1964

"Alfred Métraux, 1902–1963," *Annales de l'Université de Paris*, No. 1.

Compte rendu d'enseignement (1963–1964), in *Annuaire du Collège de France*.

"Critères scientifiques dans les disciplines sociales et humaines," *Revue internationale des sciences sociales*, Vol. XVI, No. 4.

"Hommage à Alfred Métraux," *L'Homme*, Vol. IV, No. 2.

1965

Compte rendu d'enseignement (1964–1965), *Annuaire du Collège de France*.

"The Future of Kinship Studies," The Huxley Memorial Lecture for 1965, *Proceedings of the Royal Anthropological Institute of Great Britain and Ireland*.

Preséntation du laboratoire d'anthropologie sociale, *Revue de l'enseignement supérieur*, 3.

"Réponse à un questionnaire (sur 25 témoins de notre temps)," *Le Figaro littéraire*, No. 1023, 25 novembre.

"Risposte a un questionario sullo strutturalismo," *Paragone*, numero speciale 2, No. 182, aprile, Milan.

"Les sources polluées de l'art," *Arts-Loisirs*, 7–13 avril.

"Le triangle culinaire," *L'Arc*, No. 26, Aix-en-Provence.

"Entretien avec Claude Lévi-Strauss," en collaboration avec M. Delahaye et J. Rivette, *Les Cahiers du cinéma*, Vol. XXVI, No. 4.

1966

"Anthropology: Its Achievements and Future," *Nature*, Vol. CCIX, No. 1.

Compte rendu d'enseignement (1965–1966), in *Annuaire du Collège de France*.

Interview accordée aux *Cahiers de philosophie* (numéro spécial: Anthropologie), No. 1.

1967

Compte rendu d'enseignement (1966–1967), in *Annuaire du Collège de France*.

"A contre-courant," Interview de Claude Lévi-Strauss par G. Dumur, *Le nouvel observateur*, 25 janvier.

"Entretien de Gilles Lapouge avec Claude Lévi-Strauss," *Figaro littéraire*, 2 février.

Présentation du laboratoire d'anthropologie sociale, *Sciences*, No. 47.

"Le sexe des astres," in *Mélanges offerts à Roman Jakobson pour sa 70e année*, Janua Linguarum, Serie Maior, 33, Le Haye.

"Vingt ans après," *Les Temps modernes*, No. 256.

1968

"Hommage aux sciences de l'homme," *Information sur les sciences sociales*, Vol. VII, No. 2.

"Religions comparées des peuples sans écriture," in *Problèmes et méthodes d'histoire des religions*, Paris.

INDEX